PRAISE FOR *Mud Creek Medicine*

"*Mud Creek Medicine* is a much-needed biography of a woman who succeeded through her indomitable will and raw courage in providing basic health care for low-income rural families and coal miners. Kiran Bhatraju's lively writing style and unflinching truth-telling is a compelling tribute to Eula Hall and the significant contributions she made to her home place, the Appalachian region, and to national understanding of the importance of community-based health care."

—Judith Jennings, co-editor of *Helen Matthews Lewis:*
Living Social Justice in Appalachia

"With lively prose and authenticity, Bhatraju offers more than just a gripping tale of one woman's journey—*Mud Creek Medicine* is nothing less than a full-throated critique of crony capitalism."

—Andrew Porwancher, Assistant Professor of
Classics & Letters, University of Oklahoma

"Everyone who worked in health care in Eastern Kentucky in the 1960s knows Eula Hall, and Kiran Bhatraju's incredible portrait of her life and struggle is a gripping drama. She not only saved lives, but drew the blueprint for rural community health centers that subsequently came to Appalachia and America."

—Dr. Harvey Sloane, Member of President Kennedy's
Appalachian Health Program; Founder and Director of the Park
DuValle Community Health Center; former Mayor of Louisville

MUD CREEK MEDICINE

The Life of Eula Hall
and the Fight for Appalachia

KIRAN BHATRAJU

BUTLER BOOKS · LOUISVILLE

ISBN 978-1-935497-73-8

Library of Congress Control Number: 2013952520

Printed in the United States of America

Published by:

Butler Books
P.O. Box 7311
Louisville, KY 40257
phone: (502) 897-9393
fax: (502) 897-9797
www.butlerbooks.com

For Doctor(s) Bhatraju

Proceeds from the sale of this book will be donated to the Eula Hall Patient Assistance Fund to cover health care costs for uninsured and indigent patients, and to the Eula Hall Scholarship Fund to provide financial assistance for students pursuing careers in health care or social services.

Some names and characters have been altered at Eula's request.

We have a conversation with the land here.
The land will talk to us.
It will tell us things, like nothing comes easy to people in the
Mountains.
We are a little worn.
We are a little bent.
We are a little broken.
But we are real, and we are here.
This is life for us. We ain't got a choice here in the coalfields.
We are fighting back,
'cause it's the only thing we have.

—LARRY GIBSON, "KEEPER OF THE MOUNTAINS"

I will lift up mine eyes unto the hills, from whence cometh my help.

—PSALM 121:1

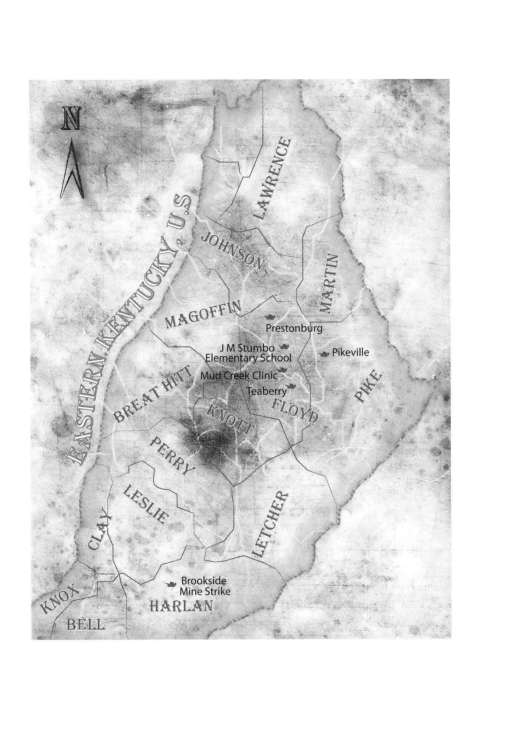

N

LAWRENCE

JOHNSON

MARTIN

EASTERN KENTUCKY, U.S.

MAGOFFIN

Prestonburg

J M Stumbo
Elementary School

Pikeville

Mud Creek Clinic

BREATHITT

Teaberry

KNOTT

FLOYD

PIKE

PERRY

LESLIE

LETCHER

CLAY

KNOX

Brookside
Mine Strike

HARLAN

BELL

A Note to the Reader about the Land and Its People

APPALACHIA HAS LONG PLAYED AN ICONIC ROLE IN America, alternating between a native frontier and, at times, a redoubt of redneck romanticism. Today, far from the bustle of city life and the quiet rudeness of suburbia, these mountains enclose a part of America often ignored, and at times forgotten. Life here is slow, always has been.

Standing for some 225 million years and stretching from Maine to Alabama, these mountains have been a refuge for those worn by modernity, a timeless and enduring testament to the nation's humble beginnings. Appalachians gave the country its first indigenous music and art, Appalachian woodsmen gave the nation timber to build its bustling cities and towns, and Appalachian coal miners trudged and labored to keep the lights on.

Observing the geography of the land, one gets the sense that the southern Appalachians are holding America together, the physical and cultural backbone of a nation wound between eastern and western ambition. If the mountains are the nation's backbone, its heart lies in Kentucky. If Kentucky holds its heart, Eastern Kentucky is where one can find the nation's soul.

In an age of rapid industrialization and connectivity, Appalachia, as historian Ron Eller writes, still reflects the enamored ideal of "a simpler, less complicated life," harkening back to America's Arcadian birth. Today, the region still plays an integral cultural and economic role, sometimes by simply challenging the conventional American dream of success and wealth.

Set in a landscape of staggering beauty, the rolling mountains of the Cumberland Plateau enclose hamlets of gritty men and resilient women. The land, like its people, is bucolic, thoroughly rustic, and worn. These mountains have bred myth and legend, and have been filled with outcast immigrants, war heroes, isolated backwoodsmen, hardworking miners, fast-moving moonshiners, religious warriors, musicians, and the occasional statesman—a rugged cast for sure. Eastern Kentucky is home to some of America's most genuine people—a place where playing the church piano loud is about as important as playing it right. Where people never wanted or asked for more than what God gave them. A place where life was tortured, but caring enough to make Eula Hall a woman of endless compassion.

While questions of *who* and *what* and *how* and *why* are no doubt useful and will serve the reader best in understanding the struggles and triumphs Eula endured, four interrogatives are a waste when just one will do. *Where*—the ultimate identifier and personification of her struggle. For Eula, and the colorful and dynamic characters who went in and out of her life, place shapes and defines them all—from the winding creek beds connecting hollows, to the sloping mountainsides echoing their twang. Place defines her struggle to give power back to the people from the hands of powerful political elites. Place defines her rugged perseverance in the face of severe domestic abuse. Place defines the holocaust survivor, the liberation theologist, the activists, doctors, elected officials, and regular folks who found hope in her mountain struggle. It is place that defines her steely feminism and resolve to continue to "raise holy hell" at the first sign of injustice. It is in this place where the most simple act—being in a land often forgotten—makes this story as unique as it is grand.

Some readers might roll their eyes and ask whether the mythmakers are at it again, deifying a region no longer in the public conscience. It is sometimes said that Appalachia was never given a chance, taken advantage of, and remembered if only for its raw American-ness and down-home culture. As in every introspective of Appalachia, fashionable social theorists, almost always on the outside looking in, quickly place blame on the people for degeneration and environmental recklessness. They claim that cultures of poverty provide causation for neediness and underdevelopment. They claim people here yearn for dependence. And they claim that Appalachia may well be hopeless.

Sentiments changed briefly in the late 1960s when the Kennedy brothers—along with a slew of scholars and historians—awakened the American conscience to the Appalachian experience. They opened a wound in America's industrial soul, exposing years of neglect and manipulation at the hands of exploitative industries. Cultures-of-poverty critiques were replaced by a reading of history showing the workers' abuse at the hand of industrial barons and crony capitalists. America learned about a new, internal colonialism taking hold and creating regions vastly different, yet within the same country. The War on Poverty, President Lyndon B. Johnson's noble war, attempted to change the trajectory of a timeless people and it gave Eula the spark to sustain a lifetime of her own brand of tough-love, bootstrapped compassion.

I grew up in the mountains, among the generous people of Pikeville, Kentucky, and I know ivory-tower pundits have for years made a haughty judgment on Appalachian culture without a thorough consideration of the people they claim to understand. Telling Eula's story using her words is an attempt to change those perceptions for outsiders, and provide a role model for the thousands of Appalachians today who may or may not have been able to find hope and inspiration for a better future.

My parents arrived in Appalachia in the 1980s to start a life of their own in their newly adopted country. As an immigrant from India, my father faced discrimination in his dream to be a doctor, *but* he faced prejudice well before he came to the mountains. Deep in Eastern Kentucky coal country, he found a home, a community, and most importantly, a place to raise his family. He encountered many interesting souls in his decades of work, but none of them inspired him as did Eula Hall. After working in her Mud Creek Clinic in the 1990s and early 2000s, he recounted her story to me once again, reminding me that the most important and the most improbable stories are of regular folks standing up for justice.

I wrote Eula's biography by interviewing her extensively, and researching people, places, and events surrounding her life. I spent many weeks with Eula in the clinic and at her home in the Teaberry holler of Mud Creek learning about her life and the unbelievable strife she faced. Many of the stories found in the following pages were recorded and written as close to Eula's remembrance as possible, with much help from outside sources. In the end, it is her life story I aimed to tell, and inevitably, this book cannot be judged as an authoritative history. But, as in the Appalachian tradition, it is a collection of memories from the horse's mouth—and Eula has quite the memory.

Whether it is the trailblazing, family feuds, coal miners' strife, moonshinin', or just folksy charm, the personal stories of individuals found in the hills of Appalachia often do rise to the heights of drama and intrigue, and reach to the depths of the American experience. Eula Hall's life is no exception. Eula's story is of a woman of remarkable strength, shaped by her community above all else. It is a story that should appeal to those with no connection to Appalachia, and to those who simply want to leave the world a better place than they found it. From a rugged mountain youth to hired girl to organizer, health care entrepreneur, and iconoclast, Eula's story echoes the story of America in the twentieth century, in all her rage and glory. She is the quintessential Appalachian-American poverty warrior combined with bucolic self-sufficiency, and she represents a dual ethos of community and individualism that is unique to the mountains.

Eula, like so many quiet civic heroes, didn't do it for fame because, in her words, "Fame ain't worth a damn"; didn't do it for accolades because "We need action, not awards"; and sure as hell didn't do it for money because she's "been rich without money since birth." She fought on, and risked her life at times, as the sign outside the clinic reads: "For the People."

Prologue

"MOMMA, WE GOT A BALLGAME OUT IN ALLEN. I'D love if you'd come by; I always play better when you do." Fifteen year-old Dean had grown up to become quite the ballplayer, and his team was in need of extra support as they competed for a countywide playoff spot. It was a hot and oppressive June evening in the Eastern Kentucky mountains, but Eula wouldn't miss the game for the world.

"Well, I'm about finished up at the clinic," she told Dean-o, a pet name she had given him years before when trying to put him at ease during the sleepless nights together in the backseat of her Ford Bronco. "I'll do my best to drive out there by six."

Eula had just put in a long, stressful day at the clinic and was finishing disability paperwork for a patient before heading out. Eula truly loved going to Dean's ballgames. Not only was Dean a solid third basemen, but those games, in a curious way, gave Eula the same fulfillment she had being at the clinic. The ballgames became potluck community picnics, bringing everyone out to enjoy the evening and cheer on the kids. Rather than bringing folks together around the illnesses and ill fate that Eula had become accustomed to, the baseball games were the clinic without ailments—just friends and family offering the medicine of the country's favorite pastime.

"You know, back in the day, our people used to celebrate farm seasons, barn raisings, sorghum stir-offs, what have ya, by gathering the community together," Eula recalled. While most of those traditions faded with time and season, families could come together and be a community again when they gathered around the children's activities.

Eula packed up her papers, rushed the nurses out, locked the doors to her trailer health clinic, jumped in her yellow Volkswagen (nicknamed "Rabbit"), and headed west out of the holler. She arrived in the hamlet of Allen, Kentucky, a little after the first inning.

Eula took a seat on the bleachers among friends she called family. She ordered a mess of corndogs, and whooped and hollered in support of Dean and the team. The ball field in Allen is set back dramatically at the foothills of a mountain, which doubles as an outfield fence. If one of the young hitters launched a ball against the mountainside, the outfielder could run up and try to make the play, but if the fielder missed and the ball hit the hillside, it was ruled a home run. Baskum, Eula's second husband, was coaching and guiding kids around third base. He turned and gave Eula a little wink between innings, a small sign of confidence in the outcome. Dean-o, as his teammates called him as well, had a smile from ear to ear, and unlike his much older brothers, his childhood was turning out more average and simpler than Eula could have ever imagined. It was a perfect night, Eula thought. Life was good and without worry—finally.

As the evening came to a close, dusk set in early over the mountain line and Dean's team celebrated their chance to play in the post-season with a three-run win. Parents grabbed their kids on both the winning and losing teams, gave them some encouragement for the next big game or season, and told them it was time to head home to get ready for school the next day. Many of the kids grew up poor in the hollers, and their parents had limited options for transportation. After most games, Baskum and Eula would split up the responsibility of taking the kids home, but that night, Baskum said he'd take as many kids as he could so Eula and her granddaughter Eulana could head home to fix Dean's favorite supper. The pair piled into Rabbit and trekked back home, joking about how ecstatic the kids were to win the game.

A beautiful Kentucky blue moon had set in above the pines as Eula made the turnoff from Highway 23 at Harold onto Route 979 to Mud Creek. Just as they pulled around the sloping curve to their small hamlet in Upper Mud, Nanetta, Eula's eldest daughter, ran out of the holler onto the road, her hair a mess, and hysteria in her eyes. She had been crying, and her dress was marked with ash and soot. Tears rolled from her eyes as she struggled to reach the car.

"Good Lord, Nanetta, what in the hell has gotten into ya?" Eula screamed as she rolled down the window.

"Momma! Go to the clinic! *Now*!

"Honey, what in the world are you . . ." She looked up, and piercing the bright moonlit sky to the right of the house was a rage of swirling flames.

"It's on fire! It's on *fire*, momma!"

Eula's heart sank. She punched Rabbit a few feet past where Nanetta was standing and looked past the trees toward the house and up to the clinic. The mountain night sky was lit up with a sickening glow. The clinic and the office she had been sitting in just a few hours before was engulfed in whipping flames and smoldering ash.

Without hesitation, the three women frantically sprinted into the house to fetch water. They raced back out, shuttling bucket after bucket, even slamming bed sheets and rugs on the flames to soften the fire's rage. The dogs barked in the fire's direction as horses fled their stables across the creek. There were no fire hydrants in the hollers, and the fire department was conspicuously absent. As the three women feverishly fought what was slowly becoming a losing battle, folks on the road stopped and tried to help, some crying along with Eula as they watched a monument in the community burn. Within twenty minutes, the roof caved in, and screams of horror rang out among the crowd. Medical records, supplies, drugs, and equipment were all gone. The desk Eula had worked at just hours before was reduced to ash. There was no help, and there would be no rescue. The clinic that she had risked her life to build was no more.

Eula knelt, motionless except for the chattering of her lower jaw. She stared into the smoke and ash, crying uncontrollably—something she hadn't done in decades.[1]

PART ONE

Born of
Suffering

Chapter 1

Greasy Creek, Floyd County, Kentucky, 1930

GREASY CREEK IS A SMALL HOLLER TOWN WHOSE NAME does a disservice to its charm. Some would say it's indigenous to these mountains, but the origin of the town's name is somewhat uncertain. Perhaps the creation of a few adventuresome long hunters in search of wild game or creek water, Greasy existed long before most elders in the area can remember. Unlike the surrounding towns of Neon, HiHat, or Blackey—all outgrowths of established coal towns named after coal barons' girlfriends—many in the area assume Greasy's history goes back much further than industrialization. Many at least hope the coal barons had better taste in women.

While the coal camps created what some call the South's first melting pot—a stew of Italian, Scots-Irish, Polish, and Russian immigrant day laborers—the early mountaineers, descendants of the pilgrims, were a homogenous clan that most likely founded Greasy sometime in the early 1800s. Slowly, these immigrants began to settle down in the rugged hollows within, and start a new life in a new world. By the 1820s, enough people had descended into the region for counties to be marked off.

Kentucky named its largest county Pike, after famed explorer General Zebulon Pike, with Pikeville as its county seat. Its neighbor to the west, Floyd County, was named after pioneer surveyor and judge John Floyd.[2]

Both nestled in the eastern-most tip of the Commonwealth, these two Kentucky counties served as the economic and political hub of the eastern region. The region is also the home of America's most famous feud between the Hatfields and McCoys. Folklorist William Lynwood Montell argues that the long, arduous years of the Civil War led to a culture of violence to settle personal and familial scores. While the feud and its cultural identity may have shaped Appalachia for a generation, Appalachia's timber and coal riches did as well. It would be against this backdrop—one of violence and the literal coal engine that powered America's ascension onto the world stage—that that would serve as Eula's home.[3]

Eula Riley was born in Joe Bonner Holler of Upper Greasy in Pike County on October 29, 1927. She was the third of five children, and her mother would later call her nearly ten-hour period of labor "an angel's arrival." Prenatal care was nonexistent; in fact, there was little in terms of care at all. Nanny delivered Eula just as she did the other six, without complaint, under the guise of serenity, on the muddied floor in the back bedroom of their four-room mountain cabin.

Eula's birth came on the heels of America's deepest and most emotionally searing depression. While historians note the late arrival of the Great Depression to the coalfields, the decade or so before Eula's birth were formative years for the Appalachian region, defining the century to come. As historian Ron Eller notes, a particular kind of modernization unfolded in the years between 1890 and 1930, best described through exploit and underdevelopment. As moneyed men from the north seeped in, they invented legally faulty deeds and found strong Appalachian backs to work the land. These moneyed and politically astute men came in fast and quietly took advantage of local folks. Often in exchange for a slightly more comforting life, generations of men and families were afflicted by black lung disease, wasted streams, and further degradation. Reconstruction, war production, and a booming American economy aided the effort, which included timber harvesting, coal mining, milling, and farming. These extractive industries made managers and CEOs in urban areas wealthy, while those in the hollers saw only a meager improvement in their quality of life. As mountain legislator, writer, and historian Harry Caudill noted, "Entrepreneurs with no real connection or empathy for the land used their capital to ravage the region, with little benefit to the local population."

However, the twentieth-century story of the mountains is more than just a sordid tale of economic colonialism. The region had not always been characterized by exploitation; in fact, Eula's ancestors in the region were sharecroppers and farmers who lived contented, subsistence lives. It wasn't until much later that the southern Appalachians evolved into company life. Although the companies brought with them significant environmental ruin, they also brought a new sense of community and lifestyle. The Appalachian worker, often seen as fiercely independent, worked hard for the coal operators and lumber mills in exchange for a bigger bulge in his wallet. Company camps sprouted up everywhere around Greasy, increasing county populations fourfold in some instances. This development, though transient and inconsistent, created a new network of communities, and brought a new formal economy and life, including better housing, road construction, grocery stores, schools, and—for good or bad—politics. These companies ushered in an era of mixed feelings for many in the mountains, as a more secure and stable life seemed to come only at the expense of the land and its people.[4]

Despite the development, life was still a far cry from

comfortable, and was by no means idyllic. Similar to the hardscrabble Appalachian life many children of the early twentieth century faced, Eula was in the yard, hoe in hand, or inside, frying and baking, doing any chores she could as soon as she was able. This often meant hard labor by age five or six. For many mountain children, life would see progress from a generation before, but bring along a host of new challenges. Almost all children went to some school, but few had money for lunch or new clothes. Almost all children could expect to live longer than their parents, but in the virtual absence of formal medical care. Families lived in a precarious balance between hope and despair. Despite the lack of material well-being, Eula recalls the sentiment of her childhood as one where "mountain children had their eyes wide open for the first time," willing to embrace the world and look at life as more than "taking care of a husband or working in the mines." She points to the Hoover years as ones giving her a thick skin, and putting the fire in her belly to fight the injustices she saw in her community.

Luckily, the Rileys were able to weather the storm of the Depression by returning to a subsistence life. Lee made a living as a tenant farmer, giving two-thirds of what he raised to the landowner. He was able to keep another half of whatever he could raise on the rocks of the mountainside, as well. In the hollers, sharecroppers like Lee practiced vertical farming, a method of clearing the mountainside to farm on what tillable land they could find. Although two sons would leave the home for years to fight in World War II, all the children were usually around to help out and learn the trade in the hope that a few of them might be able to take over one day. Lee's goal was to eventually buy the land from the owner, and keep a promise he had made to his wife Nanny years ago.

Eula doesn't recall her father as a large man, but he was strong and gentle to the touch. Lee led a charmed life, like something ripped from a Twain novel. In his younger years,

Lee sawed logs in Pike County, rolled them down to the river, and rafted them all the way to Catlettsburg, Kentucky only to catch the passenger train or bus back to Pikeville. He would use the money he made to buy barrels of sugar, meal, flour, clothes, and whiskey to take back. He grew herbs to sell, and help neighbors with their ailing pets and livestock. He also loved carving wood, and made extra money whittling together chairs to sell, along with brooms he made from corn shucks. Working with his hands was all he knew.

Lee was well past his first marriage when he courted Eula's mother. They were both grown when they first met, much different than most Appalachian affairs. According to Eula, it wasn't a reckless streak or any "hillbilly rowdiness" that kept Lee on the move, he simply hadn't found the right woman. One day while on the trail in West Virginia to sell his newest corn stock, Lee was lucky enough to quarrel with a young lady who was working him over by undercutting the price he'd set for a satchel. He took advantage of the opportunity, coyly asking her if she would like to quarrel in private sometime, because she obviously found corn prices quite the engaging conversation. She obliged.

Originally from North Carolina, and with some Cherokee ancestry, Nanny Elizabeth worked as a schoolteacher across the border in West Virginia. It was a unique role for a lady in an era when the vast majority of teachers were older and male. Eula recalls her having a "worldview of calm" but a "steely eye," stopping a child dead in his or her tracks with one glance. "You had to be one hell of a disciplinarian to be a female teacher," Eula said, and Nanny knew how to keep the classroom and her own children in line.

Together, Lee and Nanny settled on a Greasy Creek farm in 1924 and had five kids of their own, but a total of seven in the house—three girls and four boys. They sometimes housed up to eleven with cousins and family. Lee promised Nanny she would never have to work again, and although the promise was no doubt sincere, there was no way of getting around her new job taking care of a baker's dozen of her own, along with any family who decided they needed a new roof for a bit, even if the roof was much too small.

Off in the corner of their mountain farm—its size something a Great Plains farmer might instead call a "yard"—lay an honest four-room cabin. Inside its seldom-closed wooden door was a large square layout, walled off with two bedrooms, a kitchen, and a dining room. Nondescript and ordinary, the house had no couches, no indoor plumbing, and no electricity. Its pinch of modernity was represented only by its stone porch and newspaper-covered walls. The family had a cookstove in the kitchen, a coal stove or fireplace in each room, and a Bible on the dining room table. The five children shared the intimacies of daily life in a single room and on corn shuck mattresses while Lee and Nanny had the privilege of a master bedroom to themselves. An oldfangled radio served as their sole piece of entertainment. Without an appropriate idea of life outside the mountains, it was everything a mountain family desired. That is, except for the frigid winter stroll to the outhouse when nature called.

Lee and the family worked hard to keep the farm afloat. Every day as the early morning Appalachian mist crept over the mountains, he and Nanny would awake to check on their little ones and tend to the livestock before a day in the field or at the market. The family had a good lot of animals, two mules that worked hard in the field, one or two cows, and sometimes a calf, although a male calf would be the first on the selling block while the females were pampered to give birth. The family raised chickens as well, and usually a hog or two in the fall. Refrigeration had yet to arrive to Greasy, so hogs were butchered in the winter frost. The Rileys either ate the whole hog, nasty bits and all, or rendered various parts for grease, bacon, and flavoring. Eula would say that no one actually bought their food in her childhood, instead they "lived by raising supper." It was a subtle reminder to Eula today of how rapidly life had changed.[5]

For the lure of fifty cents a day, Lee would go to the market to sell his corn and any leftover cattle feed or fodder. While he made a good living, it wasn't until Eula was nine that the Rileys finally had enough chairs for everyone to eat supper together. Still, the family ate well compared to most. They kept a steady diet of the season's pickings, corn, beans, potatoes, milk, butter, bread, and pork or chicken on special occasions, depending on the quantity and quality of animals out back. Sometimes, if the clan were lucky, Nanny and Eula would bake a cake to satisfy the family's sweet tooth. When she was younger, Eula loved getting up early and helping Lee and Nanny. She would pack for market or get breakfast and lunch ready for the family. Unlike her other siblings, Eula was skilled at milking cows. She would set the bucket down and go full-bore, then strain the milk to drink, and afterward separate the cream to sell. "It was duty more than a chore," she said, a maternal instinct she carried with her from birth.

As one of the oldest children, little Eula was a motherly figure to her brothers and sisters; she helped parent and instill in her siblings the same values her parents had instilled in her. The Rileys were Baptist parishioners at Greasy Creek Regular, and despite their proud allegiance, they hardly went to church. It "certainly wasn't an every weekend thing," Eula later admitted. Life was so hard, and farm work so grueling, that sometimes they simply didn't have time or stamina for the fire and brimstone of salvation. But the church was ubiquitous in their life, a rallying point for the community to mingle and look out for one another.

It was the central tenet of mountain Christianity to look out for others, and it was a principle that deeply affected Eula. The mountain churches often held the land in religious esteem—a faith nearly equating God with Nature, and calling humanity into religious communion with the natural world. The land was as important as family. Though mountains apart, the Greasy community the Rileys lived in was incredibly intertwined, with some kinship tales going back to the pilgrims. All hardened by a rugged life, the glue of place, religion, and circumstance created a deeper community, one where neighbors didn't simply know each other, they lived and cared for each other. People knew what others were doing, they knew how they were faring, what they had, what they needed, if they were sick, if something was going on with their family, their crops, *everything*. It's true that small towns breed a certain kinship among neighbors, but it was more of a necessity in Greasy. Without knowing what the next season might hold in store, or if the mine would still be operating in the county, concerns between neighbors and family often related to life and death.

This reality was never lost on Eula. She did all she could to make life just a little easier for her neighbors. Eula remembers walking after church one night with her daddy. She asked why some houses had their cookstove going, with smoke billowing out of their chimneys, while others didn't. In the mountains, everybody had to make a fire to cook, and it was obvious which families had food and which didn't. While the Rileys always had their own food, others weren't as lucky, and often went months without staple foods such as corn, beans, and milk. Eula began taking note of different chimneys and their activity, and on days when Lee would take some corn to the mill to have it ground to make bread, Eula would steal a small bit of loaf, hide it, make some wild excuse, and take it over to houses she knew weren't cooking that night. Anything the Rileys had of abundance was fair game. Since she saw a lot of the old women take solace in smoking a pipe after a hard day's work, she would take some her daddy's green ground leaves that he grew for his own use, and without him noticing, slip it off to them at night. It was a small bit of relief she felt she could give to these women who worked hard with little reward or appreciation. Eula kept up this practice for a while until she was caught trading off milk, which was always a prized commodity. Nanny was none too happy, and brought out the switch on Eula when she found out.

Loyal Jones, famed Appalachian humorist and writer, once described Appalachian people as "independent, self-reliant, proud, neighborly, hospitable, humble, modest, patriotic, and having a good sense of humor." A fitting description, but the Rileys had all of the above and more. Whether or not they voiced it to their children often enough, they held high ambitions, even if every sign pointed to their children getting no better than their own raising.[6]

Chapter 2

"OH LORD, SHE'S ABOUT FIFTEEN MONTHS pregnant!"

Eula's granddaddy certainly had a way with words. It was mid-afternoon during a sticky Appalachian summer in 1932 and every kin of the Riley clan from up and down Pike County had descended on the Rileys' backwoods Greasy Creek home. Grandpa Ned Justice was holding court, telling tales about his daughter Nanny, most of them myths sprinkled with morsels of truth. He was struggling to put everyone at ease while he awaited the birth of his next grandchild.

Ned Riley was a snuff-dipping mountain man nearing the age of seventy who could still tell a hell of a stem-winder. He was the type of man others stopped to listen to when he spoke, his voice polished with a hint of southern aristocracy and mountain twang. Hardened by decades in the mines, he was shrewd and sociable, able to make light of a tense situation. He had seen a lot of struggle in his life, and had enough material to go all night. Laughter was the only way he knew to deal with the uncertainty of Appalachian life, and so far he was working over the rest of the family with ease.

Nanny, his youngest daughter, was in the bedroom of their small mountain home where little could be kept secret. The house was beyond modest, a four-room dwelling with a single door to keep the whispers out. With her husband Lee by her side, Nanny told her sisters to keep the family out—she didn't want them hearing her raise hell inside.

The entire holler had come out for the occasion. They hung around the yard and by the creek, talking among themselves about this and that, town gossip, any nonsense to keep from worrying about what was going on inside. Some of them came out just because everyone else seemed to be there. Some didn't even know Mrs. Riley was delivering a baby.

Eula was out in the yard too, precocious and friendly, catching crawdads in the creek with the other kids. She was all of six years old, too young to be inside the house with her mother, but just old enough to follow superstition and not talk about it. She had been through this ritual a couple of times with other families, and had picked up on the ways of childbirth. She wanted to go in and check on her mom; as the other kids would attest, Eula thought she knew everything there was to know about delivering a baby. But sensing a tinge of anxiety in the air, she decided to stay outside as the adults thought it would be best until word came. Besides, like she had told the other kids earlier, her doctoring skills were good, but not quite up to snuff yet.

Nanny had been through a tough pregnancy three years earlier during the birth of her third child, Andy, so she was keen on what to expect. She had never been to a doctor, let alone a hospital, and was perfectly happy with delivering in the comfort of her own home. She had her first two children, Eula and her older brother Buster, on this same floor, in this same room, and she wasn't one to break tradition. Luckily, she got through those births without any major help. However, because each successive pregnancy was proving to be more difficult, Nanny had decided to hire a midwife.

Midwifery was new to Appalachia, welcomed in the absence of more professional health care. Thanks to Mary Breckenridge and her Frontier Nursing Service, it simply wasn't conceivable at the time to not get some help delivering a child. Breckenridge had become acquainted with nurse-midwives in France and Great Britain during World War I and brought trained midwives from England to Kentucky. The nurses began prenatal home visits on foot or horse, and Nanny had hired one a few months back on the advice of a friend. Word had come that the midwife was on her way, but the family was worried the baby might decide to enter the world before she got there.

Eula had met the midwife earlier, a gentle woman who promised her a little brother or sister to play with. Eula, too, had wondered why "granny woman," as they called her, was so late. Eula had mentioned to her that she also wanted to become a granny woman, and the midwife had promised to tell Eula everything she knew about making medicines and taking care of others.[7]

*   *   *

The midwife finally arrived at a quarter past eight, complaining about her horse's struggle to get the buggy through the winding gravel road from Pikeville. By then, the sun had lowered past the mountainside, and the hollow was dark. Most neighbors, recognizing the weekly life-cycle ritual of keeping company for childbirth, sickness, and death, had gone home to fix supper. Only a few of the neighbors closest to the Rileys stayed to await a miracle.

Lee, with no time to quarrel, rushed the traveling midwife inside and slammed the front door behind him to make sure no one followed. Growing weary of the other kids, and impatient about her mother's health, Eula found her way inside the house, sneaking past adults and peering through the kitchen to the bedroom. In the darkness, she managed to climb on a chair and poked her head through the small window in the wall above the stove. Ned caught her out of the corner of his eye, and for reasons only a grandpa could understand, decided to let Eula be. Perhaps he thought it was about time for her to grow up, perhaps he knew Eula should be with her mom at that moment. She cricked her head up over the pane, peered down into the softly lit bedroom, and caught a glimpse of her mom being held down on both sides in the throes of pain, thrashing around a bit, hemorrhaging wildly. Eula couldn't believe her eyes.

"I can't deliver this un," the midwife cried. "I don't know why I can't get her out. There is just too much blood!"

"Well, can't you do something to stop all that bleeding?" demanded Lee, as he held on tight to his wife's hand. He had never seen so much blood, and he could feel life being torn out of Nanny as she tried to bring life to bear.

The midwife, well trained to recognize her limits, rose gently, took Lee by the hand and led him to a quiet corner of the room. Understanding his pain, she said in a quiet whisper only he could hear, "Lee, now you're gonna have to get some help or else were gonna lose her. I swear, I wish I could do something. I'm gonna try to stop the bleeding, but I can't do nothing else for Nanny."

Lee was a stoic man, hardworking till the day he died. His calloused hands and ripped forearms from a lifetime in the field and chopping timber hid a nurturing and caring soul. His family meant everything to him. Yet, when he heard those words from the midwife, he knew not to panic; it simply wasn't going to change anything to yell.

Greasy Creek, like most rural outposts, had few options for care or services, especially for medical care in calamitous situations. The Rileys knew that as a last resort, an expensive option was to go to Pikeville or Prestonsburg for a real doctor. However, without a car or a good horse, there was simply no way of getting the word out of the mountains.

Lee backed away from the midwife, and softly told everyone to keep praying. He made his way out to the yard to collect his thoughts. Eula jumped down and snuck back out to see where he was going. As he stared off into the night sky, his mind racing with doubt and fear, he knew he had to act fast, but short of running twenty miles to Pikeville, there wasn't much he could do himself. He was never keen on asking neighbors for help, always his own man who left his childhood home early in life to take care of his family. But he understood the situation was too dire to rely on fate. Each holler had its own set of elders, men who other men in town admired and relied upon during hard times. Luckily, that small hollow on Upper Greasy had a little grocery store, and Lee figured the store manager, Arthur, had connections in town. It was the only choice he had left.

Without saying much to anyone, and with Eula and other neighbors watching, Lee quietly ran off through the mouth of the holler, and nervously headed down to the store. It was late, but he was hoping he could catch Arthur right before he headed home for the night. In fact, Lee had hoped that Arthur might have closed up shop early to head to the Riley house to witness the birth himself.

Lee came up sweating to the tiny country store, watching for any signs of life, and yelled out. The store had been there, in Arthur's family name, for some time. With a broken old Coke sign and sagging porch out front, the Greasy Creek Mini-mart was a kind of gathering place to tell tales, talk politics, and buy this and that for the house and family. The lights were off, but as Lee tried the door, he was immediately greeted on the other side by a familiar face.

"Arthur! Thank Jesus I caught you before you left!"

"Son, what are you doing here? Shouldn't you be holding a new baby by now?" Arthur was a quiet, but serious, old man. The type of man who did his best to stay out of everyone's business, but couldn't help but learn about everyone's business. He was the town elder with whom everyone felt they could share their deepest secrets, knowing he wouldn't repeat them to anyone. He also had a brand new Model A Ford, perfect for getting in and out of Greasy quickly.

"I don't know Arthur, but it ain't good. The midwife says she can't do nothing and poor Nanny is just bleeding all over the damn place. I ain't never asked you for nothing free, but I need your help, Arthur. I need ya to go down to Pikeville and get us a real doctor or nurse or someone to help get the baby out."

Arthur couldn't ignore the desperation in Lee's voice, and he adored the Rileys, especially young Eula who would always come in asking if she could work the register.

"Oh, hell, that's just terrible. I wish I could Lee, but . . . you know, I know that Dr. Scott, he's a good doctor and I'm sure he'd help," Arthur said, "but I tell you, I can't get him to come all the way out to Greasy unless you pay him. Honest to God's truth. I don't know how much it'll cost, but them doctors won't come all the way out here this late unless you pay them about twenty dollars or more."

Greasy Creek was fifteen miles through a winding road to Pikeville, home to the closest hospital. A group of pioneering and influential Eastern Kentuckians built the first hospital in the region—Pikeville Methodist—which admitted its first patient on Christmas Day, 1924. It had come to be known throughout the mountains as "the house of hope and healing." At the time, Pikeville boasted a population of four thousand, far from the bustling city Lee thought it to be, but it was the big city to everyone in the mountain hollers. Besides, they had real doctors. Twenty dollars was a fortune for a sharecropper who was lucky to make fifty cents a day. Lee knew he had to give up whatever savings he had; as the midwife told him, his wife and newborn baby's lives depended on it.[8]

"Look, Arthur, you know we live 'bout as simple as it gets. I ain't got no hard money but a five-dollar bill I kept from last year's market . . . I'll tell you what, I got a healthy young milk cow and a couple hogs I can give you if you can pay the doctor what he needs. If you need more, I may have a mule I can give you, too."

Arthur stood in shock, half expecting them to just go to the house and pray for a peaceful resolution. While it was common for people in the mountains to barter in real, live things instead of money, Arthur couldn't believe Lee was ready to give up nearly all his livestock. Arthur certainly didn't want to take anything from the Rileys, especially in a moment like this, but bringing a city doctor out would cost a fortune he wasn't ready to bear himself either. The Depression took them all prisoners.

Arthur, his voice cracking on every word, replied, "Bring me the cow and a hog in the morning and we'll be square. I'll fire the truck up and head into town right now."

As they both left the store, there was no misunderstanding the consequences and urgency of the night. This was certainly out of character for Lee, and Arthur no doubt respected the trust placed in him. Lee rushed back up the holler to the house, as he didn't want to spare a moment away from his ailing wife. He made sure to stop right before he made it home to wipe the sweat from his brow and keep his appearance one of control. At the house, he broke his hustle to a stroll, saw Eula and picked her up, kissed her forehead, and brought her inside with him. Buster was outside catching fireflies and the rest of the family was left looking for indications of relief on Lee's face.

Grandpa Ned was fresh out of tales, struggling to keep everyone's mind off Nanny and the baby. Lee sauntered back into the room, didn't tell anyone about the milk cow and hog, or about Arthur, and walked straight past the family to the bedside. Nanny was quiet as the night, solemn and staring into Lee's eyes. She hadn't spoken to anyone, and with her years of strength from being a mountain mother, she knew complaining wasn't going to help the situation. She was in so much pain, she couldn't yell anyway.

Lee looked over his shoulder and saw Eula and Grandpa enter the room. Eula had quarreled so much with Grandpa that he knew none of his stories would keep her outside and entertained. Lee and Nanny knew Eula shouldn't be inside, seeing the blood and pain, but they didn't know what was going to happen. Lee didn't know if Arthur could even convince the doctor to show up. Would he even care about a mountain woman dying in childbirth? They both didn't want Eula to miss what they were realizing might be their last moments together.

Another hour passed and the moon and the mountains stood quietly. There were a few neighbors still lolling around, the kids all asleep, too tired to keep playing. The town's lay minister joined the family gathering, praying and waiting for the bleeding to stop and the baby to be born. Eula slowly walked over to hold her mother's hand. As her only biological daughter, they shared a unique relationship and closeness.

Suddenly, nearly four hours after Nanny had gone into labor, a gentle roar was heard coming from the road outside. As they ran to the yard, the headlight beams of a black Model A Ford jumped up and down, blinding everyone in its path. The good doctor from Pikeville had arrived.

"Dr. Scott!" Lee hollered as he ran to the car door to extend a warm welcome. "Dr. Scott, welcome to the Joe Bonner holler of Upper Greasy. Come on in; my wife's in the bedroom and she's been waiting."

*   *   *

The doctor was too late to save the child. Lacking any assistance or the tools he had in Pikeville, Dr. Scott delivered a stillborn who had likely died from intense internal bleeding. He later diagnosed Nanny with varicose veins and blamed them for bursting between every contraction, the blood too much for the small infant to handle.

Eula sat there, quiet and still, watching the entire event unfold. Nanny had lost so much blood the doctor told Lee that without a transfusion, he didn't know how long she had to live. His only suggestion was to give her as much water as possible and pray for her health.

The next day neighbors and family built a small coffin to bury the child. With a somber service and a quiet ballad by the local Baptist choir, Eula's newest sibling was laid to rest in the mountains she didn't even get to know. Though Eula had seen death and was surrounded by it daily, a guilt that would last a lifetime was borne out of her feelings of helplessness that night. She was angry her mother had to experience such reckless childbearing, and angry that there was no help for her family until too late.

Chapter 3

NANNY'S BATTLE THROUGH A LARGELY UNATTENDED childbirth and its mortal ambiguity was an all-too-common occurrence in the community. Her recovery after her failed pregnancy was a testament to her perseverance. The Rileys and everyone in the hollers of the mountains were no strangers to death; instead, they understood unexpected passings as a simple reality. Many folks even formed a stale demeanor in reaction to news of the departed.

By age nine, Eula had seen school friends, play friends, and elders pass away from what, in retrospect, she knew a simple, intuitive sense of well-being could have prevented. She once had a close neighbor who fell through their home stairs, lodging a nail through her foot. Without proper care for the wound, she died weeks later, leaving behind five children. After witnessing so many deaths so young, Eula quickly learned not to become too intimate with the debility of emotions she faced losing loved ones. Whether from accidents, childbirth, mining, feuding, politics, or the unknowable and undetectable specter of disease, death and poverty was all around, and its wrath was indiscriminate.

The Rileys themselves didn't have much in terms of medicine; in fact, they lacked most material things considered necessities today. Instead of shampoo, the children washed their hair with soap and after some time, when soap made their hair dull, they began using baking soda as a substitute. The baking soda made their hair shine "like a doll's hair" and would just fluff it right out. Eula absolutely loved her resulting hairstyle. It would be her signature for years to come. She enjoyed using baking soda so much she would do the hair of her little brothers and sisters like that too, a whole "clan of Rileys with afros," she joked. They learned to get by with nothing, and with baking soda being five cents a box, it was cheap enough to use as an all-purpose cleanser. They used it to brush their teeth and anytime something, or someone, needed a good scrubbing. They also used it in baking to help dough rise.

The day Clorox was introduced was significant for mountain people. Spending too much time playing in the dirty creeks on the mountainsides gave many children sores on their legs and feet. Eula remembered "kids that had so many sores it sometimes looked like their ears and nose were gonna come off" and she claimed she could still sees scars on those in Greasy who were her age. Potable well water was hard to come by then, and people added a drop or two of Clorox to well water; this method, something seen as a survival tactic to those outside Appalachia, would become a staple for purifying creek water. Eventually, the family started using a little Clorox in the bath, to wash dishes, and in the summer, Eula and the other kids would dam up the creek and bathe in the water with a little added Clorox, knowing they would be safe from lesions and scars.[9]

As a family, the Rileys adopted simple health practices, but these were by no means uniform among their neighbors. Everyone in the community had their own home medicine or ways of curing they believed were healthy or hygienic. There were so-called doctors, but they didn't have much in the way of medicine; instead, they practiced a trade called "polyfoxing," the art of homemade mountain medicine.

The polyfoxer was the holler's doctor, and something of an elder sage in the community. Some of them claimed to cure cancer, some could make your ears smaller, rid your face of freckles, or make the opposite sex consider your musk an aphrodisiac. They had a concoction for any affliction. These wizards would use everything from foxglove—a powerful diuretic—to herbs, roots, and barks in liquid form, or some combination of which was always downright unpalatable. To some of the polyfoxers, iron metal was a literal vitamin, and they would advise a patient to eat a nail for 'blood building.' Sometimes, mostly for the children, the doctor would drive the nail into an apple for a couple of days under the assumption that when the apple was eaten, a patient would receive the requisite iron boost. Often the medicinal artists would suggest patients eat carrots or wild mushrooms to heal ailments, vegetables foreign to an Appalachian diet. They explained the origin of disease from either a naturalistic sphere, or more often, a "magico-religious" domain.[10]

Some knowledgeable city doctors had tried reaching out to educate these communities, but they never could overcome the stigma, or trump the respect polyfoxers had accrued with their concoctions. In the hollers throughout Pike and Floyd Counties, there were polyfoxing prescriptions from snakeroot and poplar "teas" for diarrhea and vomiting when it was obvious to Pikeville or Prestonsburg doctors that these symptoms were simply a result of bad drinking water. In a sense, mountain people distrusted "big city" doctors because of a "fear of authority" as Eula would say, an authority that had not treated their people with respect over the years. Instead, many viewed the concoctions as something tangible—medicine as real as the earth in their fingernails. It was common for most

East Kentuckians to believe in medicines from natural fauna like bark and root because it was from the land, one of the few constants in their lives.

While mountain people had a certain kinship with the land, and certainly looked to nature to bring stasis to their lives, Nanny learned about basic health during her days teaching in West Virginia, and was positive things such as Epson salts, teas made from peach tree bark skin, and sassafras roots were not what they were using in Pikeville to make people better. She also noticed this naturalist medicinal tradition leaving a mark on the people, physical and physiological, one that she didn't find in the coal towns. Years later, Eula would recall the vast number of crippled folks with broken bodies because a broken arm in their youth only warranted a tablet wrapped with a bit of rope, or a bad cut that required some soot from the chimney, dug into the scar itself, to heal.

Eula blames the deep black mark stretching across her brother Troy's forearm to the "wise advice and counsel" of a Greasy Creek polyfoxer treating a cut from a schoolyard fight. Since dental care was nonexistent, pains like toothaches and cavities were no cause for concern. People used to tell others to keep whiskey on a tooth to ease the pain. It certainly would do the trick, but as Eula remembers, it was probably getting them just drunk enough to forget it was there in the first place.

Sadly, medical education would come slowly to the people of Greasy Creek. Almost everyone from the hollers in the early twentieth century can recall a story of using a homemade, oftentimes horrific, mountain concoction. Eula remembers once at the age of seven getting a scathing sore throat, or "croupy" as they called it, and found it a strain to breathe. Nanny took her to a local doctor who lived by his lonesome in a cabin up the holler from their home. His house was full of witchdoctor-like medical gadgets and remedies. While his diagnosis of bronchitis was spot on, his methods of healing were disturbing. Eula remembers sitting on his lap while he heated a teaspoon of kerosene poured from a Mason jar, and kindly topped it off with a little sugar for taste. Eula knew this was all nonsense. She remembers thinking "all these people just want to be taken care of when they're sick, and they're willing to listen and do anything to make it better." Eula covered her eyes, scrunched her nose, and swallowed her medicine like any well-mannered child would at the doctor's office. To everyone's surprise, the soreness actually subsided a few days later. While the doctor believed he had cured her, Nanny was certain ingesting kerosene was never a wise choice. The short-lived healthiness would give way to typhoid soon, which made all of young Eula's locks fall out. She thought she was going to die a bald nine-year-old. But weeks later she recovered, luckily this time without the help of any so-called doctors.[11]

Chapter 4

Bʏ 1935, Eᴜʟᴀ ᴡᴀs ʜᴀʀᴅ ᴀᴛ ᴡᴏʀᴋ ɪɴ ᴛʜᴇ ꜰɪᴇʟᴅ during the dense Appalachian heat. Her only solace was in the early-afternoon mountain canopy. But life wasn't all work and no play. Eula and her siblings found creative ways to pass time and have a little fun. Although they had few, if any, toys, they played with their ingenuity. The kids gathered and used everything mountain life offered.

They would follow horses that often lost a shoe traversing through winding back roads. The kids would pick up the horseshoes and fashion a homemade set to toss, bet, and play. They created homemade slingshots to take aim at partridges and would dig out sassafras roots, which they called "rosy," to use as rope for tugs-of-war. With her brothers, Eula loved playing jacks, which they called "jackstone," and since they couldn't afford a ready-made set, they created a homemade version equipped with nails or scrap metal found near the mines. Instead of tossing a ball in the air, sometimes they would catch a grasshopper, and throw the poor thing up in the air while reaching for jacks.

Although a tomboy at heart, Eula got tired at times of

playing with the boys and would instead play with her closest sister Lacy. Eula and Lacy would act out a playhouse with other girls in the holler, and do their own make-believe cooking, even when many of them actually cooked at home for the family. Instead of plastic play sets, the girls would start by patting together mud patties—into cupcakes, cakes, or loaves of bread—and then let them bake in the hot Appalachian sun until they hardened like bricks. They would set up an afternoon tea with those mud cakes and act as the southern aristocrats did on the radio.

Their industriousness came with some treacherous drawbacks. Once in the summer of 1936, Eula's older brothers Buster and Arthur were working together to construct a wagon to haul odds and ends around. Buster was the creative one, often directing the other siblings to be his factory workers—a trait that would prove to be prescient. Buster built all kinds of toys, baseballs and bats, horseshoe sets, and eventually a fully functional wagon. First, he felled a small tree, sawed the log into four round pieces, made two smaller front wheels, two larger ones at the back, and connected them with a washtub, a mattress, or whatever they could find on top. They'd take the rest of the wood, make a fire, get a piece of scrap metal white-hot in the flame, and burn a hole in the middle of the wheel. He called himself the "Henry Ford of the holler," and he eventually made a little business making wagons for any kid that could afford one.[12]

Eula saw the boys dragging that little wagon up and down the holler, hauling herbs, wood, coal, and even people who wanted a joyride.

"Buster, why don't ya make one of those wagons for us girls so we can get up and around too?" she asked. Eula wanted to haul those mud cakes around Greasy for sale.

After a bit of haggling and a guilt trip, Buster finally gave in to his little sister and they set out to make Eula a wagon of her own. They spent all day gathering wood and carving wheels with an assembly line of holler girls. By night, they were almost finished and Buster let Eula make the final cut to a piece of wood fastening the tongue to pull the wagon. Surrounded by excited little girls in muddied dresses, Buster held the piece down flat across a wooden stump, Eula took the axe back far as she could, and let her have it. As she went to chop the wood, with all the might she could muster, she slammed the axe down and damn near chopped off Buster's finger.

"Oh Lord, I thought I might have killed him!" she said. The fear of God ran through her as she shrieked, dropped the axe, and ran off into the woods. The other girls ran off in various directions while Buster sat stunned, staring at his mangled hand. Running seemed like the best thing to do for Eula and while she may not have killed him, she was in for a whooping. As she said later, "Mountain folks don't heal from those types of injuries. They just lose a finger."

Eula ran up a hillside and cried in the mountain thicket for an hour before getting up the nerve to start back. Sheepishly, she hollered every ten steps at Buster in the hope that he was still breathing. It was dark out, but Buster finally appeared, cold faced and still stunned, clutching his hand on which he had devised a homemade splint of small branches and sassafras roots.

"Sis, where the hell you run off to? Look, I ain't gonna tell on ya . . . you couldn't help it. You sure ain't do it on purpose . . . right?"

"You swear you won't tell?"

"Yeah, I swear, now follow my lead when we head on in the house."

The wound was in dire need of stitching. His finger was dangling off, being held on by only the makeshift cast and his knuckle.

As they entered the house, Buster was ready with a tale of

his own clumsiness. Out of sheer horror, Nanny didn't question either of them and quickly reached for a bottle of turpentine oil to heal the wound. Turpentine had worked in calamitous situations before—earaches, cuts, and swelling—but it was none too pleasurable to have applied. She uncorked the bottle and poured a bit on the wound as Buster cursed and wailed from the sting. Nanny yelled at Eula to find a bandage and she hurriedly undid some black electrical tape from a broken porch lamp. Nanny wrapped up the dangling finger, and said a little prayer that the finger would heal back up. Eula and Buster shared a laugh at the look of the finger, and two weeks later Buster finished the wagon for his kid sister.

*   *   *

In the weeks after the finger incident, Nanny began earnestly worrying that Eula was spending too much time loafing around the holler up to no good when she needed to spend more time becoming a proper lady. She desperately yearned to enroll the children in Greasy Middle School, but the school was a good hour and half walk out of the holler. Rural schools in Kentucky, and most of the country, lacked school buses even though they needed them the most.

Luckily for the children, the demands of the farm were slowing down a bit as Lee employed the help of laid-off coal workers, a larger plow, and a new mule. They eventually decided that not all the children needed to help at the farm, and not all of them could become farmers anyway, so it was the right time to send them off.

The Rileys kept the farm, but moved out of the house and into a trailer at the mouth of the holler—nearly on the side of US 23. From there it was only about a thirty-minute stroll to school every day, and much closer to the market for Lee to barter. The decision was made for some of the children to start school at the same time, irrespective of age or class level. The children who were old enough to go spent the summer getting ready—Buster at twelve, Eula at nine, and Cousin Lacy at eight. Lee held Jack and Arthur back to work the farm, deciding that schooling wasn't going to get the eldest any further in life.

The entire summer was wrought with anticipation. A new home, new surroundings, and an opportunity for Eula to make something of herself. At the time, the mines were slowing down, and some company towns had simply closed up. Eula knew she needed a good education even if most of women became hired help or worked as assembly line scraps—a future she was still uncertain she could escape.

On Saturday nights the summer before school, Eula and the family listened to the Grand Ole Opry, news reports from distant lands, or even took the occasional trip to Pikeville where she heard and saw a life of luxury and wealth too distant to be her own. She knew there had to be more to life than work, work, work, marriage, children, death, and burial—but she didn't know how to find it. "I dreamed a lot, oh Lord, I always wanted to be somebody," she later recalled with a tinge of desperation. "I didn't want to be trapped forever and not have nothing, and see so many others around me not have nothing. I wanted to live like you read about in the magazines and on the radio, and I wanted everyone here up the holler to have that life. I always wanted to reach as far as I could from where I was—I just didn't know how to get there."[13]

In a sticky August in 1936, Eula began her formal education at Greasy Middle School just up the holler from their new home. She was so excited to break the house and yard routine that she couldn't "keep from staying asleep."

The children proudly and promptly walked to school every day at seven thirty a.m. despite rain, snow, sleet, or cold. If they were breathing, they were walking. Thirty minutes later, they would saunter up toward a worn-out wooden house looking like nothing more than an old Appalachian barn. The schoolhouse was painted white like a church and had a small attempt at a vegetable garden in the front. It sat at the base of a steep sloping mountainside; it had a wide, plush yard and poplars hanging from the mountains over the roof. There was a tiny creek slithering behind the outhouse and a couple of picnic tables near a swing set. It was idyllic, and to Eula, it looked like something out of a movie.

The school had two rooms, a large classroom and a smaller room to the side. Both were used for instruction and both were teeming with kids ages seven to fifteen. With not much more than a single chalkboard, desks, and a wood-burning stove, the children were exposed to a world of wonder and complexity through daily teachings on science, math, grammar, geography, and history. They were sturdy, keen youth who rarely raised a disciplinary problem. Unlike modern school experiences, the mountain kids seemed eager to be there, if not to learn, to simply be out of the house.[14]

Their teacher for the first few years was a modern young man named Greenbriar Conn who hailed from Central Kentucky's stately horse country. The name was a bit foreign, so the kids called him "Green Conn" for short. While the mountains region was a foreign land to Green, he was drawn to the wilderness of Eastern Kentucky on the idealism that draws many to the profession—to teach those who would otherwise never be taught. Green quickly learned that a rural teacher worked without hierarchy, and also served as both principal and janitor. Green engendered a unique admiration from the school kids. They paid attention in class. They asked questions. They cleaned up after themselves. They even showed deference in their immaturity, agreeing among themselves that fights were strictly waged after school and off school grounds. They understood school as a privilege, far different than the children he was used to lecturing in Lexington.

When the three Riley children first started, they raised

enrollment by a grand ten percent. They had already known most of the other kids through church or playing near the creeks, while they met others for the first time. Eula was quick to make friends and wasted no time in introducing herself to each student on the first day. She subsequently introduced her siblings to each student as well.

Because of her wit, Eula was able to jump to the second grade. In fact, her siblings showed the same promise, allowing the entire Riley clan to join in either the first or second grades. While they were beginning in different levels, they all were taught in the same room with kids through the sixth grade.

Eula found an immediate inclination to study those subjects most practical to her daily life—arithmetic, science, agriculture, and most of all, health. With the numerous deaths, funerals, and diseases folks in Eastern Kentucky experienced, she was determined to understand the "right way to live." She recalled, "I loved health class because back before school you only learn what you see and hear about in the holler, things like cover your mouth, don't spit on floor, and only drink Cloroxed creek water." Sadly, even with their understanding of basic health care, six children from Greasy Middle, including her brother Buster, soon developed whooping cough. State school administrators from Frankfort deemed it unsafe for the children to attend school amid fears of spreading the vile disease to other Appalachian families, especially considering that most towns were desperate for a healthy workforce.

Eventually, every one of the children under the Riley roof would get the cough, but calling it a cough was an understatement. The infection caused the children to breathe in deep, and then convulse in a rage of coarse and beastly coughs, nosebleeds, and rounds of "whooping" and vomiting. The cough killed quite a few children in the holler that year. Eula would lose two of her new friends and school did not resume until July of the next year. It was a crushing disappointment for Eula, but one stemming from her environment that she had been used to dealing with.[15]

The county superintendent was convinced the cough resulted from cold classrooms. When school finally started, a new potbelly heating stove helped make the winters bearable in the schoolroom. Some kids would sit away, thinking it was too close to the front of the classroom. Eula, however, would "rush in on the first day and stake claim on a seat close to the heater," so she could pay attention without shivering and in hopes of never catching the cough again.

After her first three years, Eula was nearly ready for high school, an amazing feat by any generation's standards. Around that time, the mountain people first learned about the tragedy that befell the country at Pearl Harbor in the Hawaiian Islands. "Oh Lord," Eula remembered, "it was like hell was about to descend on the country. We were so scared." Though their radios had hardly enough battery power to last, they would put them on a coal shovel and set them on a grate to charge them up a bit to listen. Green knew of the consequence of the attack and wanted to teach the kids about what was happening, knowing that some of the older boys, and perhaps their parents, would be off to war themselves soon. Recognizing the cultural history of violence plaguing the region since the Civil War, Green taught the children that no generation should inherit the quarrels of their father's generation. He taught the children to be constructive and helped them develop a desire to build and shape their lives and the direction of the community, a sentiment that affected Eula deeply.

He drew a map on the chalkboard and began to sketch through the early reasoning for German aggression. Eula said, "It was terrifying, and so scary, 'cause you thought the war might come to the mountains." When Germany invaded France, Poland, and Italy, the children feared what it meant for them. With boys leaving for war every day, the news of battles in far-off lands shook many folks from their once calm hamlet. "We didn't know better, and sometimes we thought we might even be attacked in Floyd County. Even when we heard planes, we would get scared of enemy planes over the mountains."[16]

However, the beginning of the Second World War did bring an increase in coal production. Lee's farm was producing more corn than ever. In light of the newfound economic optimism, Lee and Nanny were scared that all their boys would have to go off to war, and soon they did. Buster, who was closest to Eula, and Arthur were the first to fight. In a late night good-bye, the family circled around outside the house and said a prayer before the brothers went off to war. Silently, Eula resented the fact they had to go while the children of the privileged in town would be spared.

Eula stayed up late at night in the weeks after, wondering what her brothers were witnessing and whether they would see battle. Despite the constant fear it placed on the Rileys, the family had a deep and abiding faith in the country's leadership.

"We thought FDR was the greatest thing on earth. Great man and hero," Eula said. With him at the helm, they knew everything would be resolved and the war would come to an end soon. Little did Eula know but she was soon to play a small role in the fight herself.[17]

Chapter 5

THE YEAR 1942 WAS AN IMPORTANT ONE. AMERICAN men and their allies battled ferociously across Europe against the great evil of Nazism, the Manhattan Project was launched, and *Casablanca* opened for its debut screening at a New York theater. Although it would seem a world away, that fall would also mark Eula's graduation from the eighth grade in only four years. Her graduating class consisted of twelve other students—six boys and six girls. It was one of the proudest days of her life and gave her recognition for achieving something not many in her world could stake claim to accomplishing. Only her cousin Lacy and one of her brothers, Frank, would eventually finish because her other brothers were sent off to war.

Eula still made time for having fun and even had a boyfriend, Jesse, when she graduated. She would later lament of that difficult time in her life, "If there was any happiness in my life at that point it was with him." He was like her in many ways, outgoing, attractive, and a dreamer. Jesse wanted to explore the world outside the chambered mountains. He was one of the few people Eula trusted and cared for, and he gave her no reason to doubt him. Between strict parents and the end of schooling, she had one glimmer of positivity, but due to wars bigger than the mountains, it wouldn't last long.

Since the county still couldn't afford school buses, and with the lack of a high school nearby, there was little opportunity for education beyond the eighth grade. She was fourteen and graduation would be the end of her studies. Not many women had good paying work at the time outside of the occasional service job at the local diner or the sewing factories far outside of Floyd County. Some of the graduating students had relatives in different places and many of the women found it lucrative to travel far and wide to be servants in richer homes.

One of her brothers, Andy, joined the Civilian Conservation Corps created by President Franklin D. Roosevelt during the Depression. The CCC, as it was known, was a New Deal public work relief program to help diminish high unemployment and give a younger class of workers vocational training in construction and conservation. It was a novel idea, employing unmarried men ages seventeen to twenty-three and tackling the nation's lost productivity with jobs ranging from erosion control to building bridges.

Andy learned to drive large trucks in Utah, a faraway rustic land bearing little resemblance to the mountains back home. He didn't jaunt across the country simply for his own adventure; part of the stipulation to work for the CCC was that the men had to send twenty-five dollars of their thirty-dollar monthly check back home to family. Aside from a chipper morale and increased employability, Andy gained the distinct dignity of a son giving his family financial support, something in which he took immense pride.[18]

Eula knew she couldn't access those kinds of adventures even though she was convinced a man or a woman could do the job just the same. She contemplated a different journey, one where she could make a difference in a world seeming "only to give the men a chance." With more school out of the picture, she hatched two schemes to "be somebody."

The first was to join the clergy. While the Rileys believed in God and Jesus with all their might, Eula thought the church at the time, "promised too much to a congregation just stock full of poor people." It was a logical outlet to fix the wrongs she saw in her community, but she was discouraged from getting too involved as the church was often seen as "less about salvation and more about politics." Corrupt local politicians and their graft often seeped into the Lord's home in clear view. Eula knew that when the preacher spoke about helping neighbors, he didn't mean rounding up votes for the county judge. Lee and Nanny shied away from the rampant infighting among denominations, telling their children to simply live a life serving the Lord, because "the Lord isn't gonna have one corner for the Free Wills, another for the Catholics, and a separate one for Baptists in heaven like they'd want you to believe." Besides, Eula knew she had "more faith than any of them anyhow."[19]

The second option Eula considered was to join the military. With the war raging abroad and men leaving daily to fight the villains in Europe and Asia, it seemed like the perfect outlet for an adventure. She figured with a simple haircut and a name change from Eula to good-ole-boy Euler, nobody would know the difference. Stories had trickled into the mountains about the fight and the atrocities going on in distant lands, and Eula felt a patriotic duty to help stand and fight for her country. Luckily, the decision would be an easy one to make as the fight came around to find her.

One balmy afternoon while Eula was bent over in the hot sun picking corn, a neighbor came up sweating and hollering to Eula and her brother Buster, desperate to get their attention. "Military recruiters," he said, knowing of their yearning for adventure, "are at the mouth of the holler and looking for soldiers and factory workers to send out tonight!"

Appalachians, though removed from the lofty politics of America, have given more than their fair share of sons and daughters to the cause of liberty. With the war in full swing, Eula, only fourteen at the time, knew it was as good an opportunity as ever to join the fight. She didn't hesitate.[20]

Eula ran into the house. "Momma, Daddy, I'm heading off to the war to see what I can do." Her parents shrugged, she remembers, and didn't think much of it. If she could get a good-paying factory job and bring some money back like Andy that would be just great. They knew the military would take care of her wherever they decided to send her, but only if she could convince the government she was of age. Eula hurriedly packed up her stuff and hustled up the holler with Buster. She had no idea what factory life would be like, but she smelled adventure and she knew she had to take it.

They spiritedly ran to the mouth of the holler along the gravel road, where they found a recruiting stand set up in front of a camouflaged military bus at the side of the interstate. Eula studiously grabbed a clipboard and filled out all the relevant information for her and her brother. They waited a few moments in line until a young, uniformed man looked over at Eula. Reading the excitement in her eyes, he told her, "Well, you look raring to go! Ya ever worked in a factory before?"

"Sure have," Eula proclaimed without hesitation.

"Really . . . well, you'll do just fine helping the war effort. Say, how old are you again?"

Eula stammered for a moment. She had lied on the application sheet, and though she was without even a Social Security number, she naïvely believed they wouldn't ask too many questions. Eula looked over at Buster, then turned back to the young officer and coyly replied, "Eighteen, just graduated, and ready to help defeat them Nazis!"

Buster chuckled under his breath, but that little fib was enough to send her to battle—no haircut or name change necessary. A half hour later, Eula and Buster were seated on a hot bus with windows open, heading north. However, in the rush and excitement, they forgot to even ask where they would end up.[21]

The bus made a quick stop in West Virginia to shuffle everyone onto a sleeper-train continuing to New York. With some time to kill in a new town, the two decided to explore Williamson, a thriving coal town marking the Kentucky-West Virginia border. The two were so amused by their new surroundings—eating hot dogs and window-shopping on Main Street—that they almost missed the train.

After an overnight train trip, the first of their lives, they arrived at a deployment station and canning factory in Ontario, New York, just outside of Rochester. The military issued them a room in a trailer, three meals a day, and industrial strength clothes to wear. Nearly as soon as they arrived, they were separated. Buster went to a basic training facility and Eula to a canning and munitions factory. It would be the last time Eula and Buster would enjoy each other's company for nearly a decade.[22]

The romantic appeal of the trip faded quickly. Demand for canned food skyrocketed with the war because it provided large quantities of cheap energy for the millions of soldiers abroad. While societies have been preserving and salting foods for ages, the art of canning had its origin in military campaigns dating back to Napoleon. The American military's appetite was large—nearly 70 percent of foodstuffs eaten by American soldiers would be produced from these factories.[23]

Canning fruits and food for war proved to be grueling work. The workers processed beets and potatoes by first dehydrating them and then packaging them with metal casing for shipment overseas. Eula's role was to stand at a conveyor belt where round cans would come by under a beltline shooting out potatoes every second. Another machine would grab the can and shake it to settle the contents until it was filled to the brim with mealy potatoes.

It was a fascinating process, Eula thought, but it was not equally as mesmerizing to spend an entire day watching over the machine. Her sole responsibility was to ensure the machine's proper functioning, while also placing a seal on each can that was sufficiently full. On a second shift, she would transfer to the beginning of the process where potatoes were pushed through a peeler. Often, however, the peeler didn't go deep enough to get the distasteful black spots out of the potatoes. Eula remembered that the floor supervisor, who was openly suspicious of the Appalachians, would walk up and down the platform with a "stern look and a fierce mouth." If a worker's trough wasn't full or her potatoes clear of spots, she would dress down the worker in front of everyone. She was quick to write up the "hillbillies," but was judicious in disregarding anyone's physical well-being.

Eula and the others were forced to work thirteen-hour days with little rest, and while the effort was all for the good of the country, it was breaking their backs. Eula may have fancied herself as strong as "Rosie the Riveter," but at only fourteen, and on a few hours of sleep a night, Eula's young body was hardly making it through the day.[24]

After three weeks, Eula, always personable and looking out for others, began to make friends with whom she could commiserate. She learned the workers there had been complaining all year about the squalid conditions and lack of pay. When the recruiter came to Greasy, the understanding was that transportation and lodging would be free until their first payday. However, when the paycheck finally came around, everything was held out in charges for their travel. No one was receiving their full share of money, especially the new recruits, and instead the workers were being treated like indentured servants.[25]

Eula couldn't believe that workers who had been there a year or more were doing nothing about the situation. With the floor manager's incensed demeanor, she knew it couldn't last. "I took a page out of the union playbook back home and decided to organize," she said. She spoke to some older folks she knew and, with the help of others, held a secret meeting to take a tally of where people stood. Many simply dismissed Eula as a young girl who didn't know better, but others were so mad they were willing to listen to anyone. Eula teamed up with a few older Appalachian women from Tennessee and pushed them to discuss what they could do, and whether or not they could demand some rights.

The response was overwhelming and the decision made. The first strike at the Ontario Canning War Factory would begin at six a.m. and Eula was as giddy as she was anxious. The group devised a tentative plan to "prevent anyone from entering the factory or doing their work until someone from management agreed to meet about the work and payment situation." The strategy was to leverage the frenetic pace they were producing for the front lines by shutting down productivity completely.

The next morning, Eula was out front in locked arms persuading uncertain coworkers to join the cause. She was going to make sure they got paid for the work they were doing, but what she didn't know was that striking the government was significantly different than coal strikes back home. The federal government in times of war didn't have to play nice to picketers.[26]

Within an hour, police came with riot gear and billy clubs, beating anybody who came after them. "It was scary as hell, and electrifying," Eula recalled. She grabbed a long-necked milk bottle out of fear, but without any intent or know-how on how to use it to defend herself. The police had men backed against a wall, frisking them and slapping their faces. Eula managed to get to the back of the ruckus unhurt, but evasion lasted only a short time. She was soon arrested, along with many others who were at the front of the line. The nascent strike had lasted only two hours, and by eight a.m., the factory reopened for operation with assembly line holdouts, and those who exchanged arrest for returning to work.

At the station, police charged Eula with "insinuating a riot"; she was told the charge could result in significant jail time. For a young lady from the mountains, handcuffed and fingerprinted, and who had never truly interacted with a policeman—it was beyond frightening. But she managed to hold together her demeanor and when asked how old she was, she replied as she had for the previous two months, "Eighteen and not a day older!"

One of the officers cocked his head and grinned as he asked, "Oh, is that so? I have a fifteen-year-old at home and I bet you're not a day older than her." She was speechless; her petulant attitude finally outdid her deceiving looks.

Just as he was finished writing up her notice for organizing a strike and riot, he stopped and put his pen down, aware of the absurdity of the situation. "You know what, I don't believe you. In fact, I don't know how the hell you got here. I'm not gonna lie, it's pretty damn impressive, but I'm gonna have to call your parents."

"You can try, sir, but in the mountains where I'm from, there ain't no number to dial."

The officer, half grinning, ripped up the arrest paper and made sure Eula was on the next train back to Pikeville. Eula was relieved as many of the others served time or were immediately sent to other factories where their solitude left them less likely to agitate. Her age actually came in handy, but she couldn't remember which was more frightening—the arrest or the thought of facing the switch when Nanny and Lee found out what had happened.[27]

Chapter 6

IN *The American Songbag,* CARL SANDBURG SUGGESTS THE "she" in *She'll Be Coming 'Round the Mountain* is a reference to famed labor organizer Mother Jones and her travels to mountain coal mining camps. The song, one of many great American folk ballads, was often used during union rallies to signal the vitality of the movement and its intrepid leader. While mostly content with a life of obscurity, the mountain people were getting their first taste of nationwide drama as Appalachia served as the first major southern breeding ground for unionization rallies. With coal operators staunchly and oftentimes violently in opposition, Mother Jones played a vital role in encouraging miners to look toward brotherhood in the face of industrial exploitation.

Mother Jones passed away when Eula was just four, but her legacy had already been cemented. Eula remembered reading a romanticized tale of Mother Jones and her exploits organizing her people to fight the injustices incurred on them by outsiders. Mary Harris Jones, as she was known to her kinfolk, became known as "the most dangerous woman in America," a phrase coined by a West Virginia district attorney who took her to trial for ignoring an injunction banning meetings by striking miners. "She crooks her finger—twenty thousand contented men lay down." Jones would often employ wigs and makeup to make her look older and in turn gain the trust of skeptical male miners. She spoke tirelessly and effectively for the rights of workers and unionists, often using bold rhetorical and poetic metaphors. Her mantra was, "Pray for the dead, but fight like hell for the living," and it was a phrase that informed Eula's outlook like none other.[28]

While Eula did her best to channel Mother Jones in New York, her ticket out of the mountains was dashed by the intense war effort at any costs. Eula was disappointed her adventure hadn't panned out and came back to Floyd County to face more bad news. Her boyfriend Jesse announced that he, too, would soon be leaving to fight in the war. He was one of the few people in the holler Eula trusted and cared for, and while it was inevitable for him to serve, she knew she was losing her closest friend. She had even shared with him her dreams and desires for life, which she quietly admitted were often fantasy. She had written him frequent letters in between grueling shifts canning food, and excitedly noted her triumph in leading the workers to strike just "like UMWA miners had done back home." Although he was leaving for an indefinite tour, Eula was certain he was the partner in life she would want. They vowed to keep in touch through letters and the occasional visit. Nonetheless, Eula was heartbroken; it was the first of many disenchanted relationships she would have with men.

The day of his departure, Eula declared to Nanny that it was time for her to move from the house and begin looking for hired work elsewhere. Nanny agreed, but she made certain not to let Eula stray too far.

Being a "hired girl" (domestic help) was as new as coal tipples to the mountains. Appalachia was experiencing new vigor in an old industry, bringing with it new jobs and labor. Vagrant men came looking for boarding to make a quick buck, and due to the sorry state of feminism at the time, women were required to "keep them up." It was often seen as a duty. Some girls were sent off to be hired help because they were deemed too difficult in their own families. These might have been orphans, illegitimate daughters, or daughters of widows. For some younger and older women, it was welcome domestic work, serving as a safety net to catch them if they were divorced, abandoned, or widowed without other means of support. For others, like Eula, it was a good-paying job when nothing else existed.[29]

Nearly every woman who graduated with Eula from Greasy Middle School was a hired girl for at least a brief period in her life. Eula was following the traditional route, one she had sworn to herself she wouldn't just months earlier. Luckily, Eula's half-brother from Lee's first marriage—Harvey Riley—already had a house full of children and was expecting a tenth child soon. Eula jumped at the chance to work in the family and be their granny woman of sorts.

She spent the next two months cooking, cleaning, taking care of the family, and the soon-to-be mother. She nursed Harvey's wife till she gave birth to a young son named Dallas and afterwards, on account of her aptitude, Eula was shuttled off to Toler Creek to care for Stallard and Mindy Hall's newest child as the mother had "bled like crazy." Eula loved helping these women whom she knew were struggling with so many kids. Just as when she was younger, Eula found solace in helping neighbors through tough times. She tried her best to make it bearable for the women whom no one else thought to look after.

Harvey had mentioned that sticking around Mud Creek in Floyd County would be a good idea, considering the vast number of people pouring into the area. She gave little thought to where she would settle down long-term, but the decision to work in Mud Creek would be a pivotal one in establishing the roots of her activism.

The number of drilling and mining jobs was exploding, and new wells and shafts were dug every waking hour of the day. Eula took Harvey's advice, and quickly found work outside the family as a hired girl for a well-to-do mountain clan with a nice cottage home. Her new "bosses"—Bessie and John Dean Mitchell—raised a family of miners, but were also boarding well drillers from far-off places like North Carolina, Tennessee, and Virginia. These men often didn't meddle with the community or entertain thoughts of a permanent life in the mountains; they were there simply to pull a check and enjoy some whiskey on the weekends.[30]

Eula, without any help from the lady of the house or her daughter, had to cook breakfast, pack lunch, fix supper, clean the house, and wash clothes for up to four men *and* the Mitchells. Every morning she would lurch from her bed at five a.m., make a trip to the creek, carry bucket of water back to the house, fry enough eggs and bake enough biscuits to feed a small army, and ensure the workers had their lunch ready, as well. Most of this work required hours of preparation the night before, often including slaughtering meat and baking bread until midnight. Eula, who later relished preparing food for others, vividly recalled the preparation:

"We had two or three hogs a year as a family," she recalled. "We'd have to can it, make some sausages, fry it then and there, and then put it in Mason jars, pour hot grease over it to seal it up so when you opened it, you had seasoned meat and grease to cook your beans. We didn't have mayonnaise, so I made slaw with hog grease. We'd take the skull, grind it up, add some vinegar, and make some sauce with it. Used every part of that pig just like the Indians had years ago."

"Oh, and Lord, the chickens was so pretty," she said, "but I'd have to rip the head clean off, grab some new potatoes off the vine, and make a pan of biscuits. Every. Day."

While Eula certainly didn't love the cooking process from

beginning to end, she did enjoy learning to make new desserts and recipes from the families she stayed with.

"Them boys would learn to treat me right and I'd make them jellies from wild berries, sweet custards, and walnut vanilla pies," Eula said. "I learned how to make so many different things being a hired girl I coulda' opened my own restaurant."[31]

Although she found a way to appease their appetites, the men did little to make her life easy. Their khaki and denim work clothes would come back day after day stained and abraded by oil and rocks during their days digging wells and working in the mines. Eula would spend hours scraping and clawing their clothes against a coarse washboard, callusing her already feeble sixteen-year-old hands. The men didn't care how hard she scrubbed nor did they care how dirty they got their clothes; they simply wanted to make sure they were "fixed up enough to look straight when they went out the next day."

At a tender age when most girls in America were busy stressing over high school gossip and puerile tribulations, Eula's psyche and body were being tormented. She struggled to keep up with the physical demands of the job. The host family kept their distance and took little care of her, treating her more like an indentured servant than a family friend. For them, hosting workers was a lucrative business and paying Eula was a negligible cost. "Lord, I knew how the blacks felt," Eula said. "I truly felt like a slave working that hard."

In many ways, Eula was still a child robbed of any innocence and thrown into a job that was proving to be hell. She worked through injury to her fingers, sore shoulders, and burned elbows at the stove, and sustained countless sleepless nights prepping the next day's meals. Even menial tasks took on enormous weight without any modern kitchen aids. There was no refrigerator, no plumbing, and certainly no electricity. Every meal was made from scratch and all the cleaning was on her knees and elbows with few utensils.

Nighttime would put her at her wit's end, so physically and mentally exhausted that she would "pass right out" as she hit the bed, but it was never a restful, calming sleep. Eula's friends from Greasy had warned her about the men at these houses—they were nomads with few morals and even less respect for women. Their transience was an excuse to be aggressive and depraved toward the girls who looked after them. Eula had friends who had been abused and raped without any reprieve from the host family, so she took her safety into her own hands, and claimed she was just too afraid of the dark to sleep alone. She made sure to sleep with the women of the house as a condition for working there and, luckily, it worked. The men kept their distance from the pretty young Mud Creek girl and often only asked for a sweet custard or pie.[32]

Chapter 7

AT A PIE SOCIAL MONTHS AFTER STARTING HER HIRED work, Eula caught a bit of gossip that just tore her to pieces. Her boyfriend Jesse, whose return to the United States from war was one of the few things giving her hope for a better life, was writing sweet missives to other girls. Eula was madder than hell about it.

"Oh, it just ate me alive," she remembered. "How the hell could he do me like that when I trusted him?" She had been convinced that he was the one, and hearing this news just broke her heart. Eula knew little about war aside from her brothers' stories, and she knew nothing about the mental and physical anguish war wrought on soldiers. She figured it wasn't really his fault for courting other girls under such stress, and that it might have been her fault for not getting married before his departure. No matter, Jesse would soon become an afterthought, as there was little love lost. She immediately wrote him a Dear John letter, ending her first tangle with love. When he did come back, she swore to herself she wouldn't be idly waiting on him. She needed to prove to him and herself that she was worth more than their relationship together.

Instead, she would "get established" with a husband, a family, and a house of her own.

As Eula continued to slave away at the Mitchells, a pair of new mountain boys started spending more time around the house. They were nephews of Aunt Bessie, and their father had recently died in a mine roof collapse. Both were fresh from the war and, although they were still bemoaning their father's fate, they were learning as much as they could from the boarders about mining and drilling in order to enter the profession themselves. They also helped themselves to generous portions of Eula's cooking.

The older of the two boys, McKinley Hall, had taken a liking to "Miss Riley," as he respectfully called her, and didn't waste any time making his feelings known. He was tall with an even build, his dark hair combed neatly to the side above gaunt cheeks. He had an easy smile that implied an affable nature, but also a wild streak fueled by booze and reckless abandon.

Every day without fail, McKinley would come by the house and, under the guise of helping Aunt Bessie, carry Eula's groceries, fetch her creek water, or do whatever else she needed done just to catch a moment of her time. Eula was already scared out of her wits about the men in the house and paid scant attention to him. McKinley let her know he thought it was awful how they treated her and all the work she had to do around the house. She certainly took a liking to that sentiment, and if shooting a coy smile his way every now and then could keep him doing her chores, it was fine by her.

Otherwise, in Eula's eyes, McKinley was no different than any of the other boys. Eula was an educated, hard-working, attractive young mountain girl—a catch by any standards. McKinley and his brothers were rough, heavy drinkers who lived heedlessly. Every afternoon, she'd find them hauling white lightning (moonshine whiskey) or hanging around the mines and chasing tail by night. Aunt Bessie felt sorry for her kin after their father's passing, and despite their transgressions, she made a promise to look after them no matter what.[33]

Eula repeatedly shot down McKinley's advances, but he kept right up with her. Each morning, McKinley was offering help in the hope that Eula would at least accept an offer to allow him to serenade her.

"Miss Riley," he said, "I aim to play you a little fiddle piece to see if perhaps you take a liking to me—or my fiddle. Either will do." Eula scoffed. She knew she was better than these fools who, in her mind, did "nothing but drink, dance, and play" all day. She wanted a worker, someone to be her partner, and help her establish a family. McKinley simply wasn't that. But he sure was handsome, and he sure could make that fiddle laugh, sing, or cry.

Finally, despite her better judgment, Eula agreed to see him one night after a particularly hard day keeping up the house. She came to a party McKinley and his brothers were hosting, attended mostly by folks from Upper Mud and surrounding hollers. She was captivated watching McKinley as the center of attention, and adored how he would sing a sweet tune as everyone danced around him. He commanded a presence and was the life of the party. He had a way of making everyone his friend, and Eula appreciated his carefree demeanor. She knew his father's death was difficult to accept, and perhaps his brashness was a form of grieving by forgetting.

McKinley yelled over to Eula for her to get in on the song and join the boys. She reluctantly agreed. While McKinley had a voice as sweet as pie, she had a voice that would make paint chip.

Two short songs later, she was sold. That night they were officially Mud Creek's newest couple. She wrote Jesse one last time to let him know about her newfound love. It was short and to the point—she was well on her way to being established.[34]

Chapter 8

NEARLY A MONTH LATER, EULA WAS HAULING GRAIN and meal back from the county store when, sweaty and tired, she stopped alongside the gravel road to take a break. She had continued her constant routine of cooking and cleaning as she neared her seventeenth birthday. She began the habit of taking leftovers to neighbors and sometimes felt as if she were caring for the entire holler. Pike and Floyd Counties were growing, with more and more workers pouring in, and the work was showing no signs of letting up. Usually, McKinley would be there to help her carry groceries, but that morning he was nowhere to be found. Eula saw a friend up the road a bit and yelled at him to come by and talk. Exasperated, she figured he could help her if McKinley couldn't.

"Hey, Teddy! Which way you going?"

"Just gonna cross the hill over to Mink Branch. You wanna walk over there with me?"

"Sure do." Teddy, not expecting to hold her stuff, grudgingly smiled and grabbed hold of the meal, freeing Eula's hands. They continued on chatting about life, and about whether they would see each other at the next pie social. Eula hadn't any interest in Teddy beside his willingness to hold grain, so she kept the banter light enough to make him forget what he was doing for her.

Just as they were about to split up close to Frasure Creek, they heard a loud whistle coming from down the road. They turned in unison to see who it was. Through the haze, they both recognized McKinley; he had a furious look on his brow and was bustling toward them.

"Aw, damn, Teddy," Eula said under her breath, "he ain't gonna act right."

He didn't. As he got closer, Eula could smell the cutting stench of whiskey emanating between his words. McKinley spewed a vicious rant, leaving little room between his and Teddy's faces. He accused Teddy of taking his girl, of Eula cheating on him, and everything in between. She knew this wasn't going to end well.

"Now, hold on, McKinnel," she said, using a nickname she had given him just a week earlier. "Teddy ain't doing nothing but helping me carry this heavy meal over the hill." McKinley wasn't fazed by Eula's explanation, it just escalated his anger. He slyly opened his trench coat-style jacket to show off a new, shiny pistol he was carrying. Scaring the hell out of both of them, he pulled the gun out and pointed it skyward.

"You are acting crazy!" Eula screamed as she backed away.

Not knowing what McKinley was capable of and with Teddy shell-shocked, she told him to drop the meal and he ran off emasculated across the hill without looking back. McKinley roared with laughter at his newfound ability to intimidate. Eula angrily picked up her goods and headed back toward the house, leaving him in her wake. She couldn't believe how drunk and jealous he was acting, and how brazenly he had brandished his gun. McKinley followed her all the way home, continuing to curse and accuse Eula of infidelity the entire way.

"Look!" Eula finally shouted back at him, "I'm not married

to you. You can't tell me what to do, we're just friends! It ain't no problem for me to talk to Teddy. Best thing you can do right now is put that damn gun away and get up out of this holler. I gotta get to work."

McKinley kept on quarreling, claiming the gun had no bullets and wouldn't harm a fly. He followed Eula the length of the road to the house, swinging his pistol the entire way. Finally, Aunt Bessie had to force him back down the road and away from the house. Eula had seen enough foolishness; she was through with him, she thought. She didn't want to deal with just another "hillbilly."[35]

*   *   *

Eula went about her day doing dishes and cooking, giving little thought to what had happened that morning. She was disgusted, and thought of the McKinley she had met months ago—the friendly and jovial one she had encountered at the pie social.

But the next day, as early as sunrise, McKinley showed up at the front door dead sober and pleading forgiveness.

"I'm sorry, Eula, I'm so sorry," he said. "I didn't mean to talk and act like that. I had a couple drinks and just went berserk seeing you beside him because I love ya so much." As much as she wanted to ignore and forget him, McKinley had an irresistible charm in his sobriety that Eula couldn't resist. He continued to apologize, professing his love, along with promises to stay sober. He knew exactly what to say to Eula and he made promises for a better life, a family, and home to call their own. It took Eula some time to get over his antics, but she finally gave in.

Soon after, among the heap of promises couples make after they fight, Eula and McKinley decided to make it official. On December 6, 1944, the couple went to neighboring Pike County to get a marriage license where Eula, underage and unable to marry legally on her own, forged a note from her father claiming to give permission for her to wed. A week later in a small ceremony with the lay preacher and without Nanny or Lee present, the two said their vows "for better or for worse, till death do us part." It felt right, she thought, even though she didn't feel comfortable telling her family. She was eager to get on with the productive life she had envisioned since her first days of school. McKinley promised her a house of their own and was determined to go to work soon in the mines. Eula knew this was her shot at a different life—being like the Mitchell family instead of being the help—and she wasn't going to pass it up.[36]

Chapter 9

THOSE FIRST FEW WEEKS FELT LIKE A HONEYMOON should, thought Eula, full of loving encounters and the prospect of a generous life to follow. Eula and McKinley started their life together away from Aunt Bessie's, living instead with McKinley's mother in her storefront home. The house had a grocery store on the first floor, and a basement and attic for the two of them to start a family. It was a little ways up the holler on Route 979 from Harold, in a piece of the holler named Big Mud, but Eula found it charming.[37]

McKinley was still looking for a job, but they were confident he would find something soon. Eula would keep up the house and McKinley would be the breadwinner, and they could live a life free from want. But not everyone was thrilled with their plan. When Eula finally broke the news to Nanny and Lee back in Greasy Creek, they were first shocked, then elated, but mostly worried about whether or not their precocious Eula had found an equal partner in life. They asked around about McKinley and got mixed reviews. He was from a good family, but he had his detractors, and those in the community who were fond of Eula were quick to question her judgment. She was new to Mud Creek, they said, and she should take the time to learn his reputation before making it right by God.

For Eula, however, gossip and innuendo were never to be trusted, especially in small towns. "Lord knows what they said about me anyway; can't be bothered by beauty shop biddies," she said. McKinley tested her resolve more than once early on with late night drinking binges, but she could handle it and sometimes she joined him. Besides, Eula thought, she had a house, a husband, was no longer torturing herself with hired work, and was soon to be a mother. Life was easy for once, and while she was still working hard keeping the house together, there was no reason to want anyone better. She would soon learn that even dubious gossip is rooted in some truth.

Months later on a quiet November night, Eula was spending time chatting with her mother-in-law about how much life had changed for the better. Eula mentioned the hard work she had become accustomed to growing up and how hard folks in Greasy had life compared to those in Mud Creek. The Halls had a bit more money than the Rileys, and knew little about the death and hardship Eula saw in her youth.

They spoke about the need to help neighbors as they knitted away by the fireplace, only to have their conversation on community abruptly cut by the sound of a slammed door. It was McKinley back from another night out in the woods drinking moonshine with his mining buddies.

As soon as McKinley's mother heard the door, she put down her quilt, leaned over across the fire and calmly whispered to Eula, "If he comes in here and starts quarreling with ya again, just ease down under the stairs to the basement."

Eula's face cocked immediately and her eyes widened. "Now why would I do that?"

"Eula, he's capable of hurting ya."

"Now I don't reckon . . ."

"He's capable," her voice trailed off with a certitude that Eula couldn't shake. They both stopped talking, and instinctively listened to McKinley's movements through the first floor of the house—each step and stumble on the creaky wood floor a clue to just how inebriated he was. Eula, sensing she could take whatever he had to give, got up from her chair by the crackling fire and headed downstairs to confront him. It was late and he had to look for work the next day, so Eula was going to make sure he knew it.

"What in the hell were you doing out drinkin' so late?" Eula howled as she descended the stairs. At that moment, McKinley's eyes turned to Eula and swelled with contempt. Without warning, he turned and launched an empty liquor bottle at the wall, fortunately missing Eula by a few feet. It shattered into pieces as she lurched back against the steps and shrieked in horror. They stared at one another in a silent moment pierced by heavy breathing, each wondering what the hell the other was thinking. McKinley bolted back out the door and to the backyard outhouse without saying a word. Eula, stunned, conceded to her mother-in-law's advice and descended over the broken glass and down the cold stairs to the basement where she slept that night.

The next morning McKinley acted as if nothing had happened, and he went about his business looking for a job. Eula made no mention of the night before either, assuming he didn't remember. Later that week, after tense days at home, McKinley landed a short-term stint at a nearby underground mine in Letcher County. It was the first of many mining jobs McKinley would have throughout his life, due to industry transience and his own poor work ethic. But with his first opportunity, he went to work with gusto and began a ritual of waking up early and staying late. It was as if the dignity of the job was giving him reason to do right by his wife and family. Eula thought a steady job might keep him away from his rowdy friends, too, and she was right, but only for the first few weeks.

She learned over the months how to deal with him when he had too much to drink, and the ritual became as common as the sunset. After another loose night with whiskey, Eula gently put McKinley to bed easily and without provocation. As she laid him to sleep that night, he blathered some nonsense while she tried to remind him that he had to get up early to get to the mine in Letcher County thirty minutes away. He most likely didn't hear a word before he dozed off.

The next morning Eula arose at five a.m. to tend to their new livestock, and get breakfast ready. She put some eggs and bacon on the grill and decided to check on McKinley; he was nearly comatose.

"McKinnel! McKinnel! Get your ass up. Your ride is gonna leave ya!" Eula yelled. All she got in return was a groan. She sighed, wiped her hands on her apron, and left the stove for the bedroom. The smell of eggs and bacon followed her inside where she immediately gripped the sheets from the bottom of the bed and pulled like a mother with a child trying to skip school. She started shaking his naked legs a bit, but to no avail. Then suddenly, his eyes widened and he pounced.

"Stop telling me what to do!" McKinley screamed. As he wrestled for the sheets from Eula's hands, he cocked his thin leg back and kicked out to get her away. With swollen eyes from the night before, his aim was off. His disoriented kick knocked Eula square in the stomach, her dress and apron the only protection sparing her ribs from the force of his heel. She fell back against the wall, coughing and throbbing with pain.

"I can get up myself!" McKinley announced as he jumped out of bed. Eula staggered to the ground panting for breath. The swirl of rage, emotion, and disbelief was too much for her to handle. Terrified, she slowly backed away into the corner while McKinley methodically put on his shirt. There was a short, silence as she coldly watched McKinley fix his neat black hair and leave the room. His ride honked outside and he was gone. Eula lay motionless in the corner, smelling burnt eggs and bacon, while she clutched her chest and heaved for air.

A neighbor came by soon after and quickly rushed Eula to nearby McDowell Hospital. Sad, Eula thought, that her first encounter with a hospital had to be like this. The doctor diagnosed two broken ribs; however, Eula had no money to pay for proper treatment and the doctor could only recommend time and rest to heal her ribs. To make sure it didn't happen again, the doctor recommended to Eula that she swiftly reconcile with her husband. "If only it were that easy," she sneered.

Word slowly got out through Eula's friends that McKinley wasn't treating her right, but Eula herself had too much pride to make it public or ask for help. A week later, Lee Riley heard the story from a former boarder who had stayed with Eula, and he decided to take matters into his own hands. His daughter had found a man without his permission and he decided it was time to end the charade. He went to the closet, pulled out his over-under, took the shotgun apart into pieces, placed it in a shopping bag, and caught the bus from Pike County to Mud Creek. Lee decided he was going to kill McKinley Hall.[38]

After he arrived by the interstate at Harold and began the winding walk toward Mud Creek, he slowly began reassembling his gun. He sauntered to the front door with a fully assembled shotgun in hand to find McKinley with a stunned but curious face. "I heard you was beating up on my daughter," Lee said. "Well, I've come to take her home with me if that's the way it is."

What transpired afterward is as astounding as it is a testament to McKinley's wily charm. It was a moment encapsulating Eula's future with him. Meeting his father-in-law for the very first time, McKinley put on a show and had Lee at ease, gun down, drinking and laughing within minutes. McKinley had convinced Lee he was taking good care of

Eula, and that her stomach pains were simply the result of an accident. They sat and talked for an hour, by the end of which McKinley inexplicably had Lee, who had arrived a short hour earlier with a shotgun in hand ready to kill, congratulating him on his new job.

As Lee left that day, still with a tinge of suspicion, he gave his daughter a soft kiss and whispered that he was just a bus ride away if she ever needed him. Eula couldn't believe how McKinley handled the situation. In fact, his cunning began to scare her even more than before.

"I would never in my wildest dreams think he was capable of the things he was when I first met him. I was so terrified of what might happen that day, but I didn't say nothing, because I knew my daddy would kill him and I didn't want him to go to prison," Eula said decades later.

Soon after that day, Lee passed away in his sleep, never knowing the dark fear Eula lived with in the house. "I went from being one of the prettiest girls in the creek to being tortured . . . I didn't know there was people on this earth so cruel . . . how the hell did I let this happen?"[39]

PART TWO

Pray for the Dead,
but Fight like Hell
for the Living

Chapter 10

Along Route 979 in the Tinker Fork
of Mud Creek, Kentucky, 1955

A s THE SECOND WORLD WAR CAME TO AN END, Dwight D. Eisenhower, who successfully oversaw the Normandy invasion and reshaped the war in America's favor, became the country's first five-star general president. Winston Churchill, America's staunch ally, whom many mountain soldiers referred to simply as "Church," resigned as prime minister in Britain. Waves of newly minted war veterans began the long trek home, descending on the mountains with few plans and restless souls.

The United States had proven its military might to the world, a recognition that relied heavily on Appalachian coal and labor. Some soldiers, in turn, went back home to the mines, which were booming with activity. Many, however, migrated out of the hollers to Detroit, Cleveland, Pittsburgh, and other fast-growing industrial centers, in search of new factory jobs with good pay and less danger. Appalachia would gain and lose population at a rapid pace over the next decade, and while some were forced to leave Mud Creek, the majority of folks Eula knew bucked the trend and stayed in the hollers.

While the country sat perched atop the world as its sole superpower, Eula sat agitated inside, struggling to find a middle ground between racial norms, equality, capitalism, and the common good. Labor struggles were constant in the coalfields from the end of the war to the mid-1950s with the United Mine Workers of America gaining power and prestige under the deft leadership of John L. Lewis. His efforts to organize had enlightened many folks to the injustices of their employers, and forced many to reconsider their relationship to the managers who dictated their pay and workload.[40]

The turmoil Eula observed in the mountains and the outside world only rivaled the savagery of her life at home. Eula had made few amends with her husband, maintaining a frail, unloving relationship. In a twist of irony, only weeks after Eula suffered broken ribs from McKinley, she discovered she was pregnant. Many of her neighbors acknowledged God's gift to her, but privately she worried about bringing a child into a home of little wealth and even less hope.

Despite the tumult, Eula remembered the 1955 Appalachian spring as being as pretty as the dandelions sprouting alongside the creeks. She was determined to make her life something better than what she had growing up, and she desperately wanted to raise a family. Children, as much responsibility and worry as they were, provide a reason to go on, she thought. Children sustain mountain folks just as much as their faith, and she was determined to raise good kids with kind hearts. Eula would end up giving birth to the first three of her six children in the years soon after she got married. Randy Hall was her first, born in 1954, and Nanetta in 1956. The third child, Colleen, died shortly after childbirth, much the same way Eula's lost sibling had decades ago—on the cold, wooden floor of their home. Troy, Danny, and Dean would be born years later—Danny with a birth defect that left him deaf for life.[41]

Even with deep experience of the enormous struggle of giving birth in the mountains, Colleen's death shook Eula's psyche gravely and reminded her of Nanny's struggles. She planted a vegetable garden to feed the family and give her peace of mind, a refuge of beauty in a home life replete with terror.

As always, McKinley wouldn't help with anything. "He wouldn't hoe, wouldn't help me in the garden or help with nothing, even while I was pregnant. He expected three prepared meals a day and wouldn't even go to the store to get stuff for me . . . it was terrible," Eula said. Without electricity, she was forced to cook with wood and coal, and because McKinley was too tired after a day in the mines, she had to cut the wood herself just as she had during her days as a hired girl. She began to worry about how cruel he could be.

"He would get drunk and start slapping me," she said. "I'd run my mouth, and it just made it worse. After I got pregnant, he would pull my hair 'cause I was saying that he was being lazy. He was happy-go-lucky; he just wanted to drink, party, play his music. There was no home life or getting ahead . . . I always wanted to be somebody, get ahead, not live the life I grew up in. I was beginning to see, 'Oh my god! What in the hell did I get into?' I couldn't go back to mom with two children and another on the way."

She thought briefly about leaving him, but it was a useless notion. There simply wasn't an outlet or a support system of any kind in place for women like her. Much later in her activism, she would learn that she wasn't alone in her marital struggle, but leaving was unimaginable. With children to take care of, she simply didn't know what to do but to stay and try to make it work.[42]

Despite his transgressions, McKinley did provide a roof and food for the family. With help from a GI loan, the Halls moved out of the storefront and built a house where their next child, Troy, would be born. They partitioned off one side of the house and made Nanetta a bedroom, and they had one for the boys, and a larger master bedroom for her and McKinley.

McKinley worked in the mines irregularly and it was never enough to move up the ladder. Most families either farmed or did odd jobs for neighbors to supplement meager mining wages with extra income. The Halls, too, decided they would have a side business, and one that McKinley particularly could take a deep interest in. But they couldn't brag about it openly. In fact, if anyone had known, they would have both been thrown in jail.

"Oh Lord, we made a lot of moonshine back then," Eula admitted decades later. "McKinley knew how and I learned from him. It was right after the war, and it was still a hard time to get sugar 'cause it was rationed. We had to pay fifty dollars for fifty pounds. That was so expensive, but we had to get the sugar. You could sell the whiskey for forty dollars a gallon. We sold it about five dollars a pint, ten a quart, twenty for half." Eula's schooling with numbers had finally come in handy.

The art of distilling originated with the mountaineers' Scots-Irish ancestors, who gave the Gaelic name *whiskey*—literally meaning water of life—to their newfangled brown liquor. It would become as synonymous with Kentucky as college basketball and bluegrass. While the Very Reverend Elijah Craig of Georgetown, Kentucky, produced the first bourbon in 1789, it would be moonshine, a clear elixir made from straight corn liquor, which had an even higher cultural attachment for mountain people. They fought government revenuers (whom they called "revenoors") to make it, and had to "bootleg" (hide moonshine bottles in their boots) to sell it. It was earthy and raw, like the people and the surrounding mountains, and attained a mythological stature as a cure-all. The polyfoxers regarded white lightning as a remedy for colds, anesthetic for surgery, and an antidote for venomous snakebites, among other things.[43]

Recipes were handed down for generations, and the Halls were no exception. "This wasn't no rotgut made from car radiators or acid," Eula would contend with pride. "People knew our whiskey was good, clean, and safe. We had a good reputation." Folks at the time preferred their spirits remain a household art made in small pot stills out of locally grown barley. Eula said, "If we can bake our own bread and share that with neighbors, then why shouldn't we be able to do that with liquor?"[44]

Although it paid well, moonshining was far from a simple business. The Halls had to remain covert and temporarily moved into a little known path named Bear Creek Holler to hide the smoke emanating from the still. They order copper from Sears or Montgomery Ward, and had it delivered to a post office miles away at Harold in order to deflect any suspicion from nosy neighbors. McKinley was skilled at soldering moonshine stills, a job he was happy to do as a means toward tasty ends. "If he made a rig, he made a good rig, one that would last," Eula said. Moonshine stills are copper ovens where the rye, corn, or barley is mashed, cooked, and fermented; they are blazing hot and extremely dangerous.

"It's hard work—gotta carry your barrels, carry your rig, carry your sugar, malt, corn, all of it," Eula said. "I would carry twenty-five pounds of mill, and we ain't never cooked under two sixty-gallon barrels. If we had a partner, we'd do four barrels." Despite the physical labor it took to make a batch, the Halls would sell more than they could make over the next four years. Eula's entrepreneurial spirit had found a calling, and she was busy building a business out of their impropriety.

In the cold of the winter, they would cook the corn in their house without a worry of anyone asking questions about the emanating smoke. However, in the summer, they had to make sure the still was tucked back enough in the mountainside that no one could see the smoke. While Bear Creek was the "backwoods of the boondocks," it didn't always serve as the best hideout.

"We got caught plenty of times," Eula said. "McKinley even stayed in jail a few nights. But I tell ya, if we got caught and confessed, then paid off the sheriff about seventy-five dollars, they'd just cut up your rig with axes and make a big stink about it . . . but they'd let ya go."[45]

The Halls kept at it and Eula found the constant cycle of cooking and drinking to be a welcomed habit for McKinley, who never quite found mine work as enthralling or rewarding as cooking a still. His demeanor took on a certain calm when he worked, which limited the damage he could inflict on the family. McKinley again showed Eula his lighter side she had initially fallen in love with, and he began helping out in the garden, planting tomatoes in rows "as straight as an arrow." Eula noted an irony about the way McKinley conducted himself. He had an odd way of always keeping himself clean, no matter what outdoor work he was doing. "You could throw dirt at him and it wouldn't stick," she said. Eula later lamented that she should have seen the signs of his personality through his work, but she was blinded by the adventure.

He had a finesse and playful humor that kept endearing him to Eula as they worked together the first few months. They say money can't buy happiness, but in this case, it certainly gave them room for temporary bliss. There was plenty of money to avert serious poverty, even though getting caught brought with it a slew of additional problems.

The high spirits wouldn't last long. McKinley was finding more spare time to dip into the still, starting another downward spiral he had little hope of reversing. When he was drunk—and now with more opportunity—he was as lethal as ever. He would throw things, yell at the kids, terrorize the neighbors, and accuse Eula of sleeping with old men up and down the holler. He resented Eula spending time outside of the house with others in the community. When Eula gave a free jig of moonshine to an elderly man or food to a poor mother, he thought she was showing more compassion for other families than their own. He saw Eula's selflessness as carelessness. McKinley couldn't acknowledge that he was the cause of the problem he saw in her actions.

The community took Eula in as kin upon hearing how abusive he was to her. Though she was a bit younger than most of the other women on Route 979, she kept up with them just right. Eula took the time to join knitting clubs, pie socials, church groups, anything to give her a sense of life outside of the tenuous existence she had at home. And as the holler looked after her, she began looking after them as well. Many in Mud Creek were much older than Eula and in need of food, transportation, or just a smiling face. Just as she had during her brief stint as a nanny and midwife, Eula found ways to keep giving her time and energy to others who needed it. She brought hot food to others as she had when she was younger, drove the disabled and indigent to the doctor, or sat around and gabbed for hours if someone needed company. Her compassion and patience with helping her neighbors was endless. She even on occasion helped an old lady with her insulin shots. And she always had a little extra moonshine on hand for those who needed it. Building her own community gave her a purpose outside—or perhaps more accurately, as an extension of— motherhood. It was this sense of purpose she got from doing these deeds that she had been looking for since her youth.

One of the enduring qualities Eula embodied was that even in an early life rife with poverty, she had never eschewed her circumstances. She may have wanted more from life, but she never absorbed victimhood or anger about being poor or relying on moonshine for income. "There is always gonna be someone out there with less," she said, recalling her days of moonshining, and it was that notion—a deep perspective about her surroundings—that made her actually feel privileged and want to help others.

Decades later when pressed on how she could have stayed with someone so degrading as McKinley, she reverted to this perspective. At the time, she could take the good with the bad, which to her meant, "a roof over my children's head in exchange for a marriage without love." It meant food on the table in spite of an uncertain home life. Her philosophy kept her going: "There's always someone with a worse situation than yours—*always*."

Chapter 11

E ULA REMEMBERED GETTING A CALL ONE AFTERNOON from a younger lady in Teaberry named Claydeen, who was eight months pregnant and in a similar relationship as Eula's. She was laid up in bed, "sure as coffee is black" that her baby was due. Use of midwives had faded out by that time, with older ones either dead or having succumbed to the responsibility the law placed on them. Claydeen's husband was of no help either. He was at work in the mines and had told her a week before that since his meemaw (grandmother) and momma had their children in the house, she could, too.

"It was as if men thought giving birth was like dropping an egg," Eula said later.

She had continued helping others as she raised the first of her five children, and helping Claydeen was no different. She seldom took time to herself, instead bringing food to others and providing elders in the community with companionship that too often was missing in their golden years. The seriousness of a friend's pregnancy raised the stakes. Her midwifery skills would not be enough to deal with a premature pregnancy. She had to get Claydeen up and out of the holler quickly.

McKinley had recently purchased an old pickup truck he proudly parked on the small piece of driveway they owned. However, he wouldn't allow Eula to even sit in the front seat, let alone drive. On days when he was at work in the mines, she would call up a friend she knew up the holler who could break into the car without leaving a trace of entry or use. She would use it to go to the store, take the kids around, or to head into town. She made sure to have just the right amount of gas and park it perfectly where it was left, which wasn't an issue on the nights when McKinley came home after drinking.[46]

Eula got the car jacked open and peeled out toward Claydeen's house with little Randy in the backseat. When she arrived, Eula saw time was running out, but she refused to let Claydeen give birth in the two-room house. Eula knew all too well the problems that came along with the home birth of a child from her own experience and she wouldn't dare risk another life. She gently loaded Claydeen in the truck and sped through the holler onto US 23 to Pikeville in half the usual time. They arrived at Pikeville Methodist Hospital, tucked away into a crevice of the Big Sandy Valley, and rushed inside.

"She's about to go into labor. Y'all gotta take her in," Eula cried to the emergency nurse.

"Who's her doctor?" the nurse asked, seemingly undisturbed by the situation. Eula knew Claydeen had never seen a doctor. In fact, she confessed on the drive down that she didn't even know prenatal care was necessary, that is, other than staying away from drinking and smoking.

"Well, she's about ten months pregnant. You gotta see her!"

"Sorry, ma'am. You may want to try Martin or McDowell."

Eula and Claydeen didn't argue, but loaded back into the truck, and sped through US 23 past Mud Creek and toward Our Lady of the Way Hospital in Martin, Kentucky. Our Lady of the Way was a thirty-bed hospital founded by three Catholic nuns in 1947 and renamed from Martin General Hospital. They were hoping the hospital's newfound Christian sensibility would lead them to aid in giving birth to this baby.

Sadly, they arrived to even more hostility. "You gotta see her!" Eula wailed at the emergency counter, while Claydeen lay serene and pensive behind her. It was uncommon for women to be so forceful, but Eula's tenacity assured a worried Claydeen that her baby would be taken care of that day. Claydeen had never seen a women so fired up, and she was confident she would get to see a real doctor and have the privilege of a hospital birth.

"Name your doctor, please."

"We don't have one."

"Can you pay the pregnancy charge and pharmaceutical co-pay?"

"Look, we ain't got much money on us . . ."

"Well, we're just sorry."

"Yeah, you sure as hell are!" Eula said, as she turned away.

Both women went back to the car, awaiting a miracle. Claydeen could feel the baby kick and Eula thought she might have to deliver the baby there in the backseat with Randy. *What in the world will I do? If Claydeen gives birth in the car, how the hell will I explain this one to McKinnel?*

There was one last hospital to try. McDowell had a miner's hospital that had been operating since 1953. Originally planned to aid miners and their families, the hospital slowly expanded its mission to serve everyone in the surrounding communities. The hospital had been very recently purchased by a new nonprofit organization, Appalachian Regional Hospitals (ARH), which had assumed ownership of many of the area's miners' hospitals.[47]

It was a tiny hospital with only a few beds, but it was their last best hope. They raced to the receptionist's desk and pleaded once more, but before Eula could finish, the nurse asked, "Your doctor's name, please?"

Eula was furious. "Don't you start that with me! This woman ain't going back home in this condition." She leaned in, "You better git her a damn doctor, 'cause we ain't leaving till you do. You can call the police; you can call whoever you want. And if you do, I'll call the *Floyd County Times*."

The threat of public humiliation was more than enough to get them through the double doors to see a doctor. The medical staff rushed Claydeen in, closed the curtain, and went to work. Two hours of painful labor later, she had a vibrant, healthy newborn in her arms.

*   *   *

Word of Claydeen's story swiftly spread through the holler. It was Eula's tenacity and determination that made sure the baby had a proper arrival. Upon hearing the tale, a lady in Eula's knitting club called with news she thought Eula would find interesting. She revealed details about ARH's annual retreat, taking place just up the road at Jenny Wiley State Park. The lady had worked for ARH for some time and was irked by their doublespeak about "meeting the community's health needs," and, in her mind, their failure to keep with the principles outlined in their charter.

"This fact sheet they're handing out will just blow your mind, I tell ya."

"Well, is that so? I might just sneak over there and pay 'em a visit then," Eula said.

Eula arrived at the event days later and didn't make a point to socialize. She solemnly walked through the crowd, greeting only the handful of folks she had known from around the holler. Eula fluffed out her hair a bit for the occasion and tried to fit in with what she called the "silver-spoon" crowd. The crowd was mostly men in suits and ties, and women in their Sunday best. "Eastern Kentucky's high society," she said.

As the speakers were about to go up to the podium, she

nervously wondered what the hell she was doing there. She knew she was angry, but she felt as if she had overstepped her place. She wasn't going to change anything. In fact, she had no idea what she was going to do at all. She thought, *I'm just one little lady who is upset with the way they work. Why would they ever listen to me?* Eula's confidence gave way and she slowly slid her way to the middle of the pack hoping to be unnoticed.

The meeting began by introducing all the managers, who each bragged on the services they were providing to the community. They passed out the fact sheet Eula had heard about; the third line stated proudly that ARH "provides adequate health care to everybody regardless of race, creed, color, or ability to pay."

Eula sat there, "burning right up" at the sight of those last three words—"ability to pay." She couldn't help but think of Claydeen and all the other pregnant women, disabled miners, and senior citizens who must have been turned back because of their lack of ability to pay. She couldn't help but think of Nanny, too.

As the manager of the McDowell Hospital finished his speech, Eula felt a pang of anger. Her conscience reminded her that she had to speak up. She half opened her mouth, only to shut it, realizing she had no idea what to say. The speaker accepted applause from the crowd after completing his remarks and began to walk away from the podium. Eula awkwardly stepped forward, held her copy of the sheet high in the air and said, "May I . . . may I ask who is responsible for this so-called fact sheet?" Her voice, full of doubt, cracked between every word. The crowd grew silent and slowly turned to the provocateur.

"Oh, is that Eula Hall? So glad to see you, really proud to see you over here today," he said with reluctance while walking back to the podium. Eula was surprised he had any idea who she was. He turned to the crowd. "For those of y'all who don't know, this lady Eula Hall has gone out of her way to take care of the pregnant and indigent in our community near McDowell. The staff knows her well."

There was a small, confused applause. Eula looked down and then before he could speak again she demanded, this time with force, "Excuse me, sir, I asked who wrote this?"

He cocked his head as if to ask why she was still speaking. Before he could walk away from the podium, she spoke again. "Way I see it—never no bigger lie ever printed on a piece of paper than this. You don't give a damn what color they are I'm sure, as long as they got *green*. I wish I had this fact sheet when I brought that lady in to give birth last week. You don't have a pill in that place to give to these people you claim to serve. We're living proof."

The crowd hushed, contemplating not the substance, but the fallout of what Eula had just said. The words came out without any planning. There was a newspaper reporter present, Eula had noted before the speeches began, so she made sure he could hear every word she said.

"Oh, Eula," the speaker wailed in a stricken voice as he got to the stage, "now is not the time or place, but we'd love to talk to you. We know you care a lot and we're making some changes. Thank you everyone for coming."

Eula felt emboldened. She rushed to meet him at the stage before he darted off. "Look, it's a little late, but I do wanna talk."

"Ok, Eula," he angrily said. "Now that you had your fun and created a little stir, when do you wanna meet?"

She thought for a moment, eager not to get blown off. "Tomorrow morning, seven a.m."

That evening she returned home, placed the truck just right so McKinley wouldn't notice, and sat on the couch stunned. She couldn't believe what she had done, and in front of so many important town folk. She scolded herself for going too far. She had no idea what she would say the next day, and she was equally afraid of what McKinley might do if he was aware of what she had done. She decided she had to go in the morning; it would have been a waste if she didn't, but she would do her best to be civil and polite.

The next morning she awoke early, fluffed her hair out again, put on her second set of church clothes, and made it to the hospital bright and early. As she sat down in their stately hospital offices, which looked nicer than any she'd seen before, she quickly broke her own civility promise. The director noted to her that it took courage to operate the hospital. Eula interrupted, fuming with anger. "What's courage when people are suffering?" Over the next thirty minutes, the two went back and forth, with Eula stating they had to "train those receptionists not to be bitches, allow doctors to see people in emergency situations, and do more work in the community to assess needs."

Eula had gained an intuitive sense of public health from her good deeds in the holler and it was showing. She was starting a dialogue, she hoped, and even diplomatically made a point to shower them with a few compliments on their work with local miners. She left the meeting energized, feeling as though she had made a difference, if not in the way the hospital worked, at least in making sure they knew what regular people thought.[48]

Chapter 12

I N 1963, EULA READ HARRY CAUDILL'S EPIC TOME ON
the eastern coalfields, *Night Comes to the Cumberlands: A
Biography of a Depressed Area.* The book is a caustic, anger-
fueled history of the relationship between coal, its benefactors,
and, most importantly, the brave young men who pull it
out of the earth. The dramatic changes in Kentucky's coal
industry disturbed Caudill. Labor-intensive underground
mines were losing out to highly mechanized surface mining,
employing fewer men and causing more destruction. The
coal companies' incredible machines transformed wooded
hillsides into lunar landscapes. Underground union miners
who fought throughout the years for pay and benefits were
losing jobs, and pitiful politicians were playing second fiddle
to the robber barons who owned them. *Night* was history with
emotion, a righteous diatribe describing the coal industry's role
in creating an Appalachia of two distinct populations: the rich
and powerful, and the destitute and powerless.[49]

Eula had become an avid reader, and Caudill challenged
her with a history of the region she had seldom heard before.
Caudill put words to the feelings of neglect and exploit Eula

and her neighbors experienced in their lives at the hands of the political elite. The county judges and coal executives were antagonists, keeping poor mountain folks poor, and no one had explained it so clearly and eloquently as the mountain lawyer from Whitesburg. It was intoxicating for Eula to digest Caudill's words and be able to authoritatively talk about rights and injustice, instead of simply claiming a vague "wrongness in the system." The book gave fodder and detail to her outrage and to the outrage of a generation of Appalachians who felt neglected.

It was this book and *The Other America* by Michael Harrington that purportedly convinced the Kennedys the country owed Appalachia a second chance. Only two years earlier, President Lyndon B. Johnson had followed up on President Kennedy's promise and enlivened Appalachia's poor when he professed in a speech that "current poverty problems require us to create new concepts of cooperation—a creative federalism—between the national capital and the leaders of local communities." Those were magical words, evoking a new engagement that local folks had been waiting to hear. Johnson's "creative capitalism" provided a challenge to change the relationship between the large and often impersonal federal government by using national resources to fund local solutions. It was with this idea, along with America's continued inequalities, that led President Johnson to launch a domestic War on Poverty.[50]

Initially planned by President John F. Kennedy and his associates before Kennedy's assassination in 1963, the plan promised to radically alter American life for the have-nots with community-born-and-bred innovations. Famed senator and policy intellectual Daniel Patrick Moynihan summed it up best: "The War [on poverty] is a form of controlled revolution," using existing institutions and structures to help the poor against an entrenched political system. The initiative would use community activists and locally proven methods for bettering society. This meant, for the first time, empowering the poor to improve their own destiny. It was a risky move, indeed, as corruption was as high or higher in poverty-stricken areas, leaving little room for empowerment, but it was an innovative idea perfectly suited for the hamlets and hollers of Eastern Kentucky.

As the nation mourned the death of a young and energetic president, Eula and her community did, too. Kentucky may have narrowly voted for Nixon, but Floyd and Pike Counties had overwhelmingly voted for Kennedy. Kennedy's younger brother Robert and President Johnson continued JFK's plan, and spoke deftly about the scourge of poverty. All the while, Eula was living it day to day. *It was about damn time,* she thought, *that our leaders did more than just pay us lip service.*[51]

The winter of 1964 was especially harsh, and many in Mud Creek found it increasingly difficult to brave the cold. Before the season hit, Eula spent her time plucking feathers off ducks to make thick quilts and featherbeds for her and the family. The children's shoes needed stitching as they were coming apart at the seams from the kids running up and through the hollers and hillsides. Moonshining money had all but dried up, so she took the time to stitch up each one of those shoes herself instead of buying new ones. While the house was never quite warm during the frigid nights that followed, the cookstove became their savior and best friend. But even full of coal, that tiny cookstove couldn't keep up with Mother Nature.

Despite the cold, the winter served as a time of social activity. Eula spent time digesting words of wisdom. The fame she had recently garnered when she spoke out against ARH had launched her profile among existing local activists. People were seeking out Eula not only for advice navigating the health system, but also for advice on how to get up the courage to speak out.

"People started asking me about organizing," Eula recalled. "I'd say *organizing*? You mean talking to your neighbors? Since when did that become organizing?"[52]

Eula was happy to help in any way she could. Up until that fateful day when she made her voice heard in front of hundreds, Eula simply found it routine to do things like check on the elderly neighbors of the holler. She had been a caring observer since she was a five-year-old looking for chimney smoke, and couldn't think of a reason to stop. But with her newfound prominence, timed serendipitously with the War on Poverty, she was ready to preach about empowering other people, as well.

Luckily, in this war she wasn't a Mud Creek army of only one. Two grassroots organizing groups formed in the late 1950s were only then beginning to make themselves known. One group named themselves the East Kentucky Workers Rights Organization (EKWRO), part of a national movement of union-minded folks who were tired of low wages and slave-like labor. The other, an offshoot of EKWRO founded with help from the Appalachian Volunteers (AVs), was the 979 Community Action Council (CAC). The 979 council began as an insular group composed of a small clan of sages and activists who lived along the twelve or so hollers in the winding trails of Route 979 through Floyd County. The 979 CAC even established their own newspaper, the *Hawkeye*, to break down the barriers of inter-holler communication. Unlike EKWRO, they were less interested in the monumental task of changing the system, and more intent on incremental changes in clean drinking water, paved roads, and keeping the lights on.[53]

Eula had previously heard of the two groups and the work they were doing, but was most keen on what she called the "hell EKWRO was raising among the political folks." While the Appalachian Volunteers spent most of their time building and rebuilding schools, and 979 fought parochial battles, EKWRO was fighting the system. That's where Eula wanted to direct her ire, and she knew these groups were the ones to help her do it.

"They had a rule at EKWRO—100 people write a law," she recalled, and they often made sure they got the numbers to make it happen. Soon, with Eula's help, their profiles would rise dramatically and they would be embroiled in their highest-profile quarrel yet.

That year, Randy, Troy, and Nanetta began attending the new John M. Stumbo Elementary School near the mouth of Mud Creek. The school was named after the infamous county judge executive, a scion of the Stumbo family, and it served as one of the few bright spots Eula could find in his tenure. The facility was brand new, clean, and compared to the school Eula had attended, a mansion of sorts.[54]

Shortly after the new elementary was built, Eula's kids came home one afternoon complaining of hunger. It wasn't the first time. The children had intermittently returned from school famished without an alibi. In the beginning, Eula simply chalked it up to youthful energy and playfulness, and she regularly fed the kids at four o'clock every day when they got home. However, the repeated insistences piqued her curiosity. The kids professed they were eating, but never gave details on what or when they were fed. Finally one afternoon, Eula gently nudged the children on why they were so hungry all the time and whether they were getting enough to eat during school lunch. Their story horrified Eula.

Free or reduced lunches for schoolchildren had yet to be created by the federal government, and most school districts completely controlled the amount, type, and price of food given to kids. The new Stumbo school's gym had a stage at one end, which served as both a theater and cafeteria. The school decided the best way to coordinate the children was to separate the ones who could pay from the ones who couldn't. It was under the sincerity of management, not cruelty, that the school decided to place the kids who ate on the gym floor while the others without lunch sat upon the stage glaring down at what seemed to be the daily feast they couldn't afford. The teachers would systematically collect quarters from each student lucky enough to have the funds, shaming the rest on a daily basis and secluding them to a corner of the room. In a scene straight out of *Lord of the Flies*, kids would often jump down, steal a piece of bread from a classmate's plate, and run back up to the stage.[55]

The poorest young kids, at no fault of their own, were relegated at a young age to the prejudice of their parents' fate. If they couldn't pay, they couldn't eat and had to sit while watching their peers satiate themselves. It was punishing, and every day Randy, Troy, and Nanetta who faced the same social pressures and stigmas that all schoolchildren do, had to face the additional burden of their family's poverty. "If I had known," Eula declared, her anger intensifying, "I woulda' robbed that kitchen and fed them children every day . . . Lord, it takes a devil to do what they did to those kids."

Nothing McKinley had ever done could compare to the anger Eula felt after the kids finally confessed their shame. She started asking around among other parents if they had heard the same story. Most were outraged as well, but hadn't heard a thing about it from their kids. It seemed the embarrassment wasn't confined to only the Hall children.

One parent, however, told Eula that she housecleaned as a hired girl for a well-to-do woman in Harold who was a schoolteacher, and she had noticed conspicuous gallon cans of butter, jelly, and ketchup on her countertop similar to the kind specifically made for schools. There were even rumors circulating among some parents that the principal would feed his pet beagles with scraps from the lunchroom.[56]

Eula initially thought it was the fault of a select few teachers and administrators at the Stumbo school, and that the Floyd

County School Board could easily remedy the situation. But her recent readings of systemic corruption, and the memories of the lack of school buses growing up reminded her that the school board was actually a tiny political fiefdom where the highest priority was, in her words, "who got elected, and how they would get re-elected." The AVs, EKWRO, and 979, on the other hand, might be able to cause a stir, and Eula thought it was as good a time as ever to get formally involved.

EKWRO and 979 held their meetings in an older primary school building at the mouth of the holler close to US 23. Eula decided to stop by a few nights after the conversation with her children, and see if they could live up to their reputation. Still a bit unsure of what to expect, she was surprised to find that many of the group's members were acquaintances in the community who kept their membership secret. A cowardly move, she thought, to have people come and loudly proclaim wrongs in the community, but keep their voices silent outside. EKWRO had a reputation of being radical and Eula wanted to put that to the test and see if she could "light a fire under their ass."[57]

At the beginning of each meeting, the leaders of the organization, Woodrow Rogers and George Tucker, started with a secrecy pledge followed by a recital of the mission, which focused on the primacy of people-powered politics:

> We believe people are poor because in this generation and in generations past, they have been denied equal opportunity. In Floyd County and Eastern Kentucky, this happened when coal companies bought the land and mineral rights for as low as fifty cents an acre even though they knew the true value.
>
> They set up political institutions like coal camps, company stores, and schools that would protect them and not the people. The result of this exists in the present day.

The resources of our great nation should be used to correct these injustices of the past and to give adequate income, education, and <u>health</u> to Americans whose kin have died protecting this country and whose men have given their health and lives for the growth of the industrial might of this nation.[58]

After the recital of the mission, came the rants. People would intermittingly speak up, much like an AA meeting, and voice their disgust and anger toward local businesses, doctors, and lawyers, but mostly, corrupt politicians. Members voiced their deepest frustrations while knowing that acknowledging such in public could cost some of them their jobs, or worse, their lives. Politics in Appalachia had always hewed toward a personal and informal nature, very different than formal constituencies based on issues. Most people knew the county judge or school board members personally, which made it that much harder to be open about grievances. However, this group wasn't simply representing the poor as apathetic and alienated; instead they represented the poor as aggressors and the initiators of action based on deep distrust of the ruling elite.

Eula was taken aback and refreshed by how people were willing to speak out when they didn't have to bow to pressure or intimidation. Everyone in the meeting was like her, fed up with local political bosses and upset about "the rich getting richer and the poor staying poor." She realized at her first meeting that there was a community of people who thought as she did, and this organization gave them the confidence to speak from the heart.

After a few speakers, Eula was formally introduced, but her reputation among the other members had already been cemented from her outburst at the ARH meeting. She rose and walked to the front of the room, this time without any hesitation or nerves, and offered her own grievances. "People, the schools are starving our poor little children, and we gotta do something about it," she said.

Eula used those rarefied storytelling skills she had learned from her grandpa and explained the horror she and her children felt about the lunch situation. The reaction was swift and fierce. Some of the older members stomped their feet in agreement with Eula, while others yelled retribution against specific members of the school board. The group decided that evening by a vote that something had to be done immediately. They elected a group of five individuals to sit down with the school board and write up a formal school lunch program policy.

Over the course of the next week, the group, led by Eula, met daily to gather grievances from parents to present to School Superintendent Charles Clark. They collected nearly sixty in total, not all of them concerning the undernourishment of their children, but rather regarding everything parents felt needed to change with school administration. EKWRO, a group that until then had only fumed internally or collected petitions, decided to make a real, public statement with Eula and other parents in the lead.

That next Friday morning, with a new policy laid out, EKWRO and the 979 CAC lined up outside the Floyd County Board of Education to meet with the superintendent and board officials. It became a reckoning for all the wrongs committed by the school board over the years, including the abhorrent school lunch issue. The people were ready to fight back against the political elite, Eula thought, and "it was going to start with a fight for the children." It was a powerful moment, and Eula barely managed to sneak out in the truck while McKinley was asleep. He, and arguably Eula, had no idea what she was getting into.

Close to sixty parents arrived to protest outside the board's offices in Prestonsburg, the Floyd County seat. Superintendent

Charles Clark was incredulous, and wouldn't allow them to even walk inside, let alone meet with them. It seemed someone had tipped off board loyalists as the group of protesters were greeted by a rag-tag group of board officials and supporters. Some of the officials had donned helmets and wielded baseball bats as if they were ready for physical battle. Eula was briefly reminded of her fight with military officials at the canning factory during the war, and worried about potential violence. She couldn't believe the school board members would bring weapons to intimidate parents. In fact, the sight of these 'elite' folks acting like fools put her at ease.

Woodrow, George, and Eula were furious that the board had decided to turn a blind eye to them, but Woodrow knew the crowd itself would make the difference. Previously, he had contacted a few of the new AV and VISTA workers who had been stationed in the area as part of the War on Poverty. He knew those kids were sophisticated when it came to media relations, so he made sure to reach out to them before the meeting. The juxtaposition of parents standing alongside board members with weapons was too picture-perfect to be planned.

Less than ten minutes after showing up to the site, however, someone threw a punch. One EKWRO member shoved a neighbor of his who was on the board and a full brawl ensued. The parents and board members tussled, culminating with the superintendent being punched in the face. Eula remembers it as a moment when everyone involved knew they had gone dangerously too far.

The police couldn't place everyone in jail, so they ended up taking only the man who had provoked the chaos. The school board decided they couldn't go on with so much opposition and quickly changed course by meeting with EKWRO parents. After weekly deliberations between heated parties, the board decided to change policy. All students were allowed to sit freely and the board began working toward a school-lunch policy that provided a basic amount of food for every child.

Eula couldn't believe the change of heart. Unlike the factory strike, this fight actually worked. The protest served as a catalyst in Eula's mind. She said, "Well, if we can get a school lunch program as effective as this, maybe we'll take on *anything* that we think ain't right."[59]

Chapter 13

THE EXCITEMENT AND ACHIEVEMENT OF THE SCHOOL board saga jolted Eula's spirit. She was making a real difference in her children's lives, and connecting with like-minded folks in the community who saw injustices where she did. For years, Eula had observed those few in charge who manipulated the social and political roots of her community. The political and industrial elites had all the power, while the poor and downtrodden were seen only as pawns of patronage with little influence and far less importance beyond a November election. Eula knew there was an enemy keeping Eastern Kentucky poor, and it was those folks being continuously voted into office, determined to maintain the status quo. It included the county judge all the way down to the school board, and as she lost faith in almost all of them, she found a greater faith in herself and her neighbors. This deep distrust she and EKWRO had of their political leadership extended not only to local officials, but to every politician in American since FDR who "hadn't done squat," in her opinion, "to help Appalachia's prosperity along with the rest of the nation."

Throughout the country, folks were clearly yearning for change, especially in the Deep South where racial tensions reached a roaring crescendo. Years before Rosa Parks demonstrated the most consequential act of civil disobedience in US history, a fifteen-year-old African American girl in Montgomery, Alabama, Claudette Colvin, refused to give up her seat on a bus to a white woman. The driver demanded she move, but she stood her ground only to have the police tauntingly remove her from the bus. The courage of those in the civil rights movement, and the gumption of women like Claudette and Rosa Parks was contagious to Eula. She knew many folks in Eastern Kentucky were hesitant to support the civil rights movement, but the drama and magnitude of the cause was electrifying, "at least to those with open minds and hearts," she said. The movement and the struggle for equality had less to do with race, she surmised, than with spirit.

Eula remembers questioning the origins of the heroism of these brave men and women, often asking, and seeking for herself, what exactly was it that shook these folks to fight in such brazen and dangerous ways? And why couldn't people in Floyd County and throughout Appalachia, living miserably day to day in absolute rock-bottomness, see their struggle for opportunity and equality as one in the same—against the same benefactors of power?

It was an important question for Eula to consider. With the country in such turmoil, Eula knew that the little bit of strife in the mountains was akin to the nationwide struggle. She saw kinship with herself and southern African Americans who had, in her mind, faced a similar history of neglect. Her early activism allowed her to know what it felt like to be part of something bigger, and it was intoxicating.[60]

While the buzz in the holler and across the country contemplated change against the establishment, she continually found she didn't have a willing and interested partner to talk to about it at home. McKinley was furious with Eula's impudence, and he was going to make damn sure she put an end to it.

In November 1952, Eula gave birth to her fourth child, Danny, who came into the world with a hearing problem that led to deafness. McKinley told her to focus on the children, Danny's needs, and cleaning the house—not messing around with folks who could take away his intermittent mining job. For the first time, he wasn't completely misguided. Eula had spent a significant amount of time with EKWRO and 979 activists at the expense of spending more time at home with her burgeoning family. While both McKinley and Eula had a healthy distaste for the rich and entitled, McKinley made a point to tell Eula not to "slap the hand that feeds." Every time Eula came home from a meeting, he would yell and sometimes swing at her about running around town acting "like a communist." As a result, her activism intensified as did her secretiveness. She kept her actions quiet, took care of the kids, and waited desperately every week to sneak out to EKWRO meetings. They served as her escape.[61]

Since the school board policy change, more and more Appalachian Volunteers and VISTA workers were attending EKWRO and 979 meetings to offer the group their take on what issues were the most important to fight and organize about. These groups enlivened local activists who were listening intently. The Appalachian Volunteers were not new to Floyd County, but had been helping refurbish schools and curriculum since their inception at Berea College in the early 1960s. The program envisioned a permanent regional organization of student volunteers who embarked on eight-week tours of duty. Their goal was to alter values, and encourage achievement in education through various programs. For example, one of the AV's first initiatives was an adult education program in Pike County that, in addition to its standard instructional aspects, included a motivational component to "induce in adults a

desire to learn and become aware of the value of an education."
An ambitious goal, indeed, but the implicit message was, in the
words of historian Thomas Kiffmeyer, "Educate Appalachians
so that they might take part in the wealth and prosperity of the
modern United States" extending from a proper education.[62]

Early AVs stuck to these educational goals, but the real
innovation was to include local folks as service volunteers.
Participation by locals was seen as a type of sociotherapy—
premised on the idea that poor people have been rejected
by mainstream society for so long that their inclusion will
heal psychological wounds of inferiority. It was the idea
that the downtrodden must take ownership of their fate and
development. The notion held that if you involved someone in
significant social action and gave them a hand in any decision-
making process, they would soon develop social competence to
drive themselves out of poverty. In Knott County, for example,
AVs initiated a program where unemployed fathers built a new
lunchroom for the local school. In Breathitt County, fathers
organized to build a bridge across a creek. These projects
gave locals dignity in labor, and dignity in knowing they were
directly aiding their community. Harry Caudill was credited
with claiming that the program, while still in its infancy, had
far outweighed the government's expensive studies and efforts
by "rolling up their sleeves" and hitting structural Appalachian
problems head on.[63]

A complementary program, with which the AV would
eventually merge, was the Volunteers in Service to America—
VISTA for short. VISTA provided President Johnson with
foot soldiers in the trenches of his revolution. The program,
premised on and similar to AV, promised young, wet-behind-
the-ears do-gooders an opportunity to organize and reshape
the country in the mold of the utopia they all dreamed it could
be. Armed with idealism and often naïve judgments of rural
America, these kids, mostly fresh from college, would freely

jump at the chance to 'civilize the hollers' during a year or more tour. The idea, wrote Senator Daniel Moynihan of New York, who helped usher the program through Congress, was to model the wildly successful international Peace Corps program for community building work at home. VISTAs took part in relatively benign programs to pick up trash and paint buildings, much like the AVs, but they also vigorously challenged local power structures. With this singularly bold mission, the VISTA program attracted a rather courageous bunch. As the history of the War on Poverty attested, it would take nothing less than the utmost courage to change the trajectory of Appalachia.

In the mid-1960s, in the midst of the War on Poverty, VISTA and Appalachian Volunteers merged and overlapped considerably, lending to infighting and finger-pointing as they fell in and out of favor with the local populace because of their aggressive tactics. The AVs welcomed more than 150 VISTA volunteers in 1965, and initially assigned them to help existing school projects throughout Eastern Kentucky. The VISTA mission, better funded and more assertive than the AVs, eventually took over and shook the foundation of the once careful, and pedagogically focused AV program.[64]

While these groups received mixed reviews from locals, Eula adored the young workers pouring into Appalachia. She felt like finally folks from the outside were taking the time to understand *their* problems. Eula not only admired, but also envied the volunteers she met. Here, she thought, was a collection of folks just like her, except endlessly young and idealistic. Some hailed from California and Massachusetts, spoke and acted in such different ways they seemed almost like foreigners. But Eula knew they had the right intentions at heart, even if they were a bit "snooty" in their judgments of the communities they came to change.

With a little push from the organizers, she began to entertain ideas that perhaps she too could become a VISTA.

Even at thirty-six with four kids and little money, she knew she had everything these kids had—smarts and passion—but also the good sense to know "how and when to mess with whom" in the community. On top of that, she was born and raised in the mountains, which enabled her to gain the respect many VISTAs could never achieve.

Chapter 14

LESS THAN TWO MONTHS AFTER THE SCHOOL BOARD saga, Eula found herself on a plane from Lexington heading further south than she ever thought possible. In the aftermath of the fiasco, a local VISTA sat down with Eula and aided with the application process that would take her to their southern training outpost in the red clay of Georgia. The VISTAs had recommended her and other local activists to attend their annual organizing conference; they simply needed to pay a small application fee and answer a few brief essay questions to attend.

But if Eula was going to spend days away from home, she had to tell McKinley what she was up to. Needless to say, he wasn't happy when he discovered her scheme, but the promise of a fifty-dollar-a-week paycheck helped bring him around quickly. The Halls were still poor, but in Eula's mind, this was the first step to independence, a way of gaining self worth, but also finding a path away from McKinley.[65]

While most VISTAs were college-age and thrown into new communities and cultures, the program desperately wanted people like Eula who had local connections and history with the folks they would be empowering. Eula and two veteran local Appalachian activists, Maxine Kinney and Steve Brooks, were quickly accepted and soon on their way to training.

Upon arrival, Eula took a mental picture of the Atlanta skyline—it was menacing and intimidating. "Sorta felt like the mountains, but less peaceful," she remembered. As the group settled into training, the three Appalachians, all in their mid to late thirties, were met by a room full of "kids that looked as old our own children." It was jarring for Eula to be back in a classroom, because it had been decades since she was forced to end her studies. Despite the age difference, Eula found it thrilling to meet similarly motivated community activists. She enjoyed gathering with others as passionate as she was, and discussing topics of mutual interest. However, the training itself was a different story. To her memory, it was rather mediocre and full of endless talk on tactics and strategies Eula had already implemented in Mud Creek. Eula even dosed off on occasion.

One of the more interesting training sessions, Eula recalls, gave her a foundation for understanding Appalachia's place in America. Two competing theories, both rooted in early twentieth-century progressive thinking, were presented and discussed to explain the causes and potential answers to mountain poverty. One idea squarely blamed the culture of poor education, values, and norms in Appalachian culture, which were seen as out of step with modern American society. This patronizing argument, as Eula tells it, promoted the idea that Appalachians were "dumb and simply not as bright as those born in New York or Florida." It presented a view of the triumphal American ideal of education and industriousness, and presented anything contradictory to that as a failed culture. In some respects, according to historian Thomas Kiffmeyer, the Appalachian Volunteers believed in this theory, rooting their activism in encouraging and attempting to develop a culture of learning by building libraries and promoting adult education programs.

The other theory, in which Eula clearly found more resonance, described a type of economic colonization where industrial powers extracted the region's wealth from the common people. In this view, she learned, industrial giants came from the outside, made riches on the backs of mountain labor, and left very little behind. It was the story of the industrial revolution whizzing past her ancestors; it was her father working as a sharecropper; and it was her children eventually working in boom-or-bust mining jobs that didn't provide health care or a sustainable ladder into the middle class. The colonization theory helped Eula explain the political patronage and corruption she saw at home, and described how the levers of power worked together.

The cultures of poverty theory, if true, meant that Appalachian people were forever in a hopeless cycle of generational poverty. But Eula never saw herself or her neighbors as victims; they simply weren't given a chance. There wasn't anything *wrong* with their culture, she thought, what was wrong was the lack of opportunity. What was wrong was the lack of jobs and health care. Their culture was an American culture. If they were victims of anything, it was the industrial revolution. The ideas pushed by modernization theorists, and those at her VISTA training, gave her reason to believe all hope wasn't lost.

"I saw that we were hard workers," Eula said, "that we loved our community, but there were a few folks at the top who had all the money and riches. It didn't have to be that way. All we needed was to organize, and make sure that we were at the table when the decision of who gets education and who gets good wages is made."

While AV workers tended toward the cultural answer—believing that values such as a love for education, drive, and studiousness could alone provide the panacea to change Appalachia forever—VISTA believed in a more politically radical approach. VISTA wanted to usurp power from the elite, and see industrial riches were evenly shared.

Eula took over the training, and offered guidance to volunteers by advising them on how to approach neighbors, help with poor mothers, and organize local campaigns. By the end, Eula thought she had taught more practical skills than she learned, but she was more than happy to head home a VISTA. She was ready to take on the establishment and with a paycheck to boot. The feeling of liberation, both in thought and practice, enraptured her.

She said, "I always wanted to help people, always wanted a door or window to look through and get out of. When I saw these groups organizing, I said 'here's me an opportunity to get in and see what I can accomplish or what I can do.' You were working with people suffering the same problems you were."

She had officially become a professional activist, and was ready for battle. Her return would prove to be just that, and much rougher than she expected.[66]

*   *   *

While she loved the movement she was part of, many in the community were souring on their idealism. Upon her return home, she realized more concretely why these groups were not universally loved. One of the compromises made during the passage of the War on Poverty legislation required that governors give consent before VISTAs were deployed. In fact, the compromise Republicans sought went as far as allowing governors to veto any single program they desired. The most publicized case of this came when Governor George Wallace of Alabama turned back War on Poverty funds allocated to a biracial poverty group in Birmingham. His rationale was that they were "too tolerant." Wallace and future President Ronald

Reagan of California turned out to be the most generous, and notorious, users of the veto.

In Kentucky, Governor Ed Breathitt deftly left the decision up to local county governments. He didn't want to be held responsible for their gains or losses. While AVs were welcome in their early years, as were VISTAs near the beginning of the War on Poverty, immediately upon Eula's return from training she learned she might not even start. The AV program that folded into VISTA began as a noble endeavor of local students looking to repair the communities surrounding them, but it eventually became composed of neither Appalachians nor volunteers. Thomas Ratliff from Pike County, who was running for lieutenant governor at the time, called them, "A bunch of damn long-haired barefoot beatniks and hippies running around town up to no good." He continued, "We don't want them. Let them go back to Berkeley where they belong." Not quite the kind, welcoming words from local leadership Eula wanted to hear. The Floyd County Fiscal Court, viewing the volunteers as threats to their power, voted to oust the VISTA program. During the fiscal court meeting where the local decision was made, Eula recalls members claiming AV and VISTA workers were "communists" and "undermining the power and authority of the county judge." Eula thought that undermining the power of the county judge should have been considered a positive thing.

The AVs and VISTAs entered what historian David Whisnant called their "radical" phase, which primarily involved issue-organizing against the political elites, and the elites fought back. Not only were the VISTAs kicked out, but the governor also reneged on his promises and chose to defund the Appalachian Volunteers. The two organizations' reputations as outsiders, paid organizers, and rabble-rousers—instead of community builders—was too much to overcome.[67]

Undaunted, the local VISTAs and Eula made the transition

to eventually become designated solely as Appalachian Volunteers. The AV program, while engulfed by VISTA from the start of the War on Poverty, remained its own entity at Berea College. With less funding and a lower profile, the AV found themselves Appalachians again, and the organization vowed to stick to its humble beginnings of employing the services of local people to carry out the organizing agenda.

Chapter 15

EULA HAD A JOB, A WEEKLY PAYCHECK, AND THE AV program would even find the funds to provide her with a car to get in and around the hollers for work. The car, however, wasn't much to flaunt. It was a beat-up old red and white Ford Bronco with a stick shift rising through ripped open floorboards, but it represented independence. It was rough and tough, and was perfect for getting her around the gravel roads and steep mountains throughout the county.

Now that she had taken the first step toward living the purposeful life she wanted, she faced her biggest dilemma—what issue should she tackle first? With the recent unrest over organizing, how could she do something important that wouldn't be fought tooth and nail? Eula realized that many of the problems she had grown up with didn't occur in isolation. Poverty wasn't a single issue; it was deeply intertwined, with one problem either a symptom or cause of another.

"In the mountains, if you couldn't get a job, you couldn't get health care and certainly couldn't take care of your kids. Coal jobs were good pay, but black lung was rampant and the work was physically exhausting," she said. She didn't want to focus only on education, the original intent of AVs, but rather on larger-scale problems like the ones she recently vowed to upend in Atlanta: lack of food, poor schools, and corrupt politicians. Everything seemed like part of a never-ending cycle in which one element fed into another. She deliberated for days on what was most important to the community, and what was most important to her. She would sit on the porch in the evenings with a bourbon in hand and be alone with her thoughts. As she stared across to the mountains and the creek side, she remembered her mom and the night she spent in the yard waiting for her to give birth. The hardship she and so many women faced by never seeing a doctor seemed paramount. It seemed that the foundation of a decent life was to have good health and access to health care. She remembered the woman who couldn't find a hospital to have her baby, and she couldn't forget the time her hair fell out from typhoid when she was young. Health care was central to attending school, working at a job, and even happiness—a state of being out of reach for too many poor folks. She had to make it her fight now that she had the chance to make a difference. Eula knew the afternoon she spent naïvely arguing with ARH was what set her on this path, so she decided there on the porch that access to health care was going to be her mission.

Eula, Steve, and Maxine devised a plan that their first duty as new AVs would be to survey residents on their health needs. While Eula assumed she already knew what those needs would be, running a proper survey would give her an excuse to knock on doors, get into people's homes, and learn what was really going on. What she found in the following days and weeks surprised even her.

They began the survey earnestly hoping to knock on every door up and down route 979 in Floyd County. Every day the clan would gather at Eula's, set out a game plan, and drive as far as they could through the holler, even walking the paths that weren't accessible with the Bronco. They made it through every nook and cranny of Mud Creek and found people living in abandoned barns and trailers up on cinder blocks. Eula thought she already knew everyone in Little and Big Mud Creek, but she quickly learned there were many strangers who lived extremely secluded lives, and doors were left unanswered by nearly half of those they approached. People were wary of strangers in the mountains, and oftentimes, the three of them were met at the door by a sneer or—thankfully less often—a shotgun.

When invited in, Eula asked health-related questions, but focused on listening. She asked what the parents knew about the school lunches, whether someone in the family worked, if they had seen a doctor in the past year, and even what they had for supper the night before. Some had too much pride to be honest. Some were so angry at life that there wasn't time in the day to hear all of their problems. These visits gave Eula an insight into peculiar behaviors she hadn't noticed before. For instance, if a man was home, the woman of the house would simply not talk, deferring any questions to her husband.

"You couldn't get a word out of the women," Eula lamented. "They would tell you if they'd participate or come to a meeting, but they would never tell you the truth or what was really on their mind. But if the man wasn't there, it was like a loose fire hose. You couldn't get some of the women to stop talking."[68]

After a week and a half of surveying, she was even more disheartened about the state of her community. She found that many of the women smoked only because of the depression and bondage they found themselves in. If the man of the house got sick, he would find a way to see a doctor to make sure he could continue to work. But if a woman got sick, the man would decide not to spend the money and simply tell her to bear the sickness. It was wretchedly clear for Eula, in her own life and in the lives of her mountain sisters, that they weren't equals. Women, the backbone of each Appalachian family, weren't even given a chance and disregarded during the slightest hardship. While it wasn't completely clear to Eula at the time, the lack of education worked its way into their lifestyles. Women in the mountains, unlike today, lacked any sort of exercise, and harbored terrible infant feeding practices, often giving solid food, soda drinks, and other high sugar foods in early infancy.

Most alarming, however, were the instances of domestic abuse, eerily similar to what Eula was facing at home. She found it alarming and enraging to see bruised women throughout the hollers in homes she visited, and she wasn't quite equipped to deal with it or console the victims. These revelations gave Eula an opportunity to connect with folks in an earnest way, but also served as sore reminders of the torment she faced in her own life. She had little to offer other than empathy and would later say that it was an important experience—to see abuse outside of her own life—to fully understand how awful it was in her home. The stories of abuse made her so angry, and yet not angry enough to make a real change in her life. She and so many women in Appalachia were stuck with nowhere to turn and no one to talk to but each other.[69]

Shedding new light on the community she lived in weighed heavily on her heart those first few days of surveying. She wondered at times if she could continue on knowing what she knew about the way her neighbors actually lived. Even for a small mountain holler, Eula realized that over the years, she only knew and cared for a small group of folks, and she was witnessing how the rest of them lived. These mountains made it easy for the community to remain to itself, and for families to insulate their unsavoriness from the wider world.

The survey results highlighted the simplest issue that, once clear, struck the three AVs as the most intuitive to understand. The mountains surrounding Mud Creek live and breathe only through the creeks, streams, and brooks that flow in between and around them. The water of the mountains had sustained generations, and even aided in Eula's early moonshine production. In retrospect, Eula thought it was simple to understand and core to their existence in the mountains. Creeks wove through their communities, serving as both a playground and a place of essential life. Water seemed to be the single most important resource for most families as it was commonly used in food and bathing. But for too many years, the water had been wasted, and the community faced a severe dearth of clean water. Somehow, Eula had never considered this on her own until the survey. She knew the creek water was suspect, but she just assumed her well water was healthy and safe. It was an assumption based on generations of use. However, seeing multiple families deal with dysentery and dirty wells gave her a new understanding that almost all water sources were tainted.

Her first task was learning how to test water acidity, and once she knew, she initially went home to test her own sources. After she deemed safe the well that supplied Randy, Troy, Nanetta, and Danny, Eula returned to homes she had surveyed to test their wells. The early results were dire.

"It's a wonder sometimes I think that the whole population in places like ours didn't just wipe out from drinking contaminated water," she said.

The leadership at Appalachian Volunteers was convinced—they had to fight hard for this issue. The AVs, with the help of eager undergrads from the University of Kentucky, began systematically testing water samples from various wells throughout Mud Creek. The kids were resourceful and relentless, qualities Eula admired. While Maxine and Steve's cars faced what seemed to be weekly mechanical problems, the kids were happy to bring their nicer cars from Lexington to finish the survey. They worked day and night, knowing they were directly helping the community understand its needs.

Their results matched some intuitive conclusions. Only a few houses near the interstate had indoor plumbing and the rest inside the holler depended on old, drying wells for drinking water and creeks for general use. The problem was stark—according to a final AV report, the majority of drinking water came from open wells, 75 percent of which were contaminated. Water even in exposed creek beds had fewer bacteria than water in the wells. They surmised that since the walls of family wells were built rather short, a healthy supply of water would be ruined when rain overflowed the well. The surface water couldn't help but mix with excrement of dogs, chickens, and whatever other beasts roamed the mountains, before it fell into the wells.[70]

The county needed to construct new wells, and the argument Eula and the other activists used was that if people had clean water, they could be healthy, work, and be put on a path to a more generous life. With the community's input, Eula and the volunteers developed the Mud Creek Water Board, which would serve during the following years as a place for folks to lodge their complaints and for the community to act with a single voice. It would serve as an organizing unit for the community to rally around clean water, lobby for funds, and manage the construction of new wells.

The board comprised everyday folks and more senior activists, and quickly set up meetings to speak with the Pikeville Water Department, the Floyd County Health Department, and even Kentucky state health officials. Led by Eula, the board traveled to Frankfort to meet with Governor Breathitt. With their data in hand, they successfully lobbied the governor to declare Mud Creek an emergency area, which compelled the Office of Economic Opportunity (OEO) to fund the construction of a new water system. The county health department agreed to devise an early plan, with County Judge John Stumbo's input, to get permits from the EPA and rights-of-way over land to pump water from Pikeville to the hollers.

It was a bold infrastructure project that would take time.

But as the plan came to fruition over the months, the culture of political patronage so endemic to the region reared its ugly head again. County health department officials began to site drilling areas only at politically opportune locations.

"They drilled only on special people's land, important people, in pasture fields where people had cattle, or sometimes in places where people couldn't get access," Eula said. "It was all according to *who* was friends with *whom*."

They had worked so hard, only to face the same dual antagonists that had plagued Appalachia for decades—power and corruption—but that didn't stop their efforts. Eula was elected chairwoman of the board, and began a multi-year fight against local politicians on every pipe and well that was drilled. She had taken her training and put it to work with each new well directly affecting the health of an entire family. She had to ensure transparency and effectiveness, and her perch on the Water Board gave her official status to push forward.[71]

Chapter 16

"PEOPLE WERE FINALLY FIGHTING BACK," EULA remembered, and she was at the forefront of the movement to demand jobs, health, and opportunity. Fighting for clean water and her subsequent election to lead the fight against selective drilling, made her a renowned figure in Eastern Kentucky. What she may not have known at the time, however, was that the late 1960s and early '70s also served as an inflection point in the greater fight for Appalachia, and the ennobled quest to end poverty in American once and for all.

The War on Poverty, a little past its halfway mark, bet its reputation on the Appalachian poor, and attempted to radically shift the trajectory of a historically depressed area. While the War empowered activists like Eula, Maxine Kinney, Woodrow Rogers, Steve Brooks, and others to create change with locally organized institutions such as the Mud Creek Water Board, the verdict was still out on whether the fight could actually achieve its intended goal: eradicating American poverty. With the War on Poverty legislation up for reauthorization, many of the initiative's planners were unsure if they were getting anywhere or just skimming the surface of the poverty problem. Even with gains across urban and rural America, many skeptics claimed the poor were not being utilized to solve their own problems to the extent necessary.

Sargent Shriver, director of the Office of Economic Opportunity (OEO), considered one of the federal government's prime missions to be mobilization of the poor as a political force capable of reshaping public institutions. Along with the VISTA program's mission to include the poor in their own poverty alleviation, many people thought the poor could also be a force to change political institutions from the ground up. Some cynics pilloried the notion, stating that the idea was simply a ploy by Democratic strategists and the Kennedy Administration to solidify a voting bloc. However, the idea of breaking local political fiefdoms was as commendable as it was monumental, and Shriver pushed forward to maximize local participation. Three monumental legislative words would help Sargent Shriver and his team achieve this goal—maximum feasible participation.[72]

It was revolutionary in its simplicity. Title II of the Economic Opportunity Act included this language to envision comprehensive, community-wide planning and implementation of programs aimed at combating poverty— with the impoverished at the helm. It was a powerful statement of faith in the poor, and one that had the backing of the federal largesse. In Shriver's attempt to "serve the poor, speak for the poor, and marshal America's resources on behalf of the poor," he was twisting legislative language to employ a brashly innovative approach to federal-local partnerships by placing the crux of the effort on the poor to lift themselves up.

Even among those who framed the original Economic Opportunity Act, there was little consensus about how the phrase "maximum feasible participation" was formulated or about its intended meaning. There was no public discussion of the participation clause in the bill. Committee hearings reveal that, with the exception of then Attorney General Robert F. Kennedy, there is no mention of the clause by any other government official in several thousand pages of testimony. Congressional floor debates were also void of the phrase. In some sense, it was the biggest redistribution and delegation of power since the Fourteenth Amendment—and leaders hardly mentioned its existence. However, once it was in place, Shriver used it to maximum advantage. These programs included the incredibly popular early childhood education program Head Start, Legal Aid for the poor, VISTA, Follow Through, and Upward Bound. All of these programs required folks in the community to be part of their implementation, under the assumption that power had to be wrested from local political bosses through these programs. These new agencies and activists, Eula included, were working to defy local political bosses and press forward without bowing to entrenched interests.[73]

While a few elected officials who had built fiefdoms were upset with the potential "War on City Hall," Eula and her allies preferred to call the people-powered revolution a "War on Patronage" instead of a War on Poverty. Democratic mayors Richard Daley of Chicago and Robert Wagner of New York took strong stances against the framework and so did small-town mayors throughout Appalachia. Conservative critics lambasted the idea, claiming that once in motion, it was nothing less than a blueprint for revolution. For once, Eula thought, they may have been right. In Eastern Kentucky, the Big Sandy Community Action Program, along with Appalachian Volunteers, served as national test cases for grassroots power.

Shriver ordered his lieutenants to implement the slew of legislated programs toward this end, but one major area of poverty alleviation was still lacking. Planners had yet to devise a health program for the rural poor, and Shriver wanted to create one serving as a pilot and develop best practices to mimic across the country. He also understood that power structure of health care, itself operating in a separate local political culture, had to be disrupted.

So in the midst of Eula's water battles, the minds behind the War on Poverty turned their attention to researching and developing innovative health care services in a rural and low-performing setting. Floyd County, sadly, was the perfect location.

Floyd, tucked deep into the green Eastern Kentucky mountains, was as rural as it gets and certainly disadvantaged enough. Thirty-five percent of Floyd County families had incomes under the poverty line, and unemployment was over ten percent, more than double the national rate. Child mortality was alarmingly high and health professionals in the area knew deep down that the true health care picture of the county was downright dreadful.[74]

T. P. Hipkins, then president of the ARH hospital system, with a helpful nudge from then ARC Commissioner John Whisman, used these dire statistics as ammunition to sketch together an innovative health program for the OEO to champion. He envisioned a medical access program headquartered at McDowell ARH with outposts in various hollers around Floyd County. Flexibility, access, and, above all, experimentation, were highlights of his delivery system. The key would be what he called patient program coordination teams—simple aid and screening stations with nurses who could properly diagnose ailments and then refer them immediately to a local hospital. The five-million-dollar proposal was for multiple triage clinics, of sorts, in the hollers; the proposal would meet new maximum feasible participation requirements through collaboration with the local Community Action Program (CAP). The proposal postulated that there was no better place in America to start solving dire outcomes and lack of care. They claimed even seasoned health care professionals would be "surprised by the true picture . . . about the health care status of indigents in this Kentucky county."[75]

With their patient-access model in mind, Hipkins and Russell Hall, health officer for Floyd County; Harry Eastburn, director of Floyd County CAP; and Henry Stumbo, Floyd County judge executive, made the pilgrimage to Washington to meet with their Seventh District Kentucky congressman, Carl D. Perkins. Representative Perkins, a loyal Democrat who was eponymous with the Federal Perkins Student Loans, was born in Hindman, Kentucky, and spent his nearly thirty years in Congress fighting for the most disadvantaged Eastern Kentuckians. Perkins was an early supporter and ally of the OEO and Head Start, and his name now graces the Education and Labor Committee Room in the House of Representatives, of which he became chairman in 1966 after Adam Clayton Powell of Harlem retired. He was a smooth political operator, half good-ole-boy back-slapper, and half cold political chess master. He knew whom and what it took to get something done, and he often delivered for his people back home with ease. He was also a caring man who, while wrapped up in the bare-knuckle politics of Washington, never forgot where he came from and for whom he was fighting.[76]

The four Eastern Kentuckians together hashed out a plan in the Rayburn House Office Building to submit the proposal to OEO. They changed the applicant from ARH to the more palatable Big Sandy CAP, and in accordance with the concept of maximum feasible participation, the Floyd County Board of Health would help administer the program. Stumbo was overjoyed with the arrangement. If the proposal were to be accepted, it would be yet another arrow in his political quiver—one he desperately needed after the school lunch debacle and the creation of the Water Board.

The Floyd County Comprehensive Health Services Program (FCCHSP) was funded and deployed early in 1967 to much fanfare. Eula felt "it was about damn time" people could gain access to affordable health care. Local folks seldom if ever saw federal health spending in the area of that magnitude. It was magical, Eula thought, how various parts of Floyd County's gentry came together to accomplish something for the people that, at the time, seemed to be a monumental achievement. Perhaps the local politicians were doing right by the people for once and not looking out just for themselves, she thought. It was as refreshing as it was unbelievable.

The program hired a well-respected local physician, Dr. Titzler, and opened their first coordinating clinic in a small building with multiple patient rooms and nurses on staff. The clinic wasn't exactly *in* the holler, it was at the mouth of it, near US 23, which still required a long walk or a drive for most patients. Transportation turned out to be a problem equal in magnitude to seeing and paying for a doctor. In her time off from child rearing and inspecting wells, Eula joined Steve and Maxine to volunteer and help with offering transportation to those who needed it. It was common back then for folks to pay others for rides out of the mountains, so Eula was happy to fire up the Bronco if folks needed a lift. Those early patient drives reminded Eula of her father's struggle to exit the holler in search of medical help for Nanny's pregnancy. Luckily, folks along Route 979 could access doctors quickly and be able to treat illnesses before they became severe. In only a few weeks, the requests ballooned to the point that Eula had to create a waiting list for folks who wanted to get a check-up.

As their volunteering with the new health program continued, Eula and other activists paid close attention to the management and structure of the clinics. They were a bit skeptical about all the positive comments being thrown around in the papers and among town folks. The editor of the *Floyd County Times* was chummy with the clinic doctor, and the nurses at the clinic weren't doing much treating at all, it seemed, other than informing patients of which hospital they should go to for additional care. To make matters worse, the money was slated only for patient referrals to Floyd County hospitals and not the better-equipped hospitals in Pike County or elsewhere. It operated at times like an assembly line, shuffling patients in only to shuffle them right out. Sometimes folks didn't even get needed blood pressure tests or common exams before they were sent off to a hospital.[77]

As the FCCHSP was in full swing, Eula discovered she was pregnant yet again. She decided she would find out for herself what was really going on and visit the clinic as a patient. It was a significant moment for many reasons. Not only would a visit allow Eula to observe how the clinic truly operated, but it would also serve as Eula's first encounter with professional medical care during a pregnancy.

McKinley had taken the Bronco the day she was scheduled to go, so she waited for clinic transportation and other volunteers to pick her up. She sat on her porch rocking chair for hours, and when they did finally arrive, they made her sit—six months pregnant—in the back seat.

As they drove through the bumpy and winding holler, the middle left window was left wide open, allowing gravel dust to roll in, covering everyone with whom she was huddled. They finally managed to close it, but enough dust had already entered the vehicle to make them all look like ghosts. When they arrived, Eula immediately went to the bathroom to straighten up and show a modicum of decency. Her dress was covered in dust, but she managed to wash her face and hair. Others were so filthy after the ride that they refused to be seen out of sheer dignity. Worse yet, clinic workers would yell aloud in front of the crowd about patient medical conditions, embarrassing the already undignified looking bunch.

It was a shoddy operation, lacking any sense of patient care and run by young women who "didn't know better at all" about how to operate a clinic. After a quick check-up, Eula was directed to Martin's Hospital to receive further testing and be assigned an OB/GYN. She left dejected, not only for herself, but also for the vast majority of pregnant women who would never have the means to afford the hospital service.

Eula documented her visit, and made sure to take notes of various patient stories she collected. Each week she would recite her notes at the EKWRO Health Committee Meeting, giving others the courage to chime in with their own stories of dismal service. After three weeks, the group decided they had seen enough. This was not equitable health care and folks didn't need to just be told to go to a hospital they could never afford. No one should be lauding this effort, Eula thought, and they certainly shouldn't be simply pushing folks to hospitals or giving out fifteen prescriptions when it was obvious the doctors owned the pharmacies. The clinic, they demanded, should be educating folks about their ailments and not leaving them further confused with a multitude of drugs.[78]

Not only were doctors and nurses offering poor care, but the program also lacked a robust educational mission. Family planning, nutritional lectures, homemaking, and environmental health aspects of the program—all suggestions from community activists—had yet to be fully realized. Perhaps most importantly, the experiential learning and education of the staff itself was meager. One seasoned nurse was quotes as claiming, "I've lived here twenty-two years and didn't know there were this many crippled children . . . I didn't know all of these hollers and creeks exist. Didn't know where they were or what they were about." It was a notion even Eula had to face when she began her work as an AV, and it was a reality making the task of providing care much more difficult.[79]

Soon the activists learned the Floyd County Medical Society, composed of doctors and business people whose interests were in promoting a vibrant and moneyed health system, gave the original order to send FCCHSP patients to nearby hospitals that would benefit financially. It reeked of corruption, and it surprised even the activists that they didn't see this level of manipulation coming. This region, as Eula thought, had been plagued by low expectations for so long that they should have known the program was too good to be true. They had feared the good Dr. Titzler was hired under orders from the program's managers to provide only a minimal level of care—and transfer all patients to McDowell or Martin where additional money could be poached.

Eula decided to test the system again. After an EKWRO meeting one night, a group of activists came up with a plan to prove their assumptions; they jumped in Eula's Ford Bronco and headed toward the clinic outpost. On the way, they prepped a young patient named Goldie in the backseat to ready herself for entering the clinic in dire need of care.

As they arrived, they rushed into the outpost with Eula in the lead. "We got a lady here who needs help now! She ain't gonna make it!"

A soft-spoken receptionist approached the group, took a quick look at the sickly young lady, and remarked, "She doesn't look so bad, what's wrong with her?" Then, to the receptionist's horror, Goldie's eyes rolled to the back of her head and she fainted to the ground. Goldie turned out to be a great actress.

"Oh Lord! We gotta get her to McDowell immediately!" the receptionist gasped, apparently not knowing what to do other than get her out of the clinic.

"We ain't got time for McDowell. Where's Dr. Titzler? He's gotta see her now," Eula said.

The receptionist was in hysterics; she had never witnessed a patient pass out cold in front of her. After a bit of arguing among the group about what to do, Dr. Titzler ran to the lobby to check on the commotion. Goldie snuck in momentary peeks to gauge the situation as she lay unbelievably still while the others crowded around her.

Dr. Titzler, the acting medical director and a usually calm and quiet man, rushed to her side. He paused for a moment, stood upright and said, "I can't see her Eula. You see, I'm wearing two hats right now—I'm administrator *and* doctor."

"Well, put the doctor hat on! You telling me you ain't seeing patients?"

"Not quite . . . just diagnosing and sending them on," Dr. Titlser admitted in a stupor over his competing responsibilities.

Eula roared, "If you don't see this patient, you ain't gonna have a damn head to wear a hat on!"

With that quip, Goldie couldn't help but break a smile. The others, realizing their cover was blown, mumbled something about her being a resilient young woman and shuffled her out of the office as fast as they could. They had gotten all the proof they needed. It wasn't the doctor's fault, and it sure wasn't the fault of the young receptionists who were hired to work there. The clinic couldn't treat patients because they were being forced to succumb to local political demands.

"All right, Eula, no more games," Dr. Titzler scolded.

As she walked out the door, she turned and responded, "How about we both take that advice to heart?"[80]

Chapter 17

1970

"WE'RE BEING SHAFTED!" EULA SAID AS SHE launched into a stem-winder at a FCCHSP board meeting. Eula had recently given birth to Dean at Martin Hospital, and in addition to the story of Goldie passing out in front of Dr. Titzler, she recounted to the board a multitude of stories she had collected, making the argument that folks without insurance and little income could not simply go to a hospital like rich folks could. The clinic's purpose, she argued, was to benefit the poor, but "the poor are just being shuffled and sent off, not treated."

Eula's efforts to expose the true nature of the FCCHSP proved futile. Even before the meeting started, board officials attempted to confuse Eula about the whereabouts of the meeting. Instead of hosting it at their normal location at the Board of Health offices, the members schemed to evade the activists by hosting it in the decrepit basement. When she did eventually stumble into the meeting, her arguments fell on deaf ears as the board members continued to spout seemingly absurd statistics on the program's supposed triumphs.

Despite the protests, the Board of Health and Judge Stumbo took credit where it wasn't due and deemed the FCCHSP a success. They claimed a remarkable statistic—nearly 12,610 out of 20,000 eligible Floyd Countians, more than half of the county, were identified and treated at the clinic. They were somehow claiming to have given care to more than half of the poor in Floyd County, which was farcical at best. The statistic may have referred to the number of people who stepped foot in the clinic. It was a spurious statistic to help the local medical establishment gain more money from poor and middle-income patients, while claiming to treat them. It was true the clinic itself had seen hundreds and possibly thousands of patients, but the statistics were a sleight of hand, and did nothing to account for actual health care outcomes. In Eula's opinion, the poor were simply becoming patients of one of the surrounding hospitals or consumers of pharmaceuticals prescribed at the clinics.

The board did its best to bolster the program despite two damning reports recently released by outside observers. Kentucky's new Republican governor, who already despised all "big government" initiatives in Floyd County, initiated the dual reviews of the program—the Hentschel Review and the Sparer Review—to document the clinic's progress. Sargent Shriver was a big proponent of the reviews as well; especially with the program's second round of funding due soon and with the potential of thirty-five additional programs to be established across the country in the mold of FCCHSP.[81]

These reports showed stark mismanagement, and detailed that the program's flaws were legion. By 1970, FCCHSP had spent nearly $2.5 million in becoming a referral program with little to show for quality health care. No health education was being provided and the delivery system seemed unnecessarily complicated; it was especially hampered by the lack of paramedical personnel who could triage ailments before referring patients to an already busy hospital. Even the hiring practices—a staple of maximum feasible participation—were preferential, with only twenty of the one hundred positions being filled by the poor. More than $600,000—double the original amount allotted—went to doctors, dentists, and hospitals instead of to patients. Nearly every facet of the program was underperforming—from family planning services to the hiring of local practitioners. The reports noted the clear conflicts of interest among the board, and claimed it had led to the sorry treatment of patients and the hiring of only those with political connections. The Hentschel Report even levied philosophical criticism on the program and its lack of sociotherapy by criticizing it for "doing for the poor instead of having the poor do for themselves." The report gave activists in the community fodder by reaffirming that after spending millions, FCCHSP created little more than a referral service that had yet to make a dent in the overall health of the community.

In response, Eula, the CAP board, and EKWRO created a coalition to ensure people were properly served by the generous allotment from Washington. They wanted to redefine comprehensive health care to focus more on education and provide more direct services. While they realized the clinics couldn't treat everything or everyone who walked in the door, the immediate alternative shouldn't be to ship them off to the benefit of the already rich medical elites. Her appearance at the board meeting, with both reports in hand, helped force some much-needed change. In fact, OEO demanded changes or, they stated, they would cut funding completely.

Harry Eastburn of the Big Sandy CAP, who was charged by the county judge with running the program, was forced to change direction. Eastburn couldn't simply let the program go as it represented almost 30 percent of the Big Sandy CAP's budget. At a follow-up meeting organized on July 28, 1970, to discuss the future of the program, members of the Board of Health, Big Sandy CAP, EKWRO, and others convened in Prestonsburg to bring wholesale change to FCCHSP. The status quo was about to be dismantled.

The meeting was cleverly held at the site of the county superintendent's office where many EKWRO members—including Eula—were still not welcome because of the altercation with the school board years ago. Eula and the others were a bit intimidated, but forged ahead with a few chuckles of nostalgia.

As the meeting started, many of the same refrains were heard. The CEO of the Bank of Paintsville insisted the federal largesse continue to come through his organization, and Floyd County Medical Society members were adamant about the efficacy of using their hospitals. Prestonsburg Mayor Dr. George Archer spoke out adamantly against creating a new board, citing his Washington connections, and threatening he could use his role as former president of the Kentucky Medical Association to influence doctors not to follow new rules. However, because the OEO had appointed Glen Hentschel as interim full-time director with authority to make changes, he forced the board to elect new members, implement new titles for employees, and significantly change the structure of the program. The new board included the county judge and the school superintendent, and representatives from Big Sandy CAP, the Department of Child Welfare, ARH, the nursing society, the ministerial association, organized labor, and the community, and an African American representative—even though the African American population in Floyd was hovering around two hundred people. It was as inclusive as it was unwieldy.[82]

Eula and the activists went to work, knowing that placing a community representative on the board was their chance to have their voice heard. It was Eula's first political-style campaign and she canvassed the county, knocking on many of the same doors she had knocked on years earlier during her water survey, and handed out pamphlets. It was an easy sell to make, as many folks Eula targeted had poor experiences at the clinics themselves.

When the board election took place a week later, EKWRO and other community members watched as all sorts of dirty tricks were deployed against them. Medical transportation employees were asked to hand out brochures for preferred candidates and the illiterate were allegedly given money to vote for the old board's interest. Some had even set up the nomination and election system to inhibit EKWRO from being a united front.

Despite the political elites' attempts to stifle the election, on August 15, some two hundred Mud Creek residents and EKWRO organizers elected Eula Hall to represent them on the new board of directors for FCCHSP. Eula was again honored by the trust her community placed in her and stood ready to "show those corrupt fellers a thing or two." While McKinley saw it as another distraction without a paycheck, she knew she had to withstand his criticism because her involvement was possibly the last hope for the program to succeed.

Over the next two months, the board would meet to design and approve a new budget, and Eula made EKWRO's wishes heard. On October 15, FCCHSP introduced their newly OEO-appointed full-time director, Dr. Arnold Schechter, who was to lead the march toward an effective rural health program. Peculiar, Eula thought, that after all the drama they would decide to hire a Chicago-born doctor with little knowledge of Appalachia. But perhaps, she thought, an outsider is exactly what they needed.

Chapter 18

Dr. Schecter grew up in the intellectual circles of Chicago's Hyde Park—a cultural continent away from Mud Creek. His parents were part of the great Jewish migration from Eastern Europe to America, and as people who knew injustice all too well, they instilled a strong sense of social justice in the young idealist.

The panoply of ideas and peoples in Chicago pushed Schecter to explore different cultures as a youth. After studying at the University of Chicago, he took the advice of an African American friend and attended medical school at Howard University in Washington DC. On Schecter's arrival in 1958, he was one of only ten white students. He quickly became part of the community, even dating the daughter of America's first black astronaut. While in school, he focused more on passing exams than taking part in the intense political and social debates of the day. He recalled that maybe a bit of fear kept him from getting on the buses heading south during the height of the civil rights movement, but little did he know his faith in justice would be tested less than a decade down the road.

After medical school, Schecter attended Harvard where he was drafted into the Vietnam War. He spent the next two years at Fort Knox, his first experience in Kentucky, after which he used his GI loan to finance flying lessons. He was a serious student, but also a free spirit looking for a way to make his mark on the world while having some fun doing it. He heard of a curious job offered by the OEO to run a health program in a small hamlet of Eastern Kentucky. He had an informational interview where he learned about new rural health access methods being tested and was excited about the prospects OEO had for changing the health environment in such a downtrodden part of America. What they failed to tell him was the extensive history of the program, and the reports of mismanagement and corruption. That aside, the sense of adventure had left its mark, and he decided to jump at the opportunity.[83]

Schecter's first meeting as the newly hired director was an intimidating one held in the congressional offices of Representative Perkins. Schecter remembered that the congressman sat him down in his stately office and decided to tell him the lay of the land back in his home district. Congressman Perkins began by wishing Schecter success, and laid out for him the constellation of power brokers, politicians, and egos he would have to navigate while implementing necessary changes. As Schecter walked out of the meeting that day, somewhat overwhelmed by the task at hand, he remembered the congressman's staff mentioned he should be sure to "be very nice to Judge Stumbo and the others there." He wasn't quite sure what that statement meant, and whether it was advice or a threat, but he listened intently. The looks on their faces told the story of what was yet to come.

Before his official start, Schecter studied up and toured other health clinics to get an idea of the new frontier of rural health care. He visited the community Park DuValle clinic in West

Louisville, as well as Dr. Jack Geiger's clinics in the Mississippi Delta. Geiger was famous for initiating the community health center model in the United States, founding and directing the nation's first two community health centers in the Mississippi and Boston. Schecter figured it would be wise to take lessons learned and apply them to the reorganization of the FCCHSP.[84]

When Schecter arrived in Appalachia, he and his wife found a small house in Drift, Kentucky, about ten miles east over a mountain from Route 979. They were initially very impressed with folks they met, including Eula Hall, and found Floyd County to be a much more dynamic community than they expected.

"I guess I expected to be seen as a Jewish big-city person with horns or something," he recalled. Instead, none of the stereotypes of ignorance and destitution that plague Appalachia's identity proved true. The doctor was treated with respect, even given a sixty-day extension by the board to revise the budget and incorporate any new priorities he may have. Dr. Schecter presented himself with an open mind and had plenty of innovative ideas to revitalize the FCCHSP.

The young doctor had a lot on his plate, and plenty to learn about his new surroundings that sat between the mountains and creeks. He perceived, correctly, that there was a lot more than simply a rural health program going on in the mountains. A fight was coming between the activists and the political class, and Eastern Kentucky in those years was becoming a hotbed of political activity. The FCCHSP was just the start. The War on Poverty, AV and VISTA organizing, and the intrusion of young outsiders into Eastern Kentucky, made many conservatives wary. Local officials despised the organizing, viewing the new community groups as tools to subvert local leadership. Many also believed the federal largesse was being used only to make dependent those who were formerly independent. Leading the charge was the first elected Republican governor of Kentucky in nearly twenty years (and he would be the last until 2003), Louie Nunn. "Appalachia needed help, but I can't say it needed the War on Poverty," he would say in the 1990s, when recalling his time as governor.

The state government in Frankfort created its own Kentucky "Un-American Activities Committee" molded after Senator Joseph McCarthy's infamous investigation into communist sympathizers. The Kentucky Committee was equally as perverse and investigated Eula's close friend Edith Easterling, along with many other prominent Kentuckians. Easterling, never one to shy away from a fight, wore a bright red dress to the state capitol to mark the occasion and goad communist-fearing lawmakers.

Coal strikes were a daily occurrence, strip mining was undoing mountains in a matter of weeks, and even more outspoken new community groups like Save the Land and the People were sprouting up throughout the region. This wave of free-spirited provocateurs spread throughout the country, and officials were ready to stamp it out anyway they could at home. In a famous example of the fear and irrationality that reigned during the time, a group of folks in Pikeville led by the county attorney, organized a midnight raid resulting in the arrest of three poverty workers who were later pegged with the dubious charge of sedition. The publicity from the arrests and the subsequent firebombing of their homes created a culture of fear for those who spoke out, including Eula.[85]

Eula remembers telling Dr. Schecter during their first visit not to mind the recent stories, and that "people here were ready to accept him with open arms." She also made him promise to do the right thing by the people, and if he did, Eula and EKWRO would have his back. "I really liked Dr. Schecter, but bless his heart . . ." Eula said years later, "he had absolutely no idea what he was getting into."

Dr. Schecter, with the backing of a powerful congressman

and community groups, decided this was a ripe environment for real innovation in rural health care delivery. To him, Floyd County was the ideal laboratory, a place where ideas dreamt up by academics and clinicians could be field-tested under optimal conditions. However, his plans would be short-lived as his misunderstanding of the budget and political troubles before him would throw wrenches in his ambitious path.

Schecter moved into his office in Wheelwright, Kentucky, and immediately began to study the numbers. He surmised there was room to experiment and he drew up an expansive budget request that included closed circuit television, the hiring of significantly more nurses, practitioners, technicians, medical students, paramedics, and most extravagantly, helicopter evacuation of patients in dire need of care. Schecter had learned about these effective evacuations from his time as an army flight surgeon, and thought it was a perfect antidote to the patient travel through the imposing mountains of Eastern Kentucky. In the end, his clinics would be the full-service clinics EKWRO had envisioned, with the new alternative budget costing $2.9 million, significantly more than what was expected. Dr. Schecter eagerly circulated his draft among the board for review.[86]

The doctor's ideas were dead on arrival. They were received with little fanfare from across the spectrum of stakeholders. "Poor people definitely need an airlift," Eula joked, "but not that kind of airlift. I'll drive the Bronco, but you ain't gonna see me flying helicopters through these hollers to get folks around." Initially the cost wasn't the issue; the types of technical fixes Dr. Schecter proposed were exactly what OEO directors and Washington technocrats had decided were the innovative answers to American rural health care delivery. The bulk of the new board, and others who were involved in the first patient coordinating clinics, simply thought he was overreaching with the more outlandish parts of his budget. New practitioners and a more inclusive health care delivery system were received as a welcome attempt toward better serving patients, but helicopters and closed circuit TV, while theoretically interesting methods to access geographically difficult areas, seemed outrageous. Big-city hospitals only hoped to afford one helicopter to serve their patients, and many homes in the hollers didn't even own televisions. No plans existed to manage programming for the TV station. To make matters worse, no one was consulted before being presented with the new budget items, making his ideas much more foreign among the board and activists.

Eula was one among many who got wind of Schecter's plans and told him to slow down, but he plowed ahead unfazed. With Perkins's support in his back pocket, he was determined to implement his full agenda. His budget ballooned to nearly twice as large as previous plans at a time when folks were extremely cynical about the program's previous funding and distribution. His budget was similarly bloated with ideas, and while he might have had his heart in the right place, Eula explained, "If I went to New York City to start a program, I'd first ask those folks there what they wanted before going whole hog."[87]

Over the next six weeks, the sad unraveling of his short-lived budget would play itself out. Dr. Schecter would completely alienate the fiscal court, the medical association, and even some in the activist community with his ideas for revamping the program. However, Schecter did have the backing of OHA, not to mention Congressman Perkins, and disregarded his growing opposition as he continued to push for his innovations.

Eventually, the Floyd County Medical Society, a disjointed bunch with their own internal skirmishes, would come together to fight Dr. Schecter. They agreed it was time to put past conflicts behind them, and join forces to fight the outsiders ruining their health program. In their opinion, the region had a fairly decent system already in place—cancer care in Pikeville, cardiac cases in Williamson, and a black lung clinic in Prestonsburg—that could become the basis for an expanded program beyond Floyd County, subsidizing care without siting new clinics in the hollers. They also argued that existing hospitals in McDowell might be jeopardized if the program treated more patients instead of referring. Philosophically, they continued to argue that they couldn't idly stand by while their tax dollars were being used against them—and their business interests—in the form of a wild-eyed OEO program. One board member who owned a pharmacy said, "Do you think I want them coming in here and setting up clinics with OEO money—my money! Setting up full-fledged clinics with tax money? Why, that's just socialism and its dreamers like Schecter that think the government should pay for it all."[88]

There was also a peculiar fatalism about the new practitioners. Folks were concerned that Floyd County would only be able to recruit 'rejects'—those doctors with little skill to work elsewhere. It wasn't easy to recruit medical talent to the mountains. Doctors in general looked for good schools and neighborhoods when they looked for places to practice, and even many mountain-born doctors decided to instead take their talents to Lexington or Louisville. While this scenario would later bring scores of Indian immigrant doctors to work in the mountains of Eastern Kentucky, at that particular point, no one in the medical community knew where they would find the right workforce willing to move to Floyd County.[89]

At a secret meeting led by Dr. Archer, which also included Woodrow Rogers, Eula, and Dr. Schecter, the board railed at Schecter for being a 'communist,' an outsider, and everything mean and demeaning they could come up with. Eula remembered watching board members stammer over one another trying to understand why a doctor with a degree from Washington, DC, would come down to Floyd County for such little money. They showed an extreme lack of faith in their own community, as Eula recalled, and simply couldn't understand why money didn't motivate him. They accused him of being a fake, dug up test examinations from his past, and hurled wild insults and threats. When a lady crossed the line by threatening his family directly, Eula and Woodrow rose to defend Schecter, but there was little to no room to work on a compromise. "These folks were ready to fight," Eula remembered.

The future of the program was in jeopardy, and Dr. Schecter, though standing strong in the face of severe opposition, wouldn't be able to hold on much longer.

Chapter 19

"IF IT WASN'T FOR EKWRO, THEY MIGHT HAVE KILLED Dr. Schecter," Eula said. Less than six months after he took the helm of the FCCHSP with his grand ideas for care delivery, the program was on the verge of shutting down. Articles were published in local and national newspapers; some were sympathetic to Schecter, others critical of OEO and Congressman Perkins. The OEO Office of Health Affairs sent its young director, Leon Cooper, down to Prestonsburg to sort out the mess. He held an emergency hearing involving all community partners to determine a way forward and talk through a serious budget request. The meeting quickly turned ugly, with threats and accusations flying in every direction. Cooper was disgusted and knew the community could no longer sustain a working relationship with regard to the clinic or properly disperse federal health funds. The decision was quickly made to let go of Dr. Schecter after an all-too-brief tenure, and end the once-lauded FCCHSP.[90]

The end of the program was an especially demoralizing defeat. While Eula and EKWRO fought over the previous year by Dr. Schecter's side to reallocate the funds, none of them were advocating for a complete withdrawal. Everyone was aware of the severe shortage of health care, and no one believed the problem had been solved by the wild assurances of the program's early backers. Yet, nearly three years after the program began, they were facing the demise and departure of federal funds. The entire community looked to the board—and EKWRO in particular—to lay blame.

Eula was devastated. "We went from having it all—to having all of nothing," she said. Whatever nominal level of health care residents of Mud Creek had through the program was gone, and all of the community's anger was directed toward the activists who tried to keep it.

"The community was looking at us, the activists, as the ones who ended the program. They couldn't see that the doctors were the ones who threw the first punch," Eula said.

The local physician community and politicians were quick to frame the argument to their benefit. The conflict that ended the FCCHSP made EKWRO out to be the instigators while also painting them as sympathizers with northern outsiders. It was a raw deal, Eula thought, and to make matters worse, her AV funding was in question as a result of changing priorities in the organization. In only a few short years, she had transformed herself into a community dynamo, but with the health program gone and the AV's eventual funding demise, she could be left with nothing of her own.

She refused to let this be the end, or to let EKWRO back down to powerful political interests. Although the federal government had officially shut off funds for the FCCHSP, they were far from admitting that Floyd County's health problems were solved. Luckily, Leon Cooper and other officials in Washington left open the option of entertaining another locally sourced idea if one came forward.

Eula noticed the opportunity and gathered her weary activists, along with a sympathetic lawyer from Prestonsburg named John Rosenberg, to produce a grant application for a new clinic in Mud Creek. The request was that the clinic have a board comprised *only* of community activists, and that it serve the people and would be run by the people. Activists such as Delmar Frasure, John Handshoe, Don Lafferty, Woodrow Rogers, Maxine Kinney, Thomas Lawson, and Ally Wicker were all integral partners, hoping to create a community-based clinic that—in Eula's words—would be "exactly like we had been talking about all along—for the people and by the people."[91]

While the group was busy putting together the structure for the new clinic, Eula learned that her paychecks, which had provided her with a profound level of independence from McKinley, were ending. She felt trapped again, not knowing what the future would hold and wondering if McKinley had been right all along. Was the toil of her activism worth the effort and sacrifice if it didn't ultimately help feed her kids?

Luckily, while drafting the application for the new health clinic, Eula impressed John Rosenberg so much that he decided to employ her at his legal aid clinic, AppalRED (Appalachian Research and Defense). Eula had previously met John when he and his wife, Jean, were traveling through the area deciding whether to permanently move to Eastern Kentucky. John and Jean later commented that speaking with Harry Caudill and Eula Hall made the decision to relocate "a no-brainer."

The Rosenbergs were unique to the mountains. The couple had only recently moved to nearby Prestonsburg, Kentucky, by way of Washington, DC, where John left a prestigious job in the Civil Rights Division of the Department of Justice. While John's accomplishments were impressive, his beginnings were beyond humble. John was born in Magdeburg, Germany, in the turbulent early 1930s, during the rise of the Third Reich. His father knew the five books of Moses by heart, and they lived in a house adjacent to a synagogue. One night in 1939, when John was just eight years old, German storm troopers pulled the family from the house to watch as the soldiers firebombed their temple. John thought he would die that night. His father was sent to a concentration camp, and John fled with his mother and siblings to Frankfurt.[92]

John eventually made it over to the United States from Holland in 1940 on the second-to-last boat leaving for America. He lived a rough childhood while his parents worked in the textile mills of South Carolina. Spartanburg had no religious leader for the new Jewish community, and Rosenberg's father, who escaped the camp to be with his family, became the de facto rabbi.

"Judaism is founded on the theory of justice," Rosenberg said, reflecting on his life's work. "My father instilled that in me at a young age."

While his father's teachings may have served as an influence, John's life experiences were what shaped him. When he joined the army as a navigator, he was deeply disturbed by watching his black colleagues be dismissed or overlooked on the basis of their skin color. When he attended Duke University, the school was still practicing an arcane quota program for Jewish students. In the late 1950s, Rosenberg attended law school with Julius Chambers, who later attained fame as a civil rights lawyer, and he was attracted to the newly formed Civil Rights Division of the Department of Justice. He served there eight years as a trial attorney and section chief, where he worked on some of the most consequential civil rights cases of the generation.

When Nixon was elected, the Civil Rights Division dwindled, leaving the Rosenbergs looking for their next adventure. The couple bought a used Peugeot for $800, and took off from Washington, DC, for the hills of Appalachia with their new baby, Michael. They had heard from friends that Appalachian poverty was America's next great challenge and civil rights issue. The constant drumbeat of articles and strife emanating from the mountains had made itself heard in DC, and more folks were coming to Appalachia—VISTAs, activists, and organizers—to help enact real change. It was their heart's desire to adhere to *tikkun olam*, a Hebrew phrase meaning, "repairing the world," and they knew they could fulfill it in the hollers of Eastern Kentucky.

While visiting, John and Jean spoke with author and Letcher County State Representative, Harry Caudill, to learn about the history and battles brewing in the hollers. They were also fortunate enough to meet Joe Begley, a strong strip-mining opponent who ran a country store in Letcher, and a young Mud Creek activist named Eula Hall who charmed them with her passion and authenticity. John and Jean were convinced that the next great fight for social justice was right there in the picturesque creeks, valleys, and mountains of Appalachia. The raw natural beauty, set against stark poverty, invoked awe in them and drew them in. This was where they needed to be.

John's extensive career was aimed at helping Americans realize the inalienable rights with which they were ordained. His civil rights work dovetailed easily into helping the working class and severely poor of Appalachia who too often viewed the legal system as an institution for the rich and privileged. John started AppalRED with OEO funding in 1970 as a noble endeavor seeking to provide legal services to those who for far too long had only been afraid of the law, or worse, abused by it. The AppalRED mission statement indicates that the organization exists to: "*assist in obtaining the basic necessities of life, i.e., income, adequate food and health care; decent, safe, and sanitary housing, and the protection of assets; guarding the rights of children and the protection of family members from violence and abuse. The general area of focus falls under the priorities of maintaining economic stability; ensuring safety, stability and health; preserving the home and protecting populations with special vulnerabilities.*"[93]

When the time came for John to propose his new venture to the local Floyd County Bar Association, he hoped they would either offer their support or their time and energy. However, local lawyers, yet another group of rich, insider political types, balked at his suggestion to offer services to those under a certain income. Somehow, they had never thought of perhaps helping their poorest neighbors with legal aid if they couldn't afford it.

The bar deliberated John's proposal to work alongside them, and quickly responded by telling John not only that he shouldn't practice there, but that he also should probably leave town. They were furious to think that an outsider would come in and take their business even though many of the folks John intended to help would never have the means to be paying legal clients.[94]

John, a slender man with a stark face, was the courageous type who found motivation in the face of daunting pressure. The county bar's judgment of John, and especially of his ideas to help the poor, became more reason to stay and fight. Jean began working in the community teaching childbirth classes, and John went along with his plan to start AppalRED, fighting broad-form deeds and mountaintop removal, and filing injunctions on behalf of those who had never before seen or thought to consult a lawyer.[95]

John agreed to help EKWRO and the fledging Mud Creek group put together their own bid for a health clinic, and also decided to hire Eula to help as a social worker of sorts on black lung advocacy, welfare, food stamps, and Social Security cases for his new firm. It was a perfect fit for Eula who was by then at the epicenter of Floyd County agitators. When Eula and others were picketing the hospital, for instance, John bailed her out of jail, and when John needed help finding clients, Eula had a hundred people lined up for his services. John admitted that nobody did a better job of finding and helping sick miners. He told Eula, "You're gonna have the entire black lung program defunded if you keep working this hard."

"Well, John, that money ain't doing nobody no good just sitting around in Washington," she would say.

They made a good team, but just as soon as they submitted their proposal to the federal government for the new clinic, they received a swift denial. Not because federal officials didn't think they could do a good job, but instead, Washington was convinced local officials wouldn't *let* them do a good job. Even though months earlier OEO had decided to give another group and a new director a chance, it was certain to them the atmosphere was simply too toxic to have any meaningful program established.

Dejected, the group of activists backing the clinic took another heap of criticism from the community and in 1971, many of the activists decided they might have met the end for a county health program.

It was a savage defeat. In a full year, Eula went from community hero with a paying job, to almost losing her livelihood and her dream. "It was hard, at the time, to think there would ever be hope for health care in Mud Creek," she said. "If the grand War on Poverty couldn't fix it, then why should we believe anyone ever could?"

Chapter 20

ACTIVISM CAN BE EASY TO ESCHEW DURING HARD times and for many of the activists in Mud Creek, getting by in life was hard enough. Fighting for simple justices— health care, clean water, and food—was sometimes too much to take on when there were kids to feed and bills to pay. As many EKWRO and 979 activists gave up on their dream for community-wide health care, among other priorities, Eula too turned to her home life to keep her busy.

By the mid-1970s, Troy had left the house for work, and Randy had gone off to the army for a one-year rotation. Danny was working in the mines, and Dean and Eulana, Nanetta's child who Eula took care of, were her only real preoccupation.

"Lord, Dean and Eulana were the two best kids you could ever imagine," she said later. "They didn't want or need anything more than what we had and were just the sweetest little children. They kept me strong when life was hard, and they stayed right by me when things got tough."

Eula had a hard time raising so many children, and didn't have the best relationships with all of them. She attempted to repair her relationship with Randy before he left for war. Her relationship with her son, like her relationship with McKinley, had only worsened with time. He had shown Eula love, as well as torment. Randy had more in common with McKinley than did any of the other children. They seemed more akin to one another than Eula could have imagined, and it bothered her that Randy would treat her sometimes nearly as badly as McKinley. As it had for so many who serve their country, "The war certainly changed Randy for the worse."[96]

McKinley had stopped working and was on disability through the Veterans Affairs Department, receiving a check every week. Often he would take the check and blow it on booze, which riled Eula as much as it pained her to see. His verbal abuse rivaled the physical pain he inflicted, and every day their relationship sat on a precipice with the two either outwardly fuming at one another or engaging in tiny scuffles.

In light of her new steady salary through AppalRED, Eula had contemplated a divorce. However, the weekly paychecks weren't enough money to feed the children or to ever give them a better life. Instead, with McKinley steadily becoming more physical, once twisting her arm till it came out of the socket, she decided to threaten him herself.

Providing goods or bartering was a common method of transaction for the people Eula helped. Eula aided a friend at AppalRED with his disability check in court and, in turn, he offered assistance in any way he could to thwart McKinley. He gave her a pistol—silver, shiny, and small enough to stash in the glove compartment of her Bronco—in case she really needed to strike the fear of God in him.

"There were times I coulda done it," Eula said, "but I couldn't go to jail and I couldn't live with myself not knowing what would happen to the kids." After seeing so much abuse, she was over McKinley to the point that she contemplated murder as her only escape. She knew she couldn't go on living in a forced hell. After putting the pistol away for good, she resolved that in one year she would save enough money to divorce McKinley, take the kids, and be on her own.

With her plan in motion, Eula saved every penny she could and even convinced McKinley to hold on to a few disability checks so they could buy a new place. They selected an old house with an additional trailer off to the side in a little hamlet called Teaberry in Upper Mud Creek. It was a grand set up, and while the new house and trailer were spacious, they were in dire need of repairs. Eula began major home improvements, varnishing the floor, and fixing every seam in the sheetrock. Danny and Eula put down some of the floor. Eula got a charge account at Lloyd's Hardware in Prestonsburg in exchange for bartering for the store manager's mother's health care at a local hospital. The extensive repairs went on for some time and even included upgrading the well pump. The work took Eula's mind off the turmoil of the previous year.

EKWRO continued a meek existence, but Eula continued to run the health committee and sometimes worked on the Water Board's well-siting projects. She also took part in a health fair conducted in conjunction with medical students from Vanderbilt and the University of Kentucky. In one week, the EKWRO-sponsored program gave complete check-ups to 481 Mud Creek residents, offering free follow-up care to 102 of them who were found to have ailments. The accompanying survey numbers on patient well-being were astonishing: nearly 90 percent had never seen a doctor, citing intimidation or anxiety about what they might do; 75 percent of their home surface wells were contaminated; and infant mortality was atrociously high. Transportation and the intangible intimidation factor seemed to be the biggest drawbacks for folks who actively sought proper health care. What really struck Eula was how the EKWRO-sponsored program promoted simple remedies that FCCHSP never did, such as teaching patients how to purify water, educating them about drugs and abuse, and showing folks first aid methods to treat burns and cuts.[97]

The health fair was a huge success, but the survey revealed that the same old health problems were still untreated. While Eula knew the answer was simply cheaper, accessible health care closer to home, she didn't think there was a way to make it a reality in the absence of the War on Poverty and OEO funds.

To help in any way she could, Eula allowed some of the University of Kentucky volunteers free housing in the new trailer behind her house while the students conducted the survey. She had been using the trailer as a sort of halfway house for battered women she knew in the community, or for the elderly to stay briefly if they couldn't go home. It was serving as a boarding house for adventurous undergrads who wanted to volunteer in the hollers. It was nice Eula thought, sort of a community refuge she managed that McKinley never seemed to question.

As a symbol of Eula's continued ability to affect change in her community, it didn't take long for that trailer to go through a simple metamorphosis. In a little over a month after the UK students left, inspiration struck. With some of her old EKWRO buddies in tow, Eula spruced up the trailer and made some renovations to make it a bit more welcoming. The trailer had taken on an entirely new look and feel with a small wooden stairway leading to a welcoming porch with seating.

"Now, I don't like to brag about this," Eula later confessed about the true, and possibly illegal nature of the trailer, "but the first Mud Creek Clinic was right there in that trailer out back in Teaberry." Her solution had arrived, and it was as homegrown as her moonshine.

For over a year, Eula had been scheming on how she could leave McKinley and continue the fight the FCCHSP started. "If I had half the money they gave the county health project, I could really do something. But I didn't, so I had to work with whatever I could find," she said.

That little old trailer stuck inconspicuously atop cinder blocks on a mountainside was nothing more than junk when it was purchased, which may explain McKinley's disregard for it. But when refurbished by the children and community, the trailer became the answer Eula and Mud Creek had been looking for. She didn't have a license to practice, but, in the very first days, she didn't need one, because she simply used the trailer as space to meet and counsel people who needed her help navigating the health care system, just as she had done before with friends of hers in the community. It was her own FCCHSP-style triage clinic with an emphasis on caring. It was initially a place to do the small things that didn't require a doctor, such as educating patients on simple acts of daily health care or serving as a place for people to sleep with a roof over their heads. It was all she thought it could be, that was, until she made a call to some local doctors.

After an evening spent in the trailer with a young lady afflicted with jaundice, Eula decided to reach out to two doctors who had selfless reputations. Drs. Jim Squire and Ellie Graham were a deeply caring physician pair from Our Lady of the Way Hospital in Martin who had worked with Eula in the past and as part of the health fair. They were always willing to lend a helping hand.

"I got some space in the back where she's staying, and I ain't asking you to do anything illegal," Eula remembered telling them, "but if you could take a look at her, we'd all be appreciative." The doctors did more than see a single jaundice case. They saw a few more patients later in the week, and then a stream of patients the week after. Just like that, in little over a month, the little four-room trailer built a reputation among Eula's friends in the holler, and sure enough, the doctors decided to come back weekly. Eula decided she needed to compensate them for their efforts, but initially they would only accept a dollar a day.[98]

"We didn't pretend, or do anything improper," Eula steadfastly recalled, "but we saw patients, did home visits, followed up on the health fair results, did a lot of health care work we could do *without* a license. The clinic sorta just started attracting folks and let me tell ya—the need was tremendous."

The sympathetic doctors advised Eula on the mechanics of a working clinic, and helped her begin keeping medical records and taking patient notes. She used every tiny nook of the trailer, utilizing the living area as a waiting room, the bedroom as a pharmacy, and the closet as a medical supply storage area. The kitchen counter served as a nurse's station and after the cabinets were cleaned and marbled, they too stored medical supplies. In the morning, Eula and her volunteers strategically placed partitions to make a waiting room, and then took them down to allow people to sleep after hours. Eula received help from others in EKWRO and the group set up official hours on Tuesdays and Thursdays, with Drs. Squire and Graham coming to the trailer during the day and working later shifts in Martin at night.

Their first patients were a range of folks with an even larger mix of ailments and acuity. Troy Frasure of Mud Creek had black lung, and Merv Mitchel needed help with his diabetes. There were people who had been through the FCCHSP, and others who had severe health problems, but had never seen a doctor. Eula took her Bronco up and down 979 as much as she could to shuttle people to the trailer in the early days. Many kids finally received needed care, and their parents knew the trailer clinic was their only shot at getting a proper health check-up.

Although everything was running smoothly, and the doctors were falling over themselves to offer their help, Eula remained anxious. "I worried how long I could keep this going. I was afraid that if I wasn't there every day, someone would take over and slip . . . that something terrible would happen."

She held onto her makeshift clinic like a child, ensuring McKinley didn't have access to the trailer and locking up even to use the outhouse in the yard. "I knew I was doing right, but I was scared to death we wouldn't make it. I didn't know what the hell I was getting into."

A couple of weeks in, one of the patients asked what they should call the trailer outpost. Eventually someone suggested the name Eula Hall's Medical Center.

"No," she thought, "It should be named for the people or not named at all." Besides, putting her name on it would just boost the risk of being caught.[99]

Chapter 21

"SOMETHING ABOUT WORKING IN THAT TRAILER every day fired me up, let me tell ya," Eula said. She believed that if she could start her own clinic, she could finally leave McKinley. It was time, even before her one-year deadline, to take the kids and forge a new life on her own terms. She remembered back to the early days in her marriage, when her father came by with his shotgun to wrench her from McKinley's abuse. The look on his face was one she would never forget. Her father knew she was stronger than that weak moment and worthless relationship. Eula was in such a hurry as a child to get on with her life that she hadn't taken the time to make sure she was on the right path. Make no mistake, she had some good times with McKinley, and he could be "as sweet as sugar pie" when he wanted to, but he was never a true partner like the one she dreamed about as a teenager. He provided little support, and the cruelty of his intermittent abuse had taken its toll mentally and physically.

She resolved that she couldn't back down any longer. Eula bought the biggest padlock she could get her hands on, and grabbed all essential items from the house to place inside her new home—the trailer clinic. Although she had firmly decided she was leaving, she went no farther than her own yard, at least initially.

That night, she confronted McKinley to declare she was leaving and asked her lawyer friends to help her file for divorce.

"I never want to see you again," she declared. "You can go on living in the house, but it don't matter, we ain't a pair no more." McKinley, a bit astonished and confused, didn't even put up a fight, perhaps assuming it was all a bluff or a joke. Eula recalled that he simply watched as she took her stuff and walked out the door with Dean and Eulana.

Although the trailer wasn't a complete withdrawal from home, it was enough separation to feel worthwhile. The first few days of her new life went smoothly. At night, Eula, Dean, and Eulana would deconstruct the clinic partitions to sleep on mattresses atop the cold trailer floor, and in the morning, pack all of their stuff into the closet to begin the day. Dean and Eulana would catch the bus to school, and Eula would get to work. Neighbors helped with furniture and food, often offering to watch the children when things got too busy between work at AppalRED and the clinic. The arrangement worked just fine for a time, but in two short weeks, McKinley decided he had had enough of the charade.

Randy, who unlike Troy and Danny, stayed loyal to his father, joined McKinley in harassing clinic patients and doctors any chance they could. The pair would randomly come into the clinic and raise Cain by making a scene or yelling at Eula in front of the clinic crowd. It was the first time folks in town could see, up close, how he treated and disrespected her. Patients and volunteers defended Eula and forced McKinley out of the clinic, which only temporarily ended whatever tirade he was on. At night, when everyone was gone, he would come back and continue to terrorize the family.

"After a few days, I finally brought out the hardware on him,"

Eula said. She brandished her borrowed pistol at McKinley. The pistol worked as a deterrent, but only until McKinley found out there was no ammo to back up her threats. After more handwringing, and perhaps an understanding their relationship was forever tarnished, he agreed to move back to the storefront with his kin, and leave Teaberry and the house to Eula.

"I was so relieved. I think he was finally getting the picture that I wasn't coming back," she said. But the further separation put McKinley at wit's end. He came back only a few days later, and forced Eula and the kids back into the clinic from the house. After a few weeks of this game, and with the winter approaching, spending the night at the trailer became untenable, and she had overburdened neighbors and friends with requests for a place for her and her children to crash. She was in the midst of the divorce and getting a restraining order, but her life couldn't wait for legal remedies.

"I needed an immediate refuge for Dean and Eulana's sake," she remembered, preferably a twenty-four-hour place that wouldn't mind her presence. One night soon after, before McKinley could rage, she packed the kids in the Bronco and drove through the holler to a little nursing home parking lot in Pikeville. She had heard from a sympathetic clinic patient that the parking lot was well lit, sparsely used, and quiet—a perfect hiding spot, affording them a good night's rest.

For the next few weeks, Eula's days consisted of working at AppalRED, the clinic, taking care of the kids, watching out for McKinley, dealing with the divorce, and spending the night crouched and slumped inside a Ford Bronco at the nursing home parking lot. Eula and Dean would lean the front seats back as far as they could over the backseat where Eulana was sprawled out. "If this is what leaving McKinley was going to be like," she recalled, "maybe it wasn't worth it."[100]

After a few weeks, the nursing home staff, perhaps a bit fearful about a suspicious car parked in their lot every night, called the city cops. When they arrived, Eula and the kids were half-asleep, and woke up to a flashlight glaring down at them.

"Officer, I'm not here for fun," she told the police in a daze through a cracked window. "I'm here for protection. I can't go home. I'm afraid if I go home, there will be trouble. I knew my kids and I would be protected here."

"It doesn't matter," they said. "You can't continue to park on private property at night." After a bit more bickering, the cops huddled. They got the impression that if she was willing to go to such lengths, she must live in real fear of going home, and they didn't want to seem coldhearted or risk her life. They offered her an alternative, allowing her and the kids to park and sleep in front of the police station downtown until the restraining order was in place and the divorce final.

"If your husband even dared come down there," they said, "he'll see the inside of the county jail real quick."

For the next few weeks, Eula slept in front of the Pikeville Police Department, with her two kids and a gun by her side. It was the best security and comfort Pike County could provide. If that was what it took for her to feel safe, she thought, "I was living a tragedy." The kids, who were still young enough to consider it an adventure rather than a pain, accepted that their father was worth avoiding by any means.

In two month's time, the divorce and restraining order came through, and Eula used the power of the law to separate herself from a thirty-seven-year marriage that had turned toxic. Surprisingly, McKinley obeyed the order, and attempted to absolve himself with the family by checking into the Lexington veteran's hospital to seek mental health services. Eula moved with the kids back to the Teaberry house, and received new furniture from her old friends Wanda and Homer Hamilton.

She felt liberated, but oddly sad. She was finally independent and free, without McKinley to distract her from the clinic and her kids, but thirty-seven years of good times and bad were hard to shake. It all had happened so fast with the clinic and her separation, she hadn't found time to register the new, and possibly lonely, world she was entering. The swirl of emotions concerning her new life quickly dissipated as she readied for what would be the most important moments in the young clinic's life.

The doctors working with Eula from Our Lady of the Way Hospital served as a bulwark against officials shutting down the clinic. But even in light of their help, she still worried about opposition from other regional hospitals and local private-practice doctors who believed that the clinic was taking their patients. The main issue, however, was revenue. In the early days, patients were seen and examined for free, and those who could pay did according to a sliding scale based on income.

"The more money you made," Eula explained, "the more you paid, and if you didn't make money . . . well, we'd see you anyway." Eula set up an honor system of sorts, but wanted to be able to overcome the co-pay fee that precluded the FCCHSP clinics from being truly universal. Even with the generosity of clinic patients and select donors, there simply wasn't enough money among them to keep revenue steady. The goal was to find a way to keep the clinic free and open, without placing too much of a burden on the patients.

She said, "I wanted to create a safety-net clinic, 'cause I knew I couldn't change the insurance system and I couldn't get those government dollars back—there had to be a clinic like Mud Creek that was always free for those that ain't got nothing."[101]

Few in Mud Creek had the material wealth to fund an entire clinic with doctors, although many in the community who weren't patients pitched in to help the cause. Eula thought long and hard about potential benefactors, eventually turning to folks whom she considered brothers in the fight for justice.

"I'd like to come down to the union hall and talk to the miners," Eula told the newly UMWA Local 17 president, a coal miner with black lung. Knowing they were arguing over the union's budget for next year, Eula understood it would be hard to get his attention, but she told him, "I have something important to ask and am looking to my brothers to help."

"Well, I guess so, Eula," he said. It was certainly an odd request. "Sure, why not?" Seldom had a women ever even stepped foot in the union hall, let alone asked to speak to them.

With Dean and Eulana as her audience, Eula rehearsed her lines for days before the meeting. The relationship she proposed would be mutually beneficial. The national UMWA had created a Health and Retirement Fund in 1946 after the federal government's seizures of the nation's mines. The funds had been instrumental in creating Miners Memorial Hospitals throughout the region, including one in Martin, and also made great strides in improving overall medical care in Appalachia. Sadly, many of the hospitals had closed in the previous decade due to poor money management. However, the fund continued to collect money from members to supplement the high cost of health insurance and the general lack of workplace insurance afforded by mine operators.

Eula was hoping that the local organization, which actually stretched through Eastern Kentucky into West Virginia, could provide a small lifeline for the clinic and, in turn, have Eula help miners who normally be turned away or have no access to care.

On the night of the meeting, Eula entered a union hall abuzz. Miners, some with coal dust still covering their arms and faces, were joking and fooling around before the business of the day. Although they were having a good time enjoying one another's company, they were returning from a hard day in the most dangerous profession.

Though deaths and injuries decreased significantly after the turn of the twentieth century, coal mining still accounted for nearly three hundred deaths and more than forty thousand injuries on average per year. Yet, these rough and virile workers who spent the better part of daylight underground performing some of the most difficult labor in human history, were kindhearted souls simply doing what they could to provide for their families. The union fought hard for their well-being and safety, disabusing the notion that workers had few rights, especially if they were risking their lives for management.

Eula knew she would have a sympathetic crowd, and while she normally approached speaking with confidence and few nerves, this rugged group of men intimidated her to the bone. To make matters worse, upon walking into the room it dawned on her for the first time that McKinley, who had many union friends, might be there.[102]

Eula quietly took a seat in the far back of the room. The president walked up to the stage to settle down the crowd and announced the agenda of the meeting. He soon told the crowd, "Hush up now and be gentlemen. We got a woman here named Eula Hall, who a lot of y'all probably know. She's here to speak to us about health care, so listen up, watch your language, and act right." The men, some dumbfounded by her presence, all turned their attention to the front and sat quietly as they were told. This was the first and perhaps only time a woman would run the show at the union hall.

She stood before the hushed audience, timidly cleared her throat, and began her pitch:

My name is Eula Hall, granddaughter and mother of proud miners. Floyd and Pike Counties have been my home since I can remember. I'm here because I'm tired of watching y'all not being taken care of, and tired of watching good folks like you work day in and day out without the promise of health care. Our people in the mountains have for too long given our sweat and blood with little to show for it. I'm starting the first-ever Mud Creek Clinic—free to all who come and anyone in need of care—because I can't stand it anymore.

Eula hit her stride, and went on detailing the health care problem with data from previous health surveys and the FCCHSP debacle as her ammunition. She augmented her speech with a good slice of history, reminding them they had been forgotten when it came to caring for the health of themselves and their families. She reminded them, too, that the riches they pulled out of the ground should provide more for them above ground.

She said, "I'm setting up this clinic because a lot of you are disabled and hurting, and are in dire need of care. We all wanna work, that's a fact. But we can't work if we're not healthy. It's simple to understand. The mine should want to pay for your health care to keep you working, but they don't. Hard-working folks in Eastern Kentucky need to take our lives into our own hands and that's what I plan to do—starting in Mud Creek."[103]

Eula kept on, through cheers and claps, offering a history lesson, mostly gleaned from Harry Caudill's work, describing how the country had profited from Appalachian riches while locals were left with faulty land deeds, black lungs, and low-wage jobs.

"This clinic is for our community," she said. "It will never be for the county judge or the mine operators. Please support us." Eula channeled her inner Mother Jones and worked the crowd into such a tizzy "they could have held a strike that night." After Eula left the meeting, the union voted unanimously to give a portion of their health care and retirement fund directly to the clinic. The stipulations would include a higher price paid for active miners and smaller co-pays for disabled or retired miners. The more miners they saw, the more money the clinic would receive by turning in records every month for reimbursement. It was exactly what Eula needed to hire doctors, a nurse, buy supplies, and pay herself a nominal salary.

In the following days after the agreement was signed, John helped get the clinic certified, and her team of volunteers readied the trailer to open its doors officially. One was kind enough to paint a sign on a small wooden board to hang out front on the trailer porch steps. Eula still hadn't decided on a name, but the sign made it official: The Mud Creek Clinic.

Chapter 22

THE CLINIC, OPEN TO THE PUBLIC AND NO LONGER A secret, was an immediate success. Eula greeted up to fifty patients a day at the front desk and quickly learned how to bill Medicaid and Medicare for folks who were eligible. Patients came in from as far away as northern Georgia, and the clinic's location near three state borders lent itself to regularly seeing folks from Tennessee, West Virginia, and Virginia. It was exactly what EKWRO had dreamed about years before, and they had real doctors to boot.

Drs. Jim Squire and Ellie Graham were a dedicated, but curious physician couple who became full-time doctors at the clinic after the UMWA funding. They were young, self aware, well educated, and weren't terribly worried about money, or the lack thereof, while practicing in the mountains. Eula was grateful for their early service to Mud Creek, but her sentiments on the pair remain as ambivalent today as they were then.

"Oh, Lord," Eula said, shaking her head, "you'd just love on Squire and Graham one minute, and couldn't work with them the next." They were radicals in the truest sense, both born in the northeast, but choosing to settle in scenic Appalachia to "start the revolution." Eula initially thought they were simply "kind souls doing God's work," but she quickly noticed they had an agenda not dissimilar from the criticism being directed toward all the outsiders who came running to civilize the mountains during the War on Poverty.

In the doctors' small house in Tram, Kentucky, the couple hung a four-by-eight-foot poster of Chinese Premier Mao Zedong above the fireplace, and treated visitors to lectures on the vices of capitalism. They were true children of the 1960s, living out their dreams to change American society by starting out in America's most forgotten backwoods. They didn't shy away from controversy. Squire and Graham regularly supported union strikes; in fact, they would picket anything pertaining to the government or corporations in which they didn't believe. They always had a truly radical crew with them as well, calling one another "brother" or "comrade" affectionately.[104]

"You know, I don't think they liked the city life," Eula said, contemplating their intent. "I don't think that's where they wanted to practice medicine. I know they wanted to take care of people who couldn't afford it or couldn't have it. And they wanted people they could live among and be friends with. As much as they took care of us, we had to take care of them and make sure they didn't get into too much trouble."

In the beginning, the couple didn't bring their politics to the clinic. "I could overlook their political beliefs, especially if they kept quiet and just focused on helping poor folks on Mud Creek," Eula said. They saw in the clinic the ability to practice medicine they found personally fulfilling. It was community-focused, helping the least fortunate obtain care they believed to be a human right. And without Squire and Graham, the clinic would have never grown to attract folks from neighboring states or developed its reputation. Although uncommon and brutally ideological, they were central to the clinic's early success.

Volunteers also played a crucial role in the early days.

Eula and her volunteers, most notably former VISTA Maxine Kinney, began performing home visits in earnest, hoping to cover the entire length of Route 979 and large swaths of US 23 in a few weeks to reach everyone. Maxine would go with Eula to make notes about people and their ailments, and schedule appointments for them at the clinic.

A local church gave Eula and the clinic a grant to buy a little yellow Volkswagen station wagon. "It was like a lawnmower," she remembered, "but it stood out and it was cheap on gas." They named it "Rabbit" and it became the official transportation vehicle of the clinic. With every home visit in Rabbit, Eula and volunteers scheduled appointments, and put a major focus on health education. By reaching out in such a way, Eula was pioneering a form of community health engagement never before seen in the mountains. She actively followed up with patients, and didn't wait for them to come to her. She went to them where they lived their lives and broke down walls of intimidation. By coming into their homes, scheduling their appointments, teaching basic health education, *and* giving them transportation, she was providing end-to-end service, keeping anyone from falling through the cracks. It was hard, intense work, but her efforts made for positive health outcomes.

The influx of new patients due to word of mouth and home visits was astounding. "Within just a couple of weeks, everybody knew our name and what we were about—shows you how big of a problem health care was up here," she said. Since the clinic stood in the middle of the community, more folks came out of the hollers for medical care than would have otherwise. With Eula driving around the county in her yellow VW, a patient always had access to transportation. Sometimes folks who had insurance and were regular patients at Our Lady of the Way or Pikeville Methodist Hospital would take the long trip to come to the clinic because it provided a more comforting environment. The clinic gave a sense of homelike warmth, with

Eula's kids running around playing with their friends in the yard, and old folks chatting about the weather on the porch. Most of the clinic's patients knew Eula and believed the clinic doctors had their best interests in mind.

In the early days, few patients stuck out in Eula's mind. There were just so many, and often folks with simple ailments, diabetes, black lung, and broken this or that, came to the clinic. But there were some inexplicable cases that came through the door, and one particularly anxious moment Eula remembers keenly because of its bizarre outcome.

A young woman came to the clinic with her daughter, upset about an incident that had occurred at their home. "Lord, that girl couldn't have been over fifteen when we saw her," Eula remembered. The girl was a cheerleader at nearby Wheelwright High School and her mother was a friend of Eula's. "She fell against a china cabinet last night," the mother explained, "and her side is really hurting her bad."

"Well, let's send her in the back and have the nurse take a look at her," Eula said. She wrote down some notes and walked the two to the back room, assuming it was simply a routine check-up with maybe a bump or scratch. Only a few minutes later, the volunteer nurse who had been attending the young girl came running back to Eula.

"Eula, I don't know what in the world to do. That little girl is in labor and I ain't never helped someone give birth before!"

Eula couldn't believe it. The mother came rushing out screaming, "Eula, can you believe this woman? She trying to tell me that my daughter is pregnant!" The mother's denial was apparent to all, including her daughter. "She just gained some weight and she ain't even have a boyfriend!" Eula walked over to calm her down, thinking, *Well, maybe she doesn't have one you know about . . .*

Panic quickly ensued. Jim and Ellie were at the hospital that morning, and no one else had sufficient knowledge of what to do next. Eula hadn't helped with a pregnancy in more than twenty years, but instinctively she began counseling the girl to get ready. She called Dr. Anthony Mounts, another sympathetic doctor who was quick to help in times of need, to rush down to the clinic on his day off.

As Dr. Mounts arrived and went to work, Eula sat counseling the mother. She was in a fit of rage. "Honey, sit here and listen. Let's be quiet and let's see what the doctor says first before we go saying something we might regret."

"I don't know what to tell my husband or what to do," she cried.

"Well, this little girl knows something, so you better talk to her," Eula said. "It's a child having a child—you gotta help her and be there for her. You can't carry on like this and go off the rocker."

Eula thought the woman was going to kill her with that last statement, but she eventually calmed down after hearing her daughter cry with pain. Eula continued in the role she often played—counselor and psychiatrist.

Luckily, a healthy baby was born that morning in the trailer, but the family was completely unprepared. The clinic collected diapers and other necessities for the family, and over the next week, taught the young girl the basics of childcare through home visits. They named the baby after Eula. "We called her the clinic's baby," she said.[105]

As humorous and joyous as the occasion was, it was a clear reminder to Eula of the lack of sexual health education in the mountains. After the incident, she began instructing her nurses and volunteers to weave sexual education into the general health care knowledge they preached. "The women are too important," she said, to not teach them about safe sex. They were the backbone of the community, and it was becoming clearer to Eula that women, especially in the mountains, were often abused and taken advantage of, much as she had been for so long. "It would be a duty and a dream," she said, remembering that situation, "to one day possibly open a clinic just for women."[106]

Another ailment in the early days whose frequency truly disturbed Eula and the doctors was the prevalence of pneumoconiosis—a technical term for black lung disease. Every miner who came through found themselves somewhere on a spectrum of breathing problems. Just a few years earlier, in 1969, the federal government passed black lung compensation legislation to be administered through the Social Security program. The trouble, however, was that the program Nixon signed had extremely strict regulations, preventing miners from getting the help they desperately needed. Affected coal miners required lawyers to file for their black lung compensation, and a physician check-up to prove the mines led to their illness.[107]

In her role as chair of the EKWRO Health Committee, Eula began organizing around the issue. In the previous few years, the American Black Lung Association had been created to help pass the 1969 law and included among its members miners, their wives, and sadly, their widows as well. Eula was quickly thrust into a position of leadership for the Kentucky Black Lung Association (KBLA), with her past activism and clinic creation preceding her as legend.

Beginning in early 1972, Eula was elected president of the KBLA chapter where she wielded incredible power over the large and growing network of affected miners. Along with the day-to-day running of the clinic, Eula expanded the association's rolls by bringing in lawyers and sympathetic local doctors. With the national Black Lung Association, she coordinated frequent bus trips to Washington, DC, for locals to advocate in support of amendments to make the law less onerous for those seeking help. After all, the law forced them to spend money to—in Eula's words—"ask doctors and lawyers to label a chicken a fowl." In her intuitive estimation, nearly every miner was affected in one way or another by working underground. They just needed doctors to confirm the severity of their condition and gain the proper compensation.

The trips to Washington were simply mesmerizing to Eula. In her experience, politics had been tough and at times even threatening. If her election to the FCCHSP Board or the school board fiasco was any indication, it could also be nasty. On the coal trips to DC, Eula eschewed niceties often reserved for the local political elite, and didn't balk at threats and innuendo. She knew politics solely through a prism of battle and she wanted to take that same fire to Washington.There was also something about the sheer austerity and grandeur of the city and its people, making the advocacy all that more important.

"It was on those trips to Washington that I realized what we were doing was much bigger than Mud Creek," she said. "There were associations in every state with the same problems we had, and now I was given a stage to affect it across the country."

Those rallies were viscerally powerful; with miners on the capitol steps breathing through oxygen tanks, and wives and widows trading horror stories at podiums to make the case for enhanced protections. Eula relished these events, and often brought Dean and Eulana in tow to see how uplifting it was to be an activist for justice.

Chapter 23

Later that year, as the clinic grew, Eula found herself back in Washington deliberating on what would eventually become the 1972 amendments to the original black lung legislation. She was honored to be part of the negotiation. It was a process, however, completely dominated by men. Eula traveled to DC with Jim Hamilton and former Black Lung Association president Bill Worthington, and was often the only woman at the table. She was also clearly the only one who had to bring the whole family with her to the capital. Having to walk all over the city instead of driving was another unwelcome change from life back in Mud Creek.

She had a great relationship with the Social Security Administrator Bernard Popick and would often stop by Congressman Carl Perkins's office to say hello and keep him abreast of new developments. He was always nice and welcoming to Eula and her group of activists. Most of all, he would listen, a skill many elected officials simply didn't have or only offered as a privilege to the highest bidders. The same could be said about both Kentucky senators, Wendell Ford and John Sherman Cooper. "Cooper was a great senator," Eula said.

"Even though he was a Republican, he had our back when we needed him." These three men would prove crucial to bringing together the political will to get something done for miners back home and across the country.[108]

The negotiations with lawmakers and the Department of Labor dragged on late into the night for nearly ten days, and Eula often had to keep the male miners in check. "When we went up there, a lot of those miners were heavy drinkers," she recalled. "We would sit at a table and negotiate the regulations. After about eight o'clock, we'd go down to eat, right off the hotel on Capitol Hill, [and] they would burn a whiskey bill of $200 or $300."

The miners and other representatives thought that since they were in DC doing the heavy lifting, they might as well have the association pay for their nightly merriment. Eula couldn't stand their boorish behavior, and quarreled with them to be mature and act like adults.

"Miners and their families paid for the BLA's operating costs, and it didn't square with me to be spending that hard-earned money on things like booze and steaks," she said. Despite her objections, they kept the party going late into the night.

The daily negotiations proved to be tense. Being the only woman at the table, Eula wanted to make sure that if a miner had logged twenty years underground and died, that his wife would be given an automatic percentage of his former pay. It was a story Eula heard far too often in the clinic, so much so that she didn't think the group needed to waste any more time potentially studying the issue. To her, if a miner had been a diligent worker spending decades underground only to die young, it was almost a certainty that he died of a lack of workplace safety or black lung. Doctors backed up that assertion. The wife should get paid, she thought, because she was a vital part of the man's family and working life. Again, as she would her entire life, Eula was fighting for men to realize the value of the women on whom they depended.[109]

Even in Eula's camp, some were against the rule. The fear among a few of the men was that providing supplemental income for women would cut the already small pie of funds for miners, and possibly be a lightning rod for opponents. There was a particular gentleman, Arnold Miller, the president of the West Virginia Black Lung Association, who "could argue and negotiate like a Baptist preacher," according to Eula, and he would prove to be her sparring partner. He was quick to point out that if they didn't incorporate what he wanted, he would call his cronies at UMWA and tell them to strike. To Eula, his bravado was not charming, but rather meek, because not only was he full of bluff, but she recalled that he was also "hung over every day from drinking the night before."

Near the end of the negotiation, he stood as the last holdout on Eula's provision. She took him outside for a one-on-one. As he leaned against the wall to light up a cigarette, Eula got right in his face and said, "With the way you're behaving, we ain't gonna get nowhere. Those threats you're throwing around ain't nothing 'cause you and I both know you couldn't pull your mommy to strike if you called her." Needless to say, the gentleman from West Virginia had never been spoken to like this, let alone by a lady. "Now, I want you to go in there and *shut up*! You don't know what I see in the hollers; you don't see the women who get left behind taking care of four kids. Think about what your wife would say to you."[110]

Eula knew that last line would get at his conscience. Just as Miller started to wind up a retort, she cut him short with her fist in his face. "You better straighten up or you'll get it in the mouth and I'll make sure everyone knows how you acted up here."

In retrospect, Eula admits her aggressive tactics may have

been overplaying her hand. In later years, Arnold Miller proved his power. He would pull not just his mom to the picket line, but the entire UMWA as he headed the bituminous coal strike of 1974—one of the largest and most successful strikes of the miner-reform era.[111]

Still, in that moment, Miller balked. As they walked back in the conference room, Miller told Eula he would oblige, but that she "better apologize after the deal gets done." The group quickly agreed on final terms, and the next day the final legislative language was sent to Capitol Hill for a vote where it would eventually pass a few weeks later.

"I felt as if I was helping miners breathe again," Eula said after the bill's eventual passage. The government's power in this case was astonishing to Eula. It was exhilarating for her to consider the magnitude of change resulting for so many in the mountains and throughout the United States by the simple stroke of a pen. In a post-War on Poverty era, where many ridiculed the once-important task of eradicating poverty, championing black lung benefits revived her faith in the institution of government. Her experience proved that while the group of (largely) men who ran the US government were flawed, they ultimately believed in justice. In future political conversations among cynical neighbors, she reminded them of her time in DC, and that with a little fight, it was possible to give significant aid to the men, women, and children of Appalachia.

After the euphoria, Eula came home to a rough welcome. Her house had been vandalized and the windows blown out from multiple shotgun blasts. Her porch stairs had been broken and her yard torn up. She knew it had to be the coal companies and their thugs in retribution for her work in DC. For a while, even before she went to Washington, an assortment of folks would come to the clinic to tell Eula off, claiming she was hurting the only industry in town. They called her a communist, a socialist, whatever boogieman they could think of to prove her activism on behalf of miners wasn't doing them any good and, in fact, just making it more difficult to mine in the mountains.

"I wasn't trying to hurt the industry . . . 'cause Lord knows, we need jobs," she proclaimed, but the nuance was often hard to explain. She was acting on what she had seen from the community and in her clinic. She knew with certainty that helping miners get black lung compensation was more important than coal company profits. In her mind, "even with all the black lung care in the world, the mine companies would still make money." It was a tough balancing act for Eula, especially as her own family pulled paychecks from working in the local mines.

"I never wanted my boys to go in the mines in the first place. The more I learned, the more I was against it." But Randy and Troy did work in the mines for parts of their working lives, and Danny did as well as soon as he was old enough.

Like Eula, most mountain folks at the time had an ambivalent relationship with the coal industry. There was no doubt coal had brought riches for some, jobs, and development to parts of Appalachia. But the expense of that growth was taking its toll on the streams, rivers, and most importantly, the miners who extracted the coal. While a select few were castigating the mine companies' poor treatment and working conditions, the majority felt local folks shouldn't fight against the one industry providing reliable jobs.

"It was a tough line I had to draw," she said. "On one hand, these miners needed help and were being taken advantage of. On the other, without mining jobs, what else would they do?"[112]

To make matters worse, the clinic's day-to-day operations were in shambles. Jim and Ellie's bedside manners had gotten cynical and extremely political. The pair had a group of worrisome friends who had come to Floyd County from New York to join the union and work in the mines. Instead of coming to find work and a home, they were leftists in search of trouble. These were the type of subversive folks who carried guns and ammo, and were looking for a reason to fire at the picket line. They fashioned themselves as some type of guerrilla army starting a revolution. While Eula was gone in DC, Jim and Ellie would bring some of them to the clinic, where they would hang out in the backyard, firing off shotgun blasts every few minutes for target practice. Once, one of the men came into the clinic, put his feet up on the table, and began arguing with Randy about unions and politics. Randy, who had recently come back from the army, may have given Eula and the clinic a hard time with his own erratic behavior, but he couldn't care less for these out-of-towners. He took that gentleman out back once and "beat the fire out of him."

Eula, in an attempt to maintain a modicum of professionalism, couldn't allow that kind of trouble at the clinic. She finally confronted Jim and Ellie with some harsh words. "Look here, I don't run from nothing, and don't put on no shows like y'all do, but what you're doing is your business. Just don't do it here, don't bring it here, and don't preach it to our patients. Our patients just need health care; they don't need politics and revolution."

Her tirade was enough to keep their friends from coming around, but it hardly put a dent in Squire and Graham's personal evangelism.

The couple kept on with their bedside manners, prescribing doses of Maoist history at the end of every check-up. The patients loved the doctors, but when it came to what they stood for and their actions, the patients were turned off. The final straw came when Jim and Ellie took time off from the clinic to picket the local two-person post office in Harold. It was an awfully public display of their radical politics; it annoyed clinic patients, and infuriated Eula, who felt they weren't representing the clinic's mission anymore.

"The commies thought they could just lord over the country people," she said. "We fought hard for what was right, but we were still loyal Americans. If our government wasn't doing right, we wanted to change it, but we weren't no revolutionaries, and we didn't need talk of revolution at the clinic."

Eula would get into political arguments, thinking she could change their minds, especially in light of her recent work in Washington. She thought the system allowed for change, while Jim and Ellie wanted to change the system. But it was useless; the good doctors were true believers.

"I'll be the first one to say that our system ain't perfect, but it's the best one in the world I know and I wouldn't want it any other way," Eula said.

She confronted them again one night at a board meeting, and while the two doctors tried to convince the Mud Creek Board their evangelizing was part of the clinic's educational mission, it came to light that some clinic patients had threatened the doctors, and in turn, the clinic. That was the final straw. The board agreed they couldn't have doctors who were doing anything more than their initial duty, which was to help the poor patients of Eastern Kentucky. Eula had to get them out of Floyd County for their own safety and reputation, along with hers.[113]

It was one of the more stressful moments of Eula's life. The community was fighting against her black lung accomplishments, and the clinic was heading in a direction far from what she had imagined. To make matters worse, McKinley was back from Lexington, and although he had moved to Pikeville, he made stops in Mud Creek and at the clinic multiple times where he clearly was not allowed. Randy was causing problems at the clinic, too, and Eula's bank account still wasn't providing enough to buy Dean and Eulana new clothes for school. Things were as tough, if not worse, as they had been when the FCCHSP shut down.

*   *   *

One grueling night after Jim and Ellie had departed the clinic, Eula came home to take a warm bath, relax, and reflect on the whirlwind that had been the previous few months. It was a quiet night in the mountains with a full moon piercing through the pines on the hillside. Inside the house, Dean and Danny were watching a University of Kentucky Wildcats ballgame and getting ready for bed. Eula came out to tell Dean it was bedtime, and walked Danny to the bedroom they shared. Because of Danny's deafness, his bed was positioned in such a way that Eula could always keep an eye on him in case he needed anything.

Eula tucked Dean in bed, and had gone to brush her teeth when she heard someone mumbling in the main room. She thought maybe Randy had stopped by, perhaps drunk from a long night out. She carefully made her way through the dimly lit hallway, careful to not wake Dean or Danny, and peered into the main room. There, slumped on the couch with the TV on, was McKinley, clearly inebriated, and obviously ready to start trouble. Eula just stared at him, too exasperated to tell him off.

"You shouldn't be here," she said in a soft voice. "You got a restraining order and I don't wanna see you." She took two short steps toward him to make out his face; it had been a while since she had last seen him, and she was curious whether his time in the hospital had changed his demeanor. The glow of the TV on his tame expression reminded her of the man she had once fallen in love with years before. But the empty whiskey bottle at his side reminded her of the reason she left.

She knew nothing good would come from this encounter, and backed away slowly, knowing that if she kept talking, he would want to sweet-talk her back. She had taken a few steps toward the hallway on the soft carpet and started back toward the bedroom, when suddenly she felt his presence right behind her. In the darkness, McKinley had launched off the sofa, came up behind Eula, and viciously swung the whiskey bottle across the left side of her face. She fell to the ground in horror and shock.

Dean immediately awoke from Eula's wail and shook the older Danny to get McKinley out of the house. As they rushed into the hallway, Danny took a quick look at Eula and immediately launched at McKinley. Eula lay on the ground, unable to move her jaw or open her left eye, bleeding uncontrollably. Her mind was in a blur, and she couldn't piece together the horror of the night. The pain was so intense she briefly lost consciousness and struggled to keep blood out of her mouth. She was dumbfounded by his rage, and horrified to think of how severe the injury might be.

Danny was furiously wrestling with McKinley, trading punches in between kicks to get him out of the house. After shoving him to the other side of the room, creating some space, he got down on his knees and desperately begged for him to leave them alone. Being mute and without recourse, he didn't know how to show that the family had enough. They were maddened and exasperated. Danny was bright red from Eula's blood, and clasped his hands together on his knees, praying for McKinley to go. Dean stood off to the side next to Eula with tears in his eyes.

McKinley took a deep breath, staring at the devastation he had caused. He turned and ran out of the front door and into the blue Kentucky night. Danny and Dean rushed to put a dress on Eula and get her to the car. She still couldn't open her left eye, and her jaw throbbed with stinging pain and blood. Blood was everywhere, on the wall, the carpet, and on them.

As Danny drove through the holler, Eula's thoughts swirled with regret. She couldn't believe she had put herself in this situation, and put her family in so much danger. For the previous year, she had been liberated, with the freedom to do as she pleased, but she always knew McKinley would come back one day. Although she knew he could be violent, this attack was so vicious it was unimaginable. It was the first night where she thought it was all too much, and maybe her independence wasn't worth fighting for at all.[114]

Eula Hall (Appalshop)

McKinley Hall (Appalshop)

Pictures of the family and others in the community were taken by photographer Kristen Mendenhall, who was traveling through eastern Kentucky in the early 1970s, looking to depict everyday life in the mountains. (Appalshop)

Eula at the Mud Creek Clinic, informing a miner about treatments for his Black Lung. The breathing machine in the background is one of the first medical supplies Eula purchased. (Courtesy of Earl Dotter Photography)

Scores of coal miners traveled to Washington in support of the amendments to the Black Lung Benefits Act in 1982. Eula Hall served as president of the Kentucky Black Lung Association and worked closely with policymakers to carve out benefits for widows of miners. (Earl Dotter Photography)

In the early days, patients gathered around outside the clinic doors when the waiting area was full. Eula and volunteers fixed up the clinic and painted a stethoscope with the title "Mud Creek Clinic" on the door. (Eula Hall)

Dr. Ellen Joyce was the first permanent doctor in the clinic and she grew close with Eula and the staff. Lou Ellen Hall, right, was an early volunteer and supporter who still works at the clinic today. (Eula Hall)

Eula with her children during good times when McKinley was away. Sitting from left are Dean, Eula, Randy, Danny's wife Teresa, and Danny. (Eula Hall)

A mysterious arsonist set fire to the clinic leaving nothing behind but a single smokestack. Medical supplies and patient records could not be saved and the fire department responded woefully late. This picture was taken the morning after, as volunteers gathered to assess the damage. (Eula Hall)

Eula wasted no time getting to work and raising funds for a new and improved Mud Creek Clinic. Pictured here is the clinic during construction on the plot of land purchased by funds from donors and the Appalachian Regional Commission. (Eula Hall)

In 1983, Senator Edward M. Kennedy traveled to eastern Kentucky to survey hunger in America. He was accompanied by fellow Democrat Carl D. Perkins, a loyal ally of Eula's, and a member of the US House of Representatives from Kentucky's 7th Congressional District who had built a legacy of support for the underprivileged. Eula barraged the Senator with questions about helping the poor. (Appalshop)

In 1998, Jesse Jackson kicked off a 20-city bus tour through poverty stricken parts of America to "de-racialize the issue." He stopped at the Mud Creek Clinic with UMWA President Cecil Roberts (on Eula's left) to speak to victims of black lung disease and their families.

Eula with a patient in 2012. The man stopped by to say thanks for the years of help. (Kiran Bhatraju)

In 2005, Eula was awarded an honorary Doctorate of Humane Letters from Berea College in recognition of her tireless healthcare advocacy. That day she stood alongside Archbishop Desmond Tutu, who served as the commencement speaker. (Eula Hall)

Eula presents Dr. Jagan Annabathula with a birdhouse as a gift for his dedication to the clinic. "Doc Jagan," as Eula called him, was one of many South Asian-born physicians, including the author's father, who worked in the clinic throughout the years. (Eula Hall)

Eula presents a gift to Robin Holbrook, who has worked at the clinic for nearly two decades. He started as a physician's assistant and is currently the clinic director. He calls Eula "a living legend." (Eula Hall)

Sign along Route 979 that stands in front of the clinic today.

While the staff has changed dramatically over the years, the Mud Creek Clinic still continues to attract volunteers and staff from the region who care deeply about the clinic's mission.

The modern clinic opened its doors in 1985 and includes its own laboratory, x-ray machines, and pharmacy. The clinic has expanded to include a dental clinic and a food pantry run by Eula herself, feeding over 100 families a month. Last year the clinic saw over 13,000 poor and underinsured patients.

Eula and the author in 2011, enjoying a summer day on her porch in the Teaberry holler of Floyd County.

Chapter 24

OVER THE NEXT FOUR WEEKS, EULA WAS TREATED AT Our Lady of the Way Hospital and then in Lexington for a broken jaw, cracked eye socket, and split lip. She underwent plastic surgery to make her face whole again, which required nearly thirty stitches inside and out of her cheek and mouth. Eula had decided a few months before to enroll in her first health insurance plan, which helped pay for a portion of the procedure, but didn't cover everything. As folks throughout Mud Creek heard about the attack, they also pitched in for her expenses.

The community rallied around Eula, found McKinley, and placed him briefly in jail in Pikeville. It was a horrifying few weeks, filled with anger, contempt, and sorrow. She knew she had made the right decision to leave him, but she couldn't help but imagine something this severe would have never had happened if she had stayed with him. It was a miserable feeling, and seeing the look of terror on her children's faces made it worse. She believed her selfish choices had led to the attack. It pained her deeply, and made her question the direction her life had taken. She thought she hadn't focused enough on her needs and her family. She wanted to be strong and independent, but also assumed it would have been nice to have another man in her life, too. It might possibly have saved her from the attack. She thought maybe leaving McKinley, starting the clinic, and working on black lung was too much for a poor mountain girl to take on.

By the end of her hospital stay, with visitors ranging from activists to politicians across the state, her thoughts moved quickly from regret to strength. In the dozens of people who came to console and praise her, she realized what she had done was not only fight for change in her life and her community, but she had built a new family of her own. The volunteers, the friends, the activists with whom she shared her daily struggle cared about her, because she was one in the same with the people she wanted to help. Her experience with abuse at the hand of a miserable ex-husband was similar to that of so many women she knew. She couldn't let down those women who looked to her for courage. And she had to keep up her work, because only now did she truly understand the reach and impact she was making in the lives of others. She couldn't let down the mothers who didn't have health care, or the miners who weren't taken care of. She couldn't sit idly by because she had a rough few weeks. She couldn't let this attack define her.

"I had to keep going, there was no choice," she said. By the time she was out of the hospital, she no longer questioned the life she was living. She had to and wanted to set an example as a fighter for her children and her community. It was the only thing she was sure of anymore.

Eula's face slowly healed and she eased back into clinic work. The wounds to her psyche would take some time, but being busy kept her from thinking too much about the horror she had endured. There were new doctors to recruit, and constantly more and more patients to serve. Squire and Graham left the clinic and eventually Eastern Kentucky, but not before graciously helping recruit a new doctor. They may not have been the best fit for the clinic, but that didn't mean they didn't care for the people or the mission. They recruited a young Catholic doctor named Mary Swaykus to help until Eula and the board could find full-time replacements. The staff ballooned in the following weeks to include Peggy Slone, the clinic's registered nurse; Denise Hall, the licensed practical nurse; Jim Haupert, pharmacist; Mary Williams, pharmacy assistant; Justine Kid, lab technician; Shirlene Hamilton, receptionist; Rhoda Paige and Janice Newman, billing clerks; and Lacy Henson, who handled general house cleaning.[115]

Clinic work bustled along faster every day with new patients from different states and towns. Eula worked harder than ever, and became more intrepid as a result. Armed men, most likely scabs from the mines, came by her house a few weeks after the attack, while Bill Worthington was visiting, most likely in hopes of scaring the labor leader from coming around again. She popped out of the house with a boot in hand and swung to whack those men across the face.

"Don't come around here scaring my children or I'll beat the hell outta ya!" she said.

They knew not to come back. Eula maintained her role as president of the Kentucky Black Lung Association, even as the threats continued. She had always been a testament to strength, with her deep compassion and empathy often hidden by her tough and rugged demeanor. After all she had been through, nothing could scare her or make her stop fighting for what she believed in.[116]

In the 1970s, the coal industry was changing dramatically, and looking for leaders. The Black Lung Amendments had passed, but many operators expanded strip-mining along the fertile mountaintops of Appalachia, thus spurring to action local environmental rights groups such as Save Our Land and Our People. While the new practice was certainly disturbing, spilling waste into streams and rivers, and ridding the hollers of their natural flood walls, it wasn't the reason Eula started to get involved in the picketing and strikes sprouting up throughout the mountains. She had always been concerned for miners' safety, and wanted to continue to make sure mining companies were doing everything in their power to ensure miners were healthy and safe. Many of the strikes went beyond the line of safety, and quickly turned ugly; picketers were abused and shots fired. None of this scared Eula, so she "held tight on the line." As she worked to expand the clinic over the next few months, she attended various mine strikes from Pike County to Tennessee and West Virginia to continue her fight for miners' rights. One strike, remarkable for the fear and danger it presented, changed everyone in the movement. It put her life in danger, and Dean and Eulana's, as well.

*   *   *

During a regional health fair the clinic organized in Barboursville, Kentucky, Eula first heard of the infamous Brookside Women's Club in Harlan, Kentucky. This club was unlike any citizens' group Eula encountered in the mountains, and was made up of "women as tough as rawhide." The group included miners' wives, daughters, sisters, and any woman who felt she needed to be part of the fight. By then, Eula was a legend, and the women, led by the indomitable Lois Scott, arrived at the fair specifically to enlist her in their ongoing strike against the mine company. They were desperate for help and recruited people from all over to the Brookside Mine in High Splint, Kentucky, to make their point.[117]

The fight originally erupted when Duke Energy subsidiary Eastover Coal Company insisted that workers accept a no-strike clause in their work contracts. Miners had been complaining of roof falls and accident rates significantly higher than the national average. They had also asked for a modest cost-of-living adjustment to their salaries. Eastover decided to go ahead and hire non-union workers to come in and replace the union miners who were striking in response. The fight had boiled over, with miners, their wives, and even their children standing on the line against the company to demand more power over workplace conditions. The strike had started months before, but was only then reaching a crescendo.[118]

The next morning, Eula and her family piled into the Bronco and set out for "Bloody" Harlan County before dawn to hit the picket line by five a.m. Eula decided to expose Dean and Eulana to the way mountain folks were being treated, so they could learn that "they didn't have to sit idly by if something wasn't right." The kids were overjoyed; they thought it was going to be like stuff they'd seen in movies.

When they arrived, the family parked next to a store housing folks from all over Appalachia. It was outfitted with a day care, play area, food, and sleeping stations. It was like a makeshift town, a strikers' heaven compared to the picket lines Eula had seen near Floyd County. The picketers there were busy making signs and preparing each other for another day on the line.

As they arrived to picket, they locked hands at the entrance and sang songs to keep their spirits high. One song—entitled "Which Side Are You On?"—was a famous ditty Eula remembered well. The words so deftly encapsulated the class-warfare sentiments mountain folks harbored at the time:

"Oh, workers can you stand it?
Oh, tell me, will you be a lousy scab or will you be a man?
Don't scab for the bosses; don't listen to their lies,
Us poor folks haven't got a chance unless we organize,
Which side are you on?"[119]

It was unlike any strike Eula had ever seen. Small skirmishes erupted between picketers and mine operators, and cops brandished their weapons in failed attempts to settle the crowd. A few folks who were sympathetic to the mines and mine operators fired shots into the air. It was as chaotic as a war zone, and Eula was distraught over her decision to bring the kids to such a dangerous scene. Their first day ended without any harm, or progress for that matter, and on the second day, she forced the children to stay back for their own safety.

Over the next few weeks, miners came in from everywhere to join the cause. Bill Worthington, a close family friend, was leading the charge. The coal company's scabs would stoop to any level to intimidate the chain, launching profanities and denigrations toward the women, men, and children on the line—especially toward Worthington, an African American. Bill was a dynamic man, who understood that poverty affects all—black, white, and brown. The UMWA, one of the first labor unions in American firmly prohibiting discrimination in its constitution, was his pride and joy.

"When we is down there," he said at rallies and among his fraternity, "all covered with coal dust, we is *all* black!"

At one point, Eula and some other picketers were so afraid of the gunshots, they jumped in a ditch and crawled away from the mine until the shooting ended.

"It felt like I was in Vietnam," she said. The mine operators became so vicious that on her third day they had rolled every truck down the mountainside except Eula's and five others.[120]

During the strike, Eula recalls a group of filmmakers led by Barbara Kopple who were there to witness and film the conflict. The resulting film became the Oscar-winning documentary *Harlan County USA*, which vividly captured the chaos and violence. In one spectacular scene, the mines' gun thugs physically beat the filmmakers and threw their cameras against a mountainside. Eula thought that the courageous filmmakers were crucial in helping bring an end to the strike.

"Without them, the outside world may never have known

what was happening there," she said. "It certainly put mine operators on edge knowing that their thugs were being caught in the act."[121]

After attending the strike for a week, Eula came home to Mud Creek, promising she would never put herself in such a situation again. The Brookside strike finally came to a close, but only after the unthinkable happened. A young, well-liked miner, Lawrence Jones, was fatally shot during a scuffle. His death and subsequent funeral finally brought both sides together to the negotiating table. Eula was saddened that it took the loss of life to bring people to their senses, then one day soon after the Brookside strike ended, her tortured relationship with the coal industry became her worst nightmare.

During a meeting in Prestonsburg, a young woman came and whispered in Eula's ear that she had some bad news. She pulled Eula away and told her that Danny had been in a serious accident. He was one of the best roof holders the mine had, and he found pride in his work. But in his role, a single mistake underground could claim his life. Eula feared that it might have taken his.

She broke every speed limit in Floyd County to get to Martin Hospital. She prayed to God the length of the trip to keep her son alive. Danny had nearly saved Eula's life from McKinley's rage, and she would do anything to save his.

When she arrived, she found Danny's new wife, Teresa, with him, holding his hand as he labored for air. Danny was lying on the bed, his windpipe and trachea cut in two by the coal that fell from the roof in the mine. His breathing was so loud and coarse that Eula thought he would have been "scared to death of himself if he could hear it." The doctors said he would make it, but his recovery required surgery scheduled for the next morning. The doctor allowed them to see him for a while longer, but forbade them from staying the night. When the nurse left a while later, Eula decided his injuries were so severe that she couldn't leave him. She carefully crawled under his bed and pulled a sheet down in front of her, holding his hand to let him know she was down there. After the lights were out, she came back out and stayed the night.[122]

After the surgery, which stitched his chin to his chest, Danny came home and lived with Eula, Dean, and Troy who had recently come back to be with the family. He couldn't work for weeks and, according to Eula, his throat was "swollen like a frog's neck." The mine ended up paying part of the hospital bill, and Danny was able to get some worker's compensation, but the majority of the cost fell on Eula. Despite her protests, Danny wanted to go back to the mines as soon as he was able.

"Lord, I was mad as fire! But he wanted to work and he wouldn't listen," she said. It wouldn't be until a few years later when Danny's friend was killed by a similar rock fall that he stopped working in the mines. It made Eula happy to hear him say that he would never go back, even though she knew that when Danny left the profession, a small piece of his identity was gone as well.

Chapter 25

Despite Danny's injury and the chaotic mine strikes, things around the clinic and in Eula's life were steadying. After all the turmoil, work, and sweat, Eula was finally getting the recognition she deserved. In 1975, she got her first taste of national recognition as the American Public Health Association awarded her their yearly Presidential Citation Award, given to those who exemplified the ideals of public health. She was given the award along with Betty Friedan, noted author of *The Feminine Mystique*. The APHA was impressed not only with what she was doing for her community, but with the example she was setting for other women in the mountains. She was deemed a role model for women everywhere, something she never truly considered herself until the award. Although more awards would stream in for years afterward, this one meant the most to her because it recognized her selfless work, and celebrated the fact that a woman could make a real difference in her community.[123]

Eula finally felt great pride in all aspects of her life. She had built a clinic, and a family to go with it. In retrospect, however, Eula regretted she hadn't spent more time dealing with the many issues of sibling rivalry. Dean and Eulana, who had experienced the persistence and determination it took to be an activist with Eula, were growing up to be great kids. Even with all of the hurt and trauma McKinley inflicted on the family, they never complained and supported Eula in any way they could. She, in turn, treated them with even more affection.

While Troy and the others would claim much later in life that Eula always gave preference to Dean and Eulana, Eula never thought of her kids differently. "I loved all my children the same, even the ones that brought me misery at times, I still loved them like any momma would."

The kids stayed close for the most part, as the family jointly bought enough property near Teaberry, off Route 979 in Mud Creek, to create a sort of compound where they could all live. They even had enough room for a tiny stable with two horses. Randy, who was still a nuisance in much the way McKinley had been, settled in a house down the gravel road from the clinic, and Danny and his wife lived near Eula. Troy was the only child who had briefly left for work, going as far away as Indiana.

Eula believed that she was just fine being independent and on her own with her children close by. "I thought I didn't need a man for comfort anymore." McKinley had recently gotten out of jail and had taken up with another woman from Pikeville, and he had all but forgotten about terrorizing the family. Eula could not have been happier for him.

Content with life and her family, she unwittingly found interest in yet another miner, Oliver Baskum Hall (not related to McKinley's family). Baskum would come around the house whenever the children played basketball in the clinic yard. He was an older man who had kept up with Eula and her clinic since she first approached the union for funds. He was always happy to shoot basketball with the kids, and only later did it dawn on Eula that his presence was just a sly attempt to impress the kids' mother. He was an extremely easygoing fellow "who didn't have a mean bone in his body when we first met." The kids, in turn, thought the world of him.

One sizzling summer day, Eula decided to invite him onto the clinic porch for a drink of lemonade to chat and relax. They sat and watched cars drive by on the winding Route 979 and talked about the community well into night. They were both scared of the mine agitation and where it would lead, and thought the local political establishment was to blame for the poverty. Eula soon discovered Baskum shared a similarly deep affection for his community and neighbors. She was impressed, and thought he was a supportive guy who "saw that a woman didn't have to be in the kitchen, but could be right here where I was sitting, doing what I was doing."

They continued the conversation, and Eula decided to give this gentleman a chance. He respected her deeply for what she had built, and she him for his warmth and ease. Baskum also enjoyed the clinic, and would spend time there helping out in any way he could when he wasn't working. He had a charm much more discreet than the gregarious McKinley, but it was there all the same.

Although Eula had previously sworn off men, she did get lonely on the few quiet evenings, and she understood the kids needed someone around they admired and looked up to. The two casually saw each other romantically for a short period, and Eula slowly shook off her chastity, claiming Baskum was different than the "hillbillies" she often encountered in the hollers. She thought it was worth trying to build a family again.[124]

The clinic, however, was at the precipice of an untenable situation. Since its beginning, the clinic had relied heavily on the UMWA's generous Health and Retirement Fund, which paid a monthly retainer in return for care. Along with the occasional Medicaid reimbursement, and a few philanthropic souls, the Mud Creek Clinic could get by with paying a doctor, nurses, and staff a reasonable wage. The UMWA, led by Arnold Miller, however, took a big hit from their arduous strike in 1974 and the Health and Retirement Fund faced a significant crunch in final negotiations. The fund had a long history of bad management, and the union was slowly making strides toward using private insurers. In the end, the strike proved to be one of the more lucrative standoffs in history for workers in the bituminous coal business, but health retainers took a hit, and many coal companies officially made the move to private insurance.

At first, the clinic attempted cutting salaries and hiring more volunteers, but the board knew quickly they were on a destructive financial course. A new model had to be implemented, and it required collaborating with folks they didn't completely trust.

For years, Eula and the clinic board eschewed the local medical establishment. They served as the adversary, unwilling to work on behalf of the poorest and most disadvantaged. They were also the same folks who fought, incredulously, against the FCCHSP placing its funds toward direct services. In fact, if Eula had to point to a single antagonist in her fight for universal care, it was the political and medical establishment that had fought tirelessly over the years in their own self interest. But in light of the union's steady decline, Eula and the board made the wrenching decision to seek institutional funding. The only folks they could turn to with money were those they had spent a decade working against.

The clinic board and Eula committed that if they took this route, the clinic would strive to maintain its character and mission. Clinic autonomy and maintaining the spirit of a people's health clinic were of utmost importance.

"We ain't gonna sell out," she told her troops. "No money in the world is worth your principles."

When the board approached Big Sandy Health Care (BSH),

the eventual nonprofit suitor, Eula told them upfront, "We don't want you, but we need you—and your money." At the time, BSH operated two clinics, in Wheelwright and Magoffin County, where they treated patients and referred them to local hospitals—much in the way the FCCHSP had functioned. If Mud Creek Clinic were to join, she held, it "sure as hell wouldn't turn into another referral clinic."

The initial discussions the clinic held with BSH yielded favorable results. The board would maintain 51 percent of the clinic, keep their sliding-fee scale for the poor, and perhaps most importantly, retain all board members and staff. Eula would have to change her official title to patient advocate, but she didn't mind.

"They could call me the janitor as long as they let me work," she said.

Once the clinic was part of the Big Sandy family, they had to work with the other clinics, neither of which provided transportation, one-stop patient coordination, or education in quite the same way the Mud Creek Clinic did. Neither did any of BSH's existing clinics have a food pantry, or supplemental services, but Mud Creek decided they could fill that gap for everyone.

"We helped patients in ways they didn't 'cause I saw the whole picture—health, food, legal, everything—that they couldn't see," Eula said. "Or they knew it and chose not to do anything about it." As a result, the flood of new patients became overwhelming in much the same way it was when they first opened the clinic.[125]

It was only during the negotiations and the aftermath of the merger that Eula and her staff realized they were fully implementing the concept of primary care patient coordination. The clinic's approach to the *whole* patient allowed Eula and her volunteers to oversee all of the patient's medical care needs, from general medicine, to referrals, to mental health services, transportation, food, and shelter. This was a far cry from what BSH or any other community health center was accomplishing at the time. While on a small scale in Mud Creek, the concept has since served as a model for modern efforts to reform the health care system, raise the quality of care, and reduce costs. Mud Creek Clinic had been striving to offer all of these not through any academic study of the health system or high-minded idealism, but simply out of an intuitive sense of what folks on the verge of poverty required. It was one of the determining factors leading Mud Creek in later years to recruit quality doctors, and continue to be recognized as a pioneer in community health centers.

"Merging with Big Sandy was like our protective blanket," Eula later said of the partnership. "Without them, I don't know what would have happened to our full-patient approach to care."[126]

The clinic finally had a steady financial base to support its many offerings, but was still looking for a permanent physician. Mud Creek had seen a few intermittent doctors in the years since Squire and Graham, but was in search of a long-term, full-time replacement. The doctors who came and went truly ran the gamut of professionalism. There was Dr. Beth Laine, a Catholic nun with a quiet temperament and pious demeanor. She had trouble understanding the culture and the people, but she had patience, and as a National Health Service doctor, she had the stamina and experience to stay longer than most. During her tenure, she uncovered a devastating prevalence of sexually transmitted diseases and pelvic inflammatory disease. She made sexual health one of her highest priorities.

Then there were others like Dr. Southerd, who would often come to the clinic after he had been drinking, but claimed otherwise. Eula and the board knew the clinic needed stability with a physician, and a steady medical hand to guide them through this new phase with their partner. They knew they would be under a microscope with their new co-owners and couldn't handle any discrepancies in care.

To help with the physician interviews, Eula called Dr. Julie Snyder, a psychologist in New York, for her expertise. The clinic's network by this point was expansive and always willing to help, and Dr. Snyder had become friends with Eula after making annual visits to the mountains to volunteer at the clinic. Dr. Mary Swaykus, another nun who briefly worked at the clinic, even helped post the job to the national *Catholic Reporter*. After a few interviews, some good and some terrible, there was one doctor in particular that Eula and Dr. Snyder thought had the perfect mix of passion and practicality for the clinic.

Their final choice was Dr. Ellen Joyce, a former Catholic nun steeped in liberation theology. She grew up in Watertown, Massachusetts, the oldest of five, which gave her ample early experience taking care of others much the way Eula had to care for her siblings. Once she was out of Catholic school, she spent three years in the convent at St. Catherine's in Springfield, Kentucky, vowing poverty and obedience before leaving and heading off for medical school in Boston. Just out of her family medicine residency in the Bronx, Ellen and her husband, Ron, who had recently completed his divinity degree at Harvard, decided to move somewhere where they could live out their ideals of charity and giving. The Catholic physician tradition at Mud Creek had become common knowledge in religious circles, and part of that ethos attracted Dr. Joyce to look into practicing in the mountains.[127]

Dr. Joyce and her husband first came to the rolling green mountains of Eastern Kentucky from Lexington through the scenic Mountain Parkway. They parked their car and pitched a tent near the Natural Bridge in Wolfe County to spend the night as they traveled. The young couple loved the beauty of the land, especially as snow drifted down and clumped along the pine branches covering the mountains. But as beautiful as it was, they found it utterly confusing to get around. When they would ask people how to get to Mud Creek, they often got answers detailing a puzzle of hollers and creek crossing that hardly made sense to anyone who hadn't grown up in the region. Dr. Joyce recalled that, years after moving to Eastern Kentucky, she fell into the same trap, not knowing how exactly to get anywhere except with the help of local landmarks, creeks, and hollers.

When they first entered the clinic, Dr. Joyce remembered seeing Eula spiritedly arguing with Randy. She was so incensed that she hardly noticed the new doctor had arrived. Randy had been causing problems at the clinic again, but Eula rushed him off to avoid scaring Dr. Joyce. Eula took Ellen into her side office, poured her a coffee, and chatted. They shared mutual stories of their fathers, and the examples they set to look after others. Dr. Joyce noted to Eula the unmistakable Catholic presence at the clinic. Bishop William Hughes was listed at the time as one of the clinic's biggest donors. Sister James Roach, administrator at Our Lady of the Way, sat on the board, and three members of the ten-member staff were Catholic nuns. Dr. Joyce revealed that not only were they looking to work for a couple of years in the clinic, but to actually settle in the mountains of Eastern Kentucky and start a family. It was music to Eula's ears.

"She was different, down to her heart," Eula said. "I knew it when I first met her that day." At night, Ellen and Ron spent the night with the Halls in their house across the yard from the clinic before leaving the next day.

Eula got the final approval from Dr. Snyder and staff, and quickly offered the job to Ellen. Eula didn't have much money to offer, even post-merger, so she coordinated with Dr. Gan Madiwar at Our Lady of the Way for Ellen to work a few days a week at their hospital, as well. Dr. Joyce loved how the staff worked together and—like Eula—was intent on helping the community in all aspects of their health. She took the job, and the young couple bought a simple four-room house in Allen, Kentucky, near the elementary school. Since Ron's car had been stolen in the Bronx, they decided to buy a new one with four-wheel drive before settling in.

Chapter 26

"HEY, EULA, CAN YOU HELP ME OUT HERE? I CAN'T understand what she's saying to me!"

Many patients had trouble deciphering Dr. Joyce's thick New England accent, and she certainly had trouble understanding their mountain twang. The nurses had to act as translators until Dr. Joyce picked up on the long *o*'s and dropped consonants that give Eastern Kentuckians their unique twang. Dr. Joyce encountered an entirely new people and culture at the clinic and at Our Lady of the Way Hospital, but she relished the opportunity. She was quickly dropping "y'all" and "what have ya" only a few weeks into her stint.

Joining Big Sandy Health Care had its perks, and brought the clinic and its patients a higher standard of care. The clinic was newly equipped with one fetal monitor, an EKG machine, an X-ray, ultrasound, and even a one-bed emergency room. The staff had grown as well. Janet Adkins was the new secretary, Mary Ellen, a nun, worked the lab and negotiated with vendors, and Mike McCarthy joined as a physician's assistant working through the National Health Corps. Lou Ellen Hall, who had been a volunteer at the clinic almost since its founding, also joined the staff and kept medical records.[128]

Dr. Joyce had never experienced a medical community like the one in Eastern Kentucky. Everyone knew each other and their families. The positivity and patient-centered care of the clinic was unrivaled in hospital settings. One night, Dr. Joyce noticed a family singing Christian hymns on the clinic porch. While they would have been hushed in a hospital where Dr. Joyce had trained in the Northeast, Eula told them to "take us to church" and raise their voices to comfort the other patients in the waiting room. Everyone served as an advocate, from family to family friends, and Dr. Joyce felt the community of supportive people helped keep patients on medication, coming back for appointments, and, in general, healthier.

However, the range and scope of ailments Dr. Joyce saw kept her on her toes, and in a sense, threw her to the wolves. One such emergency was a cardiac arrhythmia that she was woefully unprepared to handle. The patient's acuity forced her to frantically retreat to a medical textbook to find answers. She found herself nervously sweating on occasion, and even asking patients what they thought she should do—a tactic to lighten the mood when she didn't have the answers.

Under the tutelage of Dr. Gan Madiwar, Dr. Joyce soon learned more on the job than she had in her years at medical school or residency. Dr. Madiwar was an Indian immigrant and former lieutenant in the US Army, who, like Dr. Joyce, had come to the mountains to practice medicine. She witnessed many common colds and coughs, but also bizarre pathologies that were not immediately recognizable. Many women, she recalled, felt they had to douche every day, which took away protective liquids around the vulva. Some women who entered the clinic smelled of bleach, and Dr. Joyce had to educate folks that it wasn't safe to use on a daily basis. Chronic lung ailments and bronchitis were common, exacerbated by smoking and working in the mines. New X-ray machines made it easier to find silica deposits, as did a new radiologist in Pikeville who had special training in identifying pneumoconiosis for miners and smokers.

Another major illness, severely underreported among the population, was depression. A study completed by the Appalachian Regional Commission found there was a significantly higher prevalence of serious psychological distress or major depressive episodes among people in the mountains. Eula had long known there was an issue in the hollers made worse with chronic substance abuse and wrenching poverty. Women more often than men, she noticed, found daily struggles taking a toll on their emotional health. In part, Eula hired Dr. Joyce knowing she needed someone with her mental health training and background to heal the wounds she saw among her patients at Mud Creek.[129]

Psychological depression widely affected the population and yet was completely misunderstood. Folks in the mountains came up with anything else to explain away the emotions, low energy, and raw anxiety depression produced. Some in the hollers believed depression carried with it a religious connotation, or even involved animal spirits. While some were open to accepting their condition, many were not, and instead told by their peers their brain "simply wasn't working right." Admitting depression was all too often seen as a weakness. Dr. Joyce had to become creative in the way she spoke about the mind, incorporating an ethno-medical model into her treatment of depression, one that understood the specific culture attributed to mental and emotional problems.

The drugs used at the time to treat mental health were both a boon and a bane. Anti-depressant medications were not then what they are today; the drugs prescribed then had terrible side effects on patients, often making them feel dull or lazy. Sadly, many patients would resort to abusing these medications, creating a further dependency. Despite the efforts of Dr. Joyce and those in the clinic, Eastern Kentucky to this day is still recognized as having higher-than-average rates of depression.[130]

Comorbidities were also common and alarming. Many patients were diabetic and many came in almost weekly complaining of lower back pain. This was difficult for Dr. Joyce to treat, because she knew the vast majority of folks of both genders worked hard all day with their hands. Mountain men and women mined coal, sawed logs, worked as hired help, farmed hillsides, and did backbreaking physical labor because their economy was built on strength. Many of these folks were hurting, and needed a respite from the bodily toll. But, in retrospect, it was the early prescribing of pain pills in communities throughout Appalachia that most likely laid the foundation for the current prescription pill scourge in the mountains.

"You know, there was a doctor in Letcher County who freely gave prescriptions to those who simply asked," Eula said. "And when they were actually sick, they would come to Mud Creek, but we made damn sure not to give 'em anything." It was a tough line to draw, and it was often difficult to discern the needy from the abusive. On the other hand, there were nefarious doctors whose facilities served as "pill mills"—clinics that freely gave prescription pain meds to those who asked, creating dependency and addiction. It was a difficult balance for clinics and doctors at the time, and one that would haunt the region for years to come.

Along with handling multiple patient morbidities, Eula and Dr. Joyce began to look at patient lives outside the clinic to see how they could help. They began counseling and eventually helping complete paperwork for patients who qualified for workers' compensation or disability insurance. It was the last connection point the clinic made for patients that truly brought end-to-end patient coordination services to Mud Creek.

Jim King, the local administrative judge in charge of Social Security, gave the two a full education on how he decided whether a person was disabled or not. According to Eula, the doctors would "evaluate the patient and say what has worked, what hasn't worked, and evaluate their strength and range of motion." In the system, Workers Compensation had its own evaluative doctors who made work-eligible determinations. Many tried to game the system, but the doctors stood as a bulwark to determine who was actually disabled and who was not. While some of the tests were perfunctory, Dr. Joyce felt as if she knew who the slackers were, and who really needed help. Eula would often accompany patients to their hearings and ask Dr. Joyce to come along with her. Eula knew folks needed support because often people would get to the hearing and let their pride get in the way of telling the judge the truth about their disability. Dr. Joyce would go to spell out for the judge what was really going on, prying answers out of patients by questioning simple functions of life, like whether they were healthy enough for woodwork, hunting, or playing with their kids. Women were especially ashamed to admit they needed help from husbands or help keeping children at home.

"No one actually wanted to live off a government check, even if they desperately needed it. We aren't dependent people like a lot of folks like to paint us," Eula asserted.[131]

Folks came to the clinic because they were working-class poor or near the edge of poverty. Many were hard workers who were simply broken by years of hard physical labor, stress, and poverty. There were plenty of patients who put on their best acting jobs to exploit Eula and Dr. Joyce's assistance, but the duo knew who was faking, and over the years, convinced the judge that they brought forth only those who truly needed help. Eula had a keen understanding of people and their motivations. After all, she most likely knew their families, where they worked, and if they went to church on Sundays. She refused to help folks who didn't need checks from the government, and she made absolutely sure not to compromise her relationship with the judge. She had enough experience with government programs to know that the smallest bit of corruption corrupts absolutely—so she fought hard only for those who needed it.

*   *   *

In late 1977, Baskum asked Eula for her hand in marriage. The two wed with the slight suspicion that their relationship was purely for the benefit of fighting their separate feelings of loneliness. They weren't necessarily in love, according to Eula, but they enjoyed each other's company. Eula only had so much time to give with her children, clinic, and community all seeming to demand her attention at once. But she wanted someone to go home to, to share her day with, and to care for intimately. Baskum fit the bill. In a quiet ceremony without pomp or circumstance, the two married, and Eula began a second chance at love.

PART THREE

"You won't have a problem getting to heaven, 'cause you've already been through hell."

Chapter 27

IN THE YEARS AFTER THE CLINIC'S FORMATION, EULA experienced two competing dreams when she laid her head to rest. In one instance, she dreamt she had taken on too much to handle. These were particularly punishing dreams, forcing her to wake up and contemplate that perhaps this little girl from Greasy had overstepped her place in life. She considered her lack of a formal education beyond grade school, and regretted that maybe she had burdened the family in poverty while she chased her dream; or worse, she lamented how she brought abuse upon herself by working so much outside of the home. There was a nagging worry she wasn't providing the best care to her patients either. Eula, after all, wasn't a doctor or nurse, and she knew little about the operational functions of an expanding clinic. "Maybe I was in britches a few sizes too big," she said later.

In a contradictory set of dreams, she became similarly anxious, but instead wondered if she was doing enough. She may not have the education, or be from the right family or social class, but she knew right from wrong. She understood justice.

Most importantly, she had the tenacity and determination to pursue what was right in the face of adversity.

"I may not have a lot of sense," she said, "but what sense I got, I use it right."

In those dreams, she would be sitting quietly in her clinic office chair, talking with Congressman Perkins or luminaries like Robert Kennedy and Martin Luther King, Jr. She would discuss with them their struggles to alleviate poverty and prejudice, and then angrily scold them for not doing enough. She would yell about the hardship her parents and family had suffered, she would rage against the abusive husband she had endured, and sob over the lack of jobs, food, or medicine available to her kin in the mountains. Then her ire would turn on herself, and she would ask, "Have I done all *I* could?"

Eula's life rightfully took on a heightened sense of possibility in the years after the clinic was established, and her competing dreams pushed her to engage in any issue she could get her hands on. Black lung, clean water, union workers' rights, legal aid for the poor, school lunches, and health care were each pieces of a larger fight to give her community the respect afforded to the rest of America. Appalachia had been left behind, and she wouldn't rest until "the folks who pulled strings"—corrupt politicians and the wealthy plutocrats who supported them—were doing the right thing.

Eula did everything she possibly could for her community while raising a family by herself. At the age of fifty-five, she had touched more lives than she ever thought possible, and had truly lived up to her childhood dream to "be somebody and make a difference." Through her community work, she had made friends and enemies. The enemies, she thought, had at times gone too far by threatening her home or her family. Politicians thought she asked for too much. Doctors feared she was encroaching on their domain, and even neighbors at times wished she would keep quiet about the coal bosses. But she held strong in the face of adversity, and reassured herself by thinking most of the threats were bluffs—the chest-thumping of those fearful of ceding whatever power they had.

Then, on a quiet Appalachian night in 1982 as she was coming home from a peaceful evening with family and friends watching Dean play baseball, she found herself completely powerless. The paradox of the evening was particularly cruel. Earlier in the day, she had helped patients with their disability casework, provided food to a hungry family, then traveled to watch Dean play in a ballgame—and win—all while Baskum served as the coach and loving father the family always needed. Later that same evening, she finally understood the consequences of speaking truth to power. The bluffs had been called, and the triumphs of a remarkable life were burning that night.

*   *   *

Eula, Nanetta, and Eulana rushed feverishly to put out the flames. Eula could hardly understand what was going on; just hours before, she had locked up the clinic and made sure everyone was out before she left for the ballgame. For the next fifteen agonizing minutes, the trio did whatever they could to put out the flames, but the fire was potent. As the extended family of community members rushed toward Teaberry with water buckets and blankets to help douse the blaze, the side of the clinic crashed in, leaving a large bonfire where the porch had been. The group continued trying frantically to stop the fire from destroying the rest, but Eula had given up. She knelt down, overcome by emotion, and for the first time in decades, she wept. Family and clinic were all that had sustained her through the years of pain, anguish, and poverty, and they were the only two things giving her hope in her mountain struggle. Now, her world was burning before her eyes. As she wept for the clinic she worked so hard to build, she looked up to the heavens for an answer, but the stars of the Appalachian night sky were unrecognizable from the glow of the flames.

Nearly an hour later, the fire department arrived and left after consoling the crowd. There was nothing else they could do that night other than determining the cause of the fire. Past midnight, after everyone except Baskum and the children left, Eula stayed awake and thought deeply about the vagaries of her life. She was thankful no one was inside the clinic, but furious that no one came to stop it soon enough. The entirety of her life was on her mind that night and she considered the pain she had endured over the previous two decades to build her dream, only to have it destroyed in a fire. Eula had been through a lot of strife, but that night was simply the worst night of her life.[132]

The next morning she awoke early, feeling as if she had a moonshine hangover. She got out of bed, dressed, and walked out past the horses, into the morning mountain air. She wandered over to the smoldering pile where the clinic used to stand, and to her surprise, the clinic site was not empty. Nearly twenty men and women stood in a circle, discussing the calamity—and revenge.

Just the day before, the clinic had been up and running, its doors open to anyone who needed the comfort and warmth Mud Creek Clinic's healers could provide. It had become a community institution, and with it, a new culture of health and well-being had sprouted. But then it was gone, and everyone there knew it wasn't simply a lost clinic; the embers left by the previous night's fire were vestiges of Eula's heart and soul. The smoke and hurt were still raw, and while Eula showed contemplative calm, the others were furious.

"Somebody did this and I want justice!" yelled Lou Ellen. She learned of the fire a little past midnight the previous night from coworker Rita Hamilton. Neither knew what to do but show anger; for them it wasn't just a clinic; their jobs were at stake, as well.

The group huddled around the picnic table, near the last remnants of the nearly decade-old clinic, and debated among themselves. There was talk that the fire department had ruled the fire to be arson rather than an accident. Eula sat stoically, listening to volunteers and the board discuss who could be held responsible, and who might have been so vile.

Delmar Thacker, Ray Yates, Don Lafferty, Maxine Kinney, John Rosenberg, and many of the volunteers arrived before the work hour to kindly offer their help, and share in each other's anguish. Roger Marshall, then president of Big Sandy Health Care arrived to offer his heartfelt condolences, but also to take care of the aftermath. After briefly assessing the damage, he approached the group to announce that BSH would have to lay off all clinic workers, and put everyone on unemployment until they could figure out their next move. Groans and curses drowned out the man's voice.

"That's the least of our worries right now," Eula said softly, despite knowing that laying off staff would be the beginning of the end for the clinic. Although the Mud Creek Clinic was part of BSH's affiliation of clinics, they seldom viewed it as a part of their overarching business plan. The clinic was too isolated, too far away, and barely turned a dime. Eula spoke quietly to the crowd, "What we should be worrying about is how we're gonna contact patients. We were seeing close to a hundred patients a day before this. Some folks might die if we can't get up and running soon." She lifted her voice a bit and declared, "We can't . . . and I won't turn my back, as long as we have staff here, we'll do it."

Roger rolled his eyes, seemingly frustrated with her confidence to rebuild, and walked away, stating he would get an immediate answer from insurance about next steps. Eula circled her troops, and slowly gazed over the volunteers and the nurses around her. Beside her that day were warriors in the fight to care for the poor and heal those who had never assumed healing was something they could have. It was a gathering of family, old friends, former patients, EKWRO activists, and even some doctors. They were one big mountain family who needed to look out for one another, and she couldn't let them down. Eula took a step up on the picnic table bench, and told everyone they couldn't let patients suffer, they couldn't let their enemies win, and they had to move forward with or without BSH. She restored their lost faith with her own, and gave everyone the confidence that they could overcome this tragedy.

At that moment, a pickup truck roared up to the embers across the gravel and an old lady stepped out for her morning appointment. She had no idea what had occurred the night before, and she stood stunned, her eyes welling up at the sight of the clinic in ashes. Eula looked up at the willow tree standing strong next to the picnic table and said, "Let's get a phone line, and let's get our clinic back!"

Over the next few hours, Eula and the staff fanned out across the holler, cashing in years of favors. When the telephone company told her they couldn't run a phone line to the clinic site, she reminded them of the time she gave medicine to the general manager's brother. Within a few hours, a phone line was installed and operating on the weeping willow tree next to still-smoldering embers. Dr. Joyce was on vacation and was temporarily replaced by a visiting doctor from West Virginia who was ready for whatever came his way. Some staff members were able to drive to Pikeville and Prestonsburg to grab any supplies they could off convenience-store shelves, and for the next two days, patients steadily arrived at the picnic table while nurses and staff triaged them as best they could.[133]

Luckily, it was the beginning of summer, and administrators at the Stumbo Elementary School, the site of Eula's first battle with local officials, allowed her and the clinic staff to temporarily move their operations to the lunchroom. The Floyd County Fiscal Court provided the clinic with some emergency supplies, and the janitor's closet of the school served as a pharmacy. It was a new, unfamiliar setting, but it had the same team and compassion that had endeared the clinic to so many.

Miraculously, they didn't miss a single patient. Although the staff couldn't conduct X-rays or perform comprehensive exams, they were able to refill certain prescriptions, take blood pressure, and offer advice. They had two months before the kids came back to school—two months to get back to normal.

Implausibly, the clinic staff would face one of its biggest emergencies only two days later. Just as they moved into the school, the roof caved in at a nearby underground mine operation in Letcher County. A flood of miners came rushing to the school for immediate medical attention. Even though the contract with the miners had dried up, it was the only place they knew to go for immediate care. The staff did the best they could under the circumstances, tying up open wounds, referring severe injuries to Martin or McDowell, and providing mental comfort to families of the injured miners.

Although the first couple of days after the fire were a whirlwind, occupying everyone's time and energy, speculation about the motive and possible culprit behind the arson never left Eula's mind. A peculiar paranoia set in, and she began questioning everyone around her who could have possibly had a hand in wrecking her dreams.

"I was ready to quarrel and fight with all those folks that stood in my way for years," she said. "I was walking around looking for clues even when they didn't exist."

There were hints and suspicions from the past, that in the aftermath of the fire, seemed all too clear. Two years prior, folks looking for addictive painkillers had regularly robbed the clinic. As a result, the clinic purposely didn't stock such drugs. Subsequent break-ins, however, forced Eula and the clinic board to hire a night watchman who kept an eye over the clinic in exchange for free rent. The man they hired was "a good fellow who couldn't even harm a criminal if he tried," Eula said. The watchman successfully guarded the clinic for two years. He maintained that on the night of the fire, he had left for a few moments to get a bite to eat, only to come back to find Eula trying to put out the fire herself. Eula thought maybe someone had paid him to turn a blind eye, but his tears and extreme remorse in the days following the fire led her to believe he was innocent.

The authorities determined that the blaze had initially started in the trailer behind the main building, where the black lung clinic and the percussor machine had been. The fire department told Eula they were certain gasoline had been poured on the black lung clinic, and that it was the first to go before the entire building went up in flames. Even though she had seen her share of intimidation and harassment from the mine companies over the years, she couldn't believe mine operators or their thugs would go as far as doing something so egregious. Burning the clinic was akin to killing somebody, she thought. They may have wanted to scare her, but the fire was beyond fair game.

Then there was the most bizarre element of the night, the lack of response from the local fire department. The Floyd County Volunteer Fire Department was just outside the holler, and they could have easily made it to the site before the roof caved or significant damage was done. Delmar Frasure and Ray Yates were both on the fire department board, and Eula couldn't help but wonder if they had held back the first responders. Could they have had a hand in this? While they had their disagreements about the management of the clinic, they were her friends and confidantes in the struggle to give care—but maybe envy had gotten the better of them.

"It all just looked and felt political," Eula later said. "We always tried to keep the judges and politicians off our board 'cause I wanted folks who wouldn't easily be bought or sold."

All of the questions and allegations swirling in her head about people she had known for essentially her entire adult life weighed heavily on her. Everyone around her was pointing fingers, and the police had no real leads, making the speculations even more potent. When most others approached Eula to discuss whom to hold responsible, she usually balked, pointedly talking about the future instead of the past. She would tell everyone, "What happened, *happened*, and the focus now should be on rebuilding what we built together."

But Eula couldn't help but consider another possible culprit, one that made her heart hurt—a possibility that her conscience continually told her to set aside for eternity. But she couldn't shake the thought.

In the previous few years, her relationship with her eldest son, Randy, had deteriorated significantly. So much so that he once got in a fistfight with Dean in front of Eula and directly threatened her on occasion. Randy aggravated the family relentlessly in the 1970s, and even owned up to having his prison buddies from Arkansas come up to rob the clinic once before. The clinic received random calls from time to time in the months before the fire, asking about what drugs they had in stock. Clinic staff would give the standard response about the lack of painkillers at the clinic, but the callers never listened and the calls kept coming. Randy took McKinley's side in family fights, and had been recently hanging around folks who encouraged increasingly bad behavior.

Late the night of the fire, Eula, yearning for revenge on the perpetrator, stormed alone to Randy's house to interrogate him. She found him drunk and sheepish.

"I swear," Eula said, "I'll shoot you right now and take you out of your misery if you did this." He promised her he hadn't done anything, but Eula couldn't let the possibility die. Could her own son have ruined what she had worked so hard to build?

Walking back to her home that night, she tried her hardest to convince herself otherwise. "I hoped it was somebody away from here, who thought we were just some hillbillies out in the boondocks and didn't know better . . . I want to think it's just some criminals who had been in prison, or were looking for drugs." But the gnawing feeling just wouldn't go away.

Every time Eula thought about the possibility, she reminded herself that it didn't matter. It didn't matter how it happened. It didn't matter who did it. It never mattered. What mattered, Eula knew, was what she would do in response.

Whoever did it would just have to live with their shame, and whoever did it should have to know they had messed with the wrong woman.[134]

Chapter 28

B Y THE TIME OF THE CLINIC FIRE, EULA HAD FRIENDS everywhere, even across the world. In some ways, the clinic fire was a call for something bigger, better, and grander than circumstances previously allowed. She started to secretly plot the Mud Creek Clinic's return; not only with the supplies and facilities they had before, but with the idea of a facility just a notch below a hospital. Luckily, Eula had taken out a $20,000 insurance policy well before the fire, which she secretly held onto as she designed the new clinic in her mind.

Some day-to-day considerations had to be made immediately. Since BSH let go of the staff immediately after the clinic fire, it would be an understatement to say Eula's relationship with the organization had deteriorated. While they made repeated overtures to her, even offering to buy her land at a premium, she didn't trust them to properly rebuild the clinic as it was envisioned—*for the people*. Besides the obvious differences, BSH was rumored to be in bad financial shape; they had recently closed their formerly successful Magoffin County Clinic and fired Director Roger Marshall.[135]

She had heard from board member Ray Yates that BSH

was planning on rebuilding the clinic with funds from a matching grant that the Appalachian Regional Commission was sponsoring. She dug a bit deeper, enlisted her old friend at AppalRED, John Rosenberg, and researched her own viability to apply for the grant.

At the same time, Delmar Frasure was quoted in the *Floyd County Times*, claiming the funds had already been awarded to BSH. "The [ARC] might as well send us the funds, because we're going to build it!"

County Attorney Arnold Turner donated $1,000, and State Senator Benny Ray Bailey from Hindman gave $400, challenging others to match or exceed them. Eula was proud that the community was coalescing around the idea of rebuilding, but she couldn't let them control what was taken from her. It was a lesson clearly learned from FCCHSP, and she wouldn't resign the future clinic to a tepid fate.

Eula, Maxine, John Rosenberg, and some sympathetic folks at the Big Sandy Area Development Agency quietly went to work preparing an application. They went as far as recruiting doctors from a primary care center in Frankfort to ensure word didn't get out, even to members of the Mud Creek Board, such as Delmar Frasure. BSH had already submitted their application and, it seemed, were all but certain to receive funds. Eula was far from naïve about her prospects of winning the grant herself. She didn't see how ARC would entrust her instead of an institution like BSH with a solid reputation and the means to raise additional funds. Her experience applying for the OHA grant years before had told her they wouldn't take seriously a woman without education. But she had to give it a shot, and she knew her best chance to compete for the grant would be to go to the top.

The day Eula and her team filed the application, she picked up the phone and called Governor John Y. Brown to ask for one of the biggest favors of her life—to force BSH to pull their application to the ARC and support Mud Creek's. Her argument was as simple as it was devious. She explained that it was in the state's best interest to win the grant, but in order to do that, Kentucky could field only one application. The application had to be one from the Mud Creek Clinic to make sure there wasn't another FCCHSP-style debacle. She knew a lot of feelings were still raw on the national level, as well as locally, about the War on Poverty health program, so she made sure to remind the governor not to repeat the same failure. She also mentioned she would be more than happy to get all of Floyd County out to help the Democratic Party in the upcoming November elections.

Her call did the trick. The next day, as expected, the BSH Board summoned Eula and her co-conspirators to come and explain why BSH was being forced to pull its application.

At a meeting the next day in Salyersville, the BSH and Mud Creek boards showed up, both groups fuming, to decide what their next step would be and whose application would eventually stay with the ARC. Carol Prater, the chairwoman of the BSH Board, immediately threw a fit, scolding Eula that she was in violation of previous agreements. She also maligned Eula's efforts, claiming she could never gain the respect or admiration of the ARC. She asked Eula bluntly, "How could you betray us after all we've done for you and Mud Creek?"[136]

Eula launched into her own diatribe. "Well, it's because I want a clinic *for the people* and I don't want this clinic to go the way of Magoffin." She told the board about her earlier struggles with the health program during the War on Poverty. She was careful not to accuse anyone of bad intentions, because she knew in their hearts, they wanted what was best for the community, as well. However, she stressed to them that they were thinking small. The community could run its own clinic if given the chance, and the clinic could be bigger and provide more services.

Despite her arguments, her oratory failed her for the first time. Both boards were still furious they weren't consulted, and BSH particularly was embarrassed to be told by the governor to step down. After a bit more wrangling, a doctor from Frankfort who served on the BSH Board—but was relatively unknown to most folks around Floyd County—spoke up just as the board was ready to vote.

"Now, Eula may be violating the rights of an earlier agreement, but I'm gonna say I have to side with her," the doctor said. "What Eula built was special. I'm not sure she can get the funds from ARC, but I'm gonna vote for the Mud Creek Community Corporation and formally ask BSH to withdraw." Eula had no idea who he was, but she was grateful he had spoken up.

Other people, however, continued to hurl accusations at Eula, and the room boiled over with anger. Many sided with BSH, while a few, including some of her old board members, were backing Eula to continue with her bid. However, the conversation was soon out of control, and kept returning to how implausible it was for Eula to successfully apply and win such a large grant. The meeting ended without any resolution, instead leaving it up to Blaine Cotter, a BSH employee who was spearheading their effort on the ARC grant, to decide what would be the best way to move forward in the interest of actually receiving money for a clinic.

That evening Blaine gave Eula a call and said he would come by the picnic table to talk. The table was the last remaining piece of the old clinic. Eula agreed, half-expecting and preparing for an offer to make a deal on clinic ownership. When he arrived, Blaine and Eula sat at the picnic table face to face, with the clinic ruins, still untouched, next to them. Eula knew he wanted to win the grant, as much for the community as for his own career, so she turned on her charm by giving him a short tour of what used to be clinic exam rooms, supply closets, and waiting rooms. As they finished touring the ruins, he looked her dead in the eye and whispered as if he were committing a sin. "Eula, I'm gonna tell you something you already know, but you got two strikes on you. Two. You better watch your step, watch what you do, because one more strike and you're out."

"Well, Blaine," Eula said without hesitation, "throw me a strike and I'll hit a homerun. Just give me the chance, Blaine. I won't disappoint."

*   *   *

Because of the dust-up, the ARC allowed both parties to collaborate before resubmitting a final application. Eula had John Rosenberg look over the application and Blaine made edits as well before it was shipped off. In the days following, she called everyone and pulled every string she knew how to pull. The next two weeks were a miserable mix of uncertainty and anxiety. The community was evenly split. The gentry assumed she had no chance, while the majority of folks who attended the clinic and lived on Route 979 quietly prayed that Eula would succeed.

Three weeks later, in the middle of a busy workday at the clinic's newly donated trailer home, Eula received a call with the final verdict. She quietly walked over to the fax machine without telling the staff, and pulled out the letter from the ARC. She studied it carefully, made a copy, and immediately faxed it to Blaine. When he received it at BSH headquarters, he could hardly notice the ARC header for the big bold handwriting covering the text: "HOME RUN!"[137]

Chapter 29

THE TERMS OF THE ARC DEAL REQUIRED THE grantee to raise in three months a fifth of the total $400,000 toward the construction of a new clinic. To Eula, a woman who hardly ever had more than a few thousand dollars in her bank account, this lofty goal never seemed insurmountable, just difficult. In 1982, the per capita income in Floyd and Pike Counties hovered between $7,000 and $8,000, so while folks could pitch in here and there, she knew the vast majority of the funds wouldn't come from the people of Mud Creek, or the surrounding area. She had to go big, and get every dollar she could find from wherever she could find it.[138]

Her strategy wouldn't simply be to sell the new clinic and all of the fancy bells and whistles she envisioned for it. The pitch, she thought, had to reflect the emotions and compassion that made the clinic so precious to the folks served by it. It had to embody the sentiments that brought John Rosenberg and Dr. Joyce to her side early on. It had to be thoughtful of the struggle for health care, but, most importantly, it had to be about the people the clinic was meant to serve when no one else would.

At the first meeting with those who volunteered to help raise money, she stressed that every donation had to be attached to a name or it wouldn't be counted toward the goal. She made everyone promise that if they didn't build the clinic themselves, donors would get their money back, no questions asked.

Her insistence led some volunteers to question whether Eula had officially lost it. The fire was a great tragedy, and perhaps, some thought, she couldn't think straight about herself or her future. The clinic was her home, it was where Dean and Eulana were raised, and while people who knew her best still didn't quite know the horrid details of her marriage, it had also been her sole source of income allowing her to live a life independent of McKinley. The volunteers were not offering to help simply to build a clinic, but to ensure that the woman they loved so much could continue her life.[139]

"You know, even after I got the letter, many folks thought I couldn't do it," she said. "That I'd run back to Big Sandy asking for money after a few weeks. But I was never going to lose what I built. I didn't ever know what I was capable of . . . that is, until I tried."

With that rock-solid mentality, Eula went to work, dedicating the next ninety days to nothing but phone calls, potlucks, door knocking, yard sales, and good old-fashioned fundraising.

Eula began by calling every "silver-spooned mouth" she had encountered in her life. The staff put together potlucks at the Stumbo School nearly every week; one dumpling dinner cooked by Eula netted nearly $1,300. Eula and her volunteers also pioneered some in-your-face tactics never before seen in Eastern Kentucky. She staged roadblocks on US Highway 23, one of Eastern Kentucky's main arteries through the mountains, and Eula stood proudly on the yellow dividing line between guardrails. As cars slowed down to read the clapboard signs plastered to their chests and backs, two volunteers collected money in buckets on each side. The stunt brought in a couple of hundred dollars every rush hour, and local officials were so supportive of Eula that they simply turned a blind eye to the traffic jams and obvious danger.

Early in the fundraising push, local Pikeville radio station WLSI, located next to Pikeville High School, allowed Eula and volunteers take to the airwaves for a twenty-four-hour telethon. People called in from all over Eastern Kentucky, offering things to donate ranging from homemade quilts to used shotguns. One old man even called in earnestly offering homemade moonshine for sale. Eula chuckled at the man's offer, remembering her own days of living off moonshining, but kindly declined. The outpouring of support was non-stop, and by the end of just two days on the air, the clinic had raised nearly $17,000, a huge haul for the nascent fund.[140]

The wider news media caught on to the fund drive and began pouring into Mud Creek to highlight the clinic's struggle to rebuild. Eula remembered the immense power the news media held in getting the word out from her days fighting the Floyd County School Board, so she was more than happy to tell everyone who would listen about her vision for the new clinic. Reporters and media representatives from West Virginia and Tennessee did pieces on the former clinic and the arson. Pictures of the smoldering ashes were plastered on the pages of the state's two biggest newspapers, the *Louisville Courier-Journal* and the *Lexington Herald-Leader*. As a result, checks started pouring in from around the state, including a stunning $10,000 donation from the archdiocese in Covington, Kentucky. Catholics had always played a large role in the clinic's development, providing a steady stream of doctors such as Ellen Joyce and Mary Swaykus. Their empathy and drive for social justice continued to resonate with Eula through their generous gift.

Different community organizations and sympathetic individuals poured checks into the tiny P.O. box she kept for donations at the Harold Post Office. Letters, describing why the donor felt compelled to give, often accompanied the donations. Some, like her, were warriors in the fight for universal health care. Others simply loved the story of a proud, independent woman leading the way for her community. Some couldn't believe that there still was such agonizing poverty in America.

Local banks donated money, and John Rosenberg, by then one of the most respected individuals in the county, rounded up local lawyers and doctors to give generously. County Judge Executive Jerry Lafferty, Jr. made a public announcement, offering the clinic a $60,000 loan to immediately begin buying new equipment. It was election season, after all, so Eula made sure to hit up every politician she could find. Even some previously angry folks who worked for BSH, caught up in the excitement and celebration, decided to donate to the new Mud Creek Clinic.

Six weeks into the drive, Eula went national. ABC's *Good Morning America* sent producers to Mud Creek to do a piece on Eula's life and the clinic. The segment referred to Eula as a "diamond in the coal" and was an immediate hit with national audiences, prompting a slew of letters of support and donations. In an effusive letter dated that fall, the executive producer of the show, Mellen O'Keefe, who admittedly never wrote to any of the show's subjects, wrote to Eula that her story "soothes people's aching spirits," and that she "lives the true American dream."[141]

In less than ninety days, Eula, her board, and her dear volunteers raised nearly $120,000, well above what they needed for the matching grant. With the loan, and the additional money, the board immediately purchased a plot of land in Big Mud for $45,000, had contractors place dirt against the mountain to raise it above flood level, and began construction.

"If the fire were a funeral or a death in the family," she said years later, "the day we bought the land felt like giving birth."

Chapter 30

THE CONSTRUCTION OF THE NEW CLINIC WAS NOT without its own drama. Five board members were elected to the new Mud Creek Community Health Center Board immediately after the award was received. John Handshoe was the chairman, giving Eula some needed rest, but he was not afforded a vote unless there was a 2–2 tie. In the early days of the clinic, there was almost always a tie, even on trivial matters.

The biggest dust-up between the community-elected members of the board actually developed over what to name the new clinic and ultimately who owned the funds. A loud and vocal contingent of community folks, many who had given significant amounts of money to the clinic, wanted to name the clinic the Vietnam Veterans' Clinic of Mud Creek. Some folks advocating for the name change even brought guns with them to the meetings, possibly in the hopes of rattling Eula and her board confidante Hi Mitchell, who were hoping to keep the clinic as it was. Eula was a major supporter of the local veterans' community; in fact, some of her most loyal volunteers and fundraisers were veterans. However, she was concerned that such a specific name might cause the clinic to lose a bit of its independence, and might keep some folks away who thought the name meant exclusivity. In addition, two members of the board wanted control of funds without having to go through votes. Yet, Eula knew that many county organizations, such as fiscal court and the fire department, had run into money trouble because of the lack of oversight. She couldn't leave decision-making up to herself and four others. She knew power corrupts and she wanted a safeguard set up even against her own board. Additionally, she knew she wasn't getting any younger; she had to consider the long-term viability of the clinic beyond her years.

Eula rose at the opening of the next meeting to let her feelings be known. She was being backed into a corner, and had to reassert herself against what was becoming staunch opposition, with some folks asserting they would leave the board if changes weren't made.

"Nothing y'all say or threaten will scare me," she said. "I'll tell ya another thing—this clinic ain't gonna be no Vietnam clinic. Anyone, regardless of who they are, where they're from, where they've fought, or what they've done, will be served here. This will be the Mud Creek Clinic, for Mud Creek and its people." The vote would be held a week later among the five of them and with the other board members showing continued resistance, Eula needed to come up with a plan to keep the operation of her clinic transparent and to continue to provide services to all.[142]

Luckily, Hi Mitchell had a plan. The board rules were set up to not allow any board member to vote by proxy. To keep the vote 2–1, they had only to keep one member away from the meeting. Eula knew Ray might be a good target; his wife and he didn't have the best relationship and she might help if the price were right. Ray's wife worked at the Dairy Queen and according to town gossip ran around on him. The two surmised she might conspire with them to keep Ray away.

The day before the vote, Eula and Hi went to the Dairy Queen in Pike County where Ray's wife worked, ordered themselves two Blizzards, and offered Ray's wife a proposition. If she could fake car trouble between the hours of five and seven, they'd give her a hundred dollars, fifty now, and fifty if she could keep him away. She happily obliged.

The next day at the meeting, Ray was conspicuously absent and the others nearly went crazy trying to find him. John Handshoe's wife came with a gun, and sat right next to Eula with the weapon in her lap. Eula later laughed at the memory. "I was just tickled to death watching them argue about where Ray had been and trying to intimidate us any way they could."

Eula started the vote, first bringing out the bylaws and reading them to make sure no one broke the rules. The other board members and their posse were livid, again threatening to leave the board, and claiming they had power to stop the money at the bank.

"They were throwing papers, acting like children, stomping, cursing, and ranting," Eula said. She finally erupted. "Stop acting like heathens and start acting like adults! We're here for a clinic, not your ego." In the end, the other members quit the board, and Eula and Hi helped elect Linda Carl, Tina Vance, and Carl Stratton from the local community to replace them.

Two days later, Ray and John went to the bank and told the teller they needed an overdue check signed and they couldn't find Eula to sign it. The bank manager was suspicious since Eula had always made herself available for anything involving the clinic. He went in the back and called her. "Eula what's this talk about a check and taking your name off the account?"

"Oh Lord, we're just getting started to build; don't let those guys fool ya." Eula knew they had crossed the line. When the teller asked if he should call the cops, she waved him off, telling him "they weren't worth the police's time."

A few weeks later, the entire $400,000 was deposited to the clinic, and construction started immediately.

*   *   *

In November 1982, across the front of the *Lexington Herald-Leader*, the headline read, "It's now Official: Eula Hall is a "Wonder Woman." Eula was honored by the Wonder Woman Foundation and given a $7,500 award. The award was given in honor of the fortieth anniversary of the DC Comics' Wonder Woman character to celebrate her real-world equivalents. Eula's life work had again been recognized as a triumph. Actress Jean Stapleton and feminist activist Gloria Steinem presented the award to Eula in New York City. It was Eula's first trip to the city and she started her speech to the crowd with the quip, "I've been called a wild woman . . . but never a wonder woman."[143]

Chapter 31

THE NEW CLINIC WAS BEING BUILT WITH STATE-OF-the-art examination rooms, a food pantry, X-ray machines, and an attached pharmacy; it was slated for completion in late 1984. In the meantime, Eula made some improvements to their temporary trailer quarters. Baskum was consistently one of the hardest workers for the clinic. He completed much of the carpentry work for the temporary clinic and finished the septic system. However, he was also a bit upset that Eula was diving right back in.

On the surface, Baskum was a "great feller" as Eula called him, a partner to her and a great father figure for teenagers Dean and Eulana. He was always ready to lend a helping hand. When Eula was away organizing or lobbying on public policy, he looked after the children and he would be there when they came home from school, too. Even though he didn't necessarily agree with all the time and effort Eula invested in the clinic, he supported it. But over time, he realized she may have loved the clinic more than him.

"You know, Baskum is a good worker, not a lazy bone

in him," she recalled. "If you ever met him, you'd a thought sugar never melted in his mouth. But he was only the lesser of two evils." While Baskum never laid a finger on Eula, and was supportive of her work in the beginning, he found it easy to sling nasty words and was verbally caustic at times. After the second clinic construction began, he started loathing Eula's work outside the home. Baskum wanted to grow old with Eula, spend his days with her, and not see her only when she came home late from work. While he knew how much the clinic meant to her, he wanted to mean that much as well, but he was asking for more than she could give.

Baskum also showed some odd behavior as his animosity grew. He often wore Dean's new college clothes and got them rough and dirty without remorse. He even once stole two of Dean's guns and sold them at a local pawnshop, later telling Dean and the family he had nothing to do with it. Eula chalked up his antics to his loneliness at home, but it wouldn't be long before she found out he had been regularly stealing money from her, too.

"You know, Baskum's family never lived as hard as we had; he didn't quite understand compassion either, so he didn't understand why I did what I did," she said. Baskum had stooped so low as to steal money from his own mother, who stored her savings among the pages of her favorite Bible passages. While his demeanor and affect gave the impression of a stark departure from McKinley, Eula said, "He was a devil in disguise . . . he was a liar and a deceiver wrapped in sheep's skin."

One day, soon after she learned of his thefts, Eula inquired at the bank to see copies and verify her recent history of deposited checks. She found his handwriting on a number of checks she had never seen, nor endorsed.

"I went home and got my gun. I pointed it at him and said 'you better come up with my money or I'll kill you. I'm not gonna work hard and let you steal from me.'" She got most of her money back, but things didn't get better. A week later, Baskum approached Eula in a fit of rage with a screwdriver in hand.

"If you come at me with that screwdriver, I'll leave you to the cats!" she said as she pointed the gun at him yet again. Soon after, Baskum gave up and moved out, leaving Eula on her own once again—except this time leaving her with a wholly satisfied conscience.[144]

* * *

Baskum's departure only briefly occupied Eula's mind. Their relationship had been more of convenience than love, and while she did care for him, she was fed up with trying to make men treat her right. Her whole life she had searched for a partner, especially one who respected and cared for her. She had her children, her clinic, and her community—but only with Baskum's deception did she finally come to understand she didn't need a man for comfort. It was difficult to think she had wasted so much time, but she thanked God she finally knew she could live by herself.

While she was dealing with Baskum leaving, her confidante and colleague in healing—Dr. Ellen Joyce—was ready to make her next move, as well.

"I loved Ellen like a sister," Eula said, but she recognized it was time for the doctor to move on. Ellen had been Eula's partner at the clinic and had made it much of what it is today—a place that stops at nothing to care for a patient. Ellen had become medical director of Big Sandy Health Care, and was very well thought of in the community. However, her work at the clinic became more and more demanding, forcing her to work until midnight on many occasions. The mix of a new family and a tough schedule pushed the couple closer to their next adventure. Ellen's husband, Ron, had created a niche for himself in the local news industry, alternating work for the Johnson County newspaper and for the *Floyd County Times*, reporting on everything local and political. Ron was an intellectual, and the news was his way of talking to the community about its ills in an attempt to change it. The goal was to make sure people knew the vast power that political elites held. Ron remained neutral, like a good journalist, but like a bulldog he attended every school board and city council meeting that had never been reported on before. He faced severe backlash for some of his articles, which only served to tell him he was doing the right thing. After years of writing, he felt his work wasn't sufficiently moving the people to action the way he had hoped it would.[145]

Ron decided to attend law school at the University of Louisville, and after spending six years following Ellen's dream, they both moved to the River City to pursue Ron's.

"You know, we had a lot of doctors, but I never hated to see anyone leave until Ellen left," Eula said. Over the following years, a slew of doctors came to the clinic; many of them were foreign-born (including the author's father), and they wanted to work in settings where all that mattered was providing access to care for those who didn't have it.

In the days shortly after Dr. Joyce left town and Eula split from Baskum, McKinley made a surprise appearance at the clinic, asking for help with his severely labored breathing. "The irony was rich," Eula remembered. She couldn't believe he would have the audacity to enter the clinic he had loathed for so long. Eula was with another patient when he came and she quietly inquired about his condition, but decided not to see or speak to him while he was there. Dr. Doris, who was the lead physician at the time, saw McKinley, and not knowing of their tortured history together, asked Eula if she would take him to the hospital. Eula was stunned and didn't know how to react. She was furious at McKinley for even showing up, but she couldn't help but feel compassion for a man who looked like half the person she remembered.

"The Lord taught me to do unto others as you would have them do unto you," she said. "In that moment I couldn't help but treat him like any other patient, no matter what he had done to me."

If there were ever a moment to test Eula's compassion, that was it. Despite all the pain and hurt McKinley had caused her and the family, she couldn't stand to watch him in such agony, struggling to breathe. She didn't wish that on anyone, and it was exactly why she started the clinic in the first place. She loaded a weak and feeble McKinley into the car and drove him to McDowell. They didn't speak a word the entire way.

After a few tests, he was diagnosed with lung cancer and given only a little while longer to live. "You know, I always thought I would love to see him gone, and spit in his face," Eula said later. "I had so many cruel thoughts over the years. But in that moment, I just couldn't bring myself to be as evil as he was to me."

Sadly, McKinley's new wife did little to care for him, and he admitted to Eula that he often went hungry at home. In the following weeks, Eula brought food to him at his home because she couldn't stand the thought of him starving. She felt like his life was in her hands. She still didn't understand why she could show kindness to him after all he had done to her, but the clinic had given her a compassion that could even overcome the evil he had brought to her life. She did what she would do for any patient.

Dean, Troy, Randy, and Danny went to the hospital together to see him one last time before he passed away. He was, after all, their father and no matter what he did, the children had pride and felt like they owed him a final burial. His death was especially hard on Randy and Troy who knew their father in good times and bad—and knew he played a large part in making them the men they were.

When McKinley died, his wife failed to claim his body. Eula and the children put money together to give him a proper burial. "It was respect for another human being," Eula said. For her, it was good to know he was gone, but she knew she could never erase the mark he had left on her life.[146]

Chapter 32

Eula's days were packed with the makeshift clinic, making plans for the new clinic, and being a mom to Dean and Eulana. On an almost weekly basis, she received awards and honors from community groups, churches, and colleges, and made trips all over the region to speak. The country was in the midst of a recession, and politicians from all over were seizing the opportunity to speak for the poor and the economically disenfranchised. Eula found it amusing. "The only time they seem to remember us is around November."

While a bit jaded by local politics, Eula had a profound faith in the power of federal officials. Her black lung advocacy, along with the well-funded ARC, gave her hope that many outside of the mountains were still concerned with the plight of those in the hollers and creeks. A special young senator from Massachusetts was interested in Appalachia as well, and planned a fact-finding trip to Floyd and Letcher Counties to understand the causes for Appalachian poverty himself. Camelot was coming to Mud Creek.

On November 23, 1983, a day before Thanksgiving, Senator Ted Kennedy arrived in Floyd County to much fanfare. After surveying hunger issues in Pittsburgh, Detroit, Minneapolis, and San Francisco, he noted, "Economic distress isn't confined to one region." His brother, the late President John F. Kennedy, was a hero to many in the mountains. He was young, idealistic, and along with his brother Bobby, spoke poetically and with affection toward the poor. They spoke with empathy in a way few politicians had since Roosevelt. Ted Kennedy came to reclaim that love, and wanted to see firsthand the great poverty and beauty of the mountains. Congressman Carl Perkins invited him, knowing his family's past, but also with an eye to please the young senator who held a desire for a higher and more powerful office.

After Congressman Perkins and local Democratic leaders paraded the senator around town, Kennedy was scheduled to have a tour of the now-famous Mud Creek Clinic by its founder, and to host a field hearing later in the day. Volunteers and clinic staff anxiously crowded the clinic porch to catch a glimpse of the senator, prompting the porch to give way and volunteer Juanita Compton to tumble to the ground. "She was fine," Eula remembered, "but we joked that we were so excited, we couldn't stand up straight!"

After Eula whisked the senator around the exam rooms, he rushed off to Stumbo School, the site of so many pivotal moments in Eula's life, where the hearing was to be held. The room was hot and packed with activists, supporters, clinic patients, and curious folks from around the hollers. Shabby old water jugs sat next to microphones on the table where speakers were prepping, and policemen and political types chatted in the back. Everyone was in their Sunday best as they grabbed seats under the fans waiting to see the senator and hear him speak. A very young and terrified-looking Patrick Kennedy arrived first and sat down behind the senator's seat as a neatly coifed staffer settled in next to him.

Kennedy started the hearing by recalling the events of the

day, and the great poverty he saw around him. He thanked Congressman Perkins and took a few digs at President Ronald Reagan's lack of action. A woman from Mud Creek was the first local to speak, and she detailed her personal struggle to feed her kids and herself. She desperately wanted to keep her family intact, but she had lost eighty pounds and had no idea how long they could go without food. Then, at the Mud Creek Clinic, she received her first real meal in months.

"Eula said 'this house is a community,'" she told the senator.

Kennedy responded to her with amazement, commenting to Congressman Perkins, "Makes you wonder, congressman, how many places there are in Eastern Kentucky or across the country, where there aren't those Eula Halls . . . and those very special places we saw run by a very special person . . . just makes you wonder."

The next to speak was a father with seriously ill children. Kennedy said, "As I understand it, you can't get the health care for your children who are sick. Well, as Congressman Perkins and I can tell you, there's no member of Congress that has to worry about that because we've got ourselves a real good health insurance program . . . And I think if it's good enough for the members of Congress, it ought to be good enough for the people of Kentucky. And the rest of this country."

The local man finished his testimony, and the senator thanked him, and then invited Eula to the dais to speak: "Thanks for the tour, Eula, and for introducing us to the families. Obviously, you've heard what your center meant to them and what *you* mean to them. I know you've faced a lot of hardship, but I must say, you ought to receive some well-deserved recognition."

Eula, dressed in a purple blouse with matching earrings, quickly fixed the microphone and began her comments. Instead of responding to the senator's flattery, she launched into her prepared testimony.[147]

EULA HALL: "Thank you for coming to our area. Thank you to your son Patrick and your staff. And thank you to Congressman Perkins; he's always been there when we need him. No one in the Congress knows more about this area than him.

It was a pleasure to give you a tour. It was sad to show you the problems that exist in our area. I know you're not to blame.

It's a sad thing the day before Thanksgiving to talk to people who haven't eaten for days. You know I come talk to these people due to my position at the Mud Creek Clinic. What we've seen today is a drop in the bucket. People are suffering, hungry, cold, and sick.

It's because of cutbacks in the safety net intended to help people. The unemployment rate is high. Jobs are scarce. Food stamps are minimal. People don't want to live on food stamps. They want jobs. It's either you get sick on fixed income and you can maybe go to the doctor, or you stay home sick.

There is no prediction of sickness or problems. You can't predict health.

The Mud Creek Clinic charges according to income, but nobody is turned away. We're a primary care center, we don't have an emergency room after closing hours, and we're closed on weekends. We do everything we can on nights and weekends, and we do emergency care.

People here don't have insurance and can't afford it. Pregnant women have no prenatal care. We can only see them up until delivery, then we try to sneak them to the hospital. No pregnant woman should sneak around to have a baby. But if they don't pay, they won't be delivered.

SENATOR KENNEDY: You know, in Philadelphia, you have to put $2,200 down in cash in order to just get in the hospital. That's what's wrong with this society.

EULA HALL: It's not that much here, senator, but they do require it. There was a seventeen-year-old . . . end stage of pregnancy. They told her you need $350, then they said $400. They refused to see her on last visit. The child was so scared. She called me and said, "What do I do?" I made a home visit. This woman was living in a barn, with a bed in it. No nothing, just a bed in a barn. [I asked] "Why are you living here?" [She said,] "Our only income is food stamps and we can't get them if we stay in the house with his mother. So we have to stay here to get food."

SENATOR KENNEDY: What sense does that make to you, Eula?

EULA HALL: It makes no sense. No one should suffer such degrading. Makes me angry and sick. In our country of plenty, why should they face such suffering?

The housing situation is critical.

Unemployment—if you're on unemployment, you're over the income guidelines for Medicaid. What kind of sense does that make?

These people want jobs.

Eula and the senator continued back and forth, and eventually turned to the subject of healthy drinking water and dental care.

SENATOR KENNEDY: In Boston, we have twelve cavities per child because of raw minerals in water. We put fluoride in just for that reason.

EULA HALL: Well, that sounds like something simple we could do here, doesn't it, senator?

SENATOR KENNEDY: Why, yes it does . . .

By this point, the senator's face was distraught and tired. Perhaps the enormity of the day—in all he had witnessed—had taken a toll on his psyche. He had never before seen poverty on such a scale, and everyone was quick to remind him of the earlier promises his brothers Jack and Bobby had made to mend this beautiful American territory. The look on his face made it clear that it pained him to see a region so far removed from the American story of progress.

He interrupted Eula again, to remind her that they needed time to hear from the rest of the panel. But Eula was never one to follow traditions of etiquette—even to political royalty. She summed up her desires with the same tenacity and vigor she had had since her youth.

EULA HALL: So, senator, is it the government's responsibility to give health care to its people—or not?

Kennedy concluded the hearing by telling folks he met in Eastern Kentucky that "the powerful interests and the wealthy interests have the high-powered lobbyists. Their interests are well represented. But what this country is truly about is caring for each other—and that's what I saw here today . . . The people of Kentucky care about each other. What they need is just a helping hand."

Twenty-five years later, at the 2008 Democratic National Convention, Ted Kennedy would declare health care to be the "cause of my lifetime." Perhaps it was in the beautiful winding hollers and hamlets of Eastern Kentucky—with Mud Creek's favorite daughter Eula Hall—where he first made that commitment.

Epilogue

ON A CLEAR AND SUNNY DAY IN 1984, THE NEW clinic opened its doors for the first time. Located just a short distance from the Stumbo School, the brick structure sat neatly at the slope of a mountainside and covered nearly 5,200 square feet of space. The clinic had a small parking lot across the creek from the winding Mud Creek Route 979. Some commented that the clinic looked like a newly built home, which suited Eula just fine.

The morning of the unveiling brought together dignitaries from across Kentucky and the country to take part in the festivities. Congressman Perkins, former doctors, activists, Republicans, Democrats, and nearly every speaker engaged in a competition to see who could shower Eula with the highest adulation. Eula had her hair done up the night before and wore a brand new blue dress for the occasion. She sat on the stage with a wide smile and a heavy heart; she would have loved for her parents to see what she had achieved for her community.

From its humble beginnings in a trailer off Tinker Fork, the new modern clinic stood as a monument to the community and was Eula's legacy. In the next three decades of her never-ending work, she saw friends die from illness, and fought bouts of her own. She continued to fight for women's issues and community empowerment, only to be stymied by powerful local officials. But Eula's day-to-day clinic life, beyond the fire and rebuilding, took on a separate air of calm. There was less drama, less public confrontation, and less familial fighting. She worked hard every day for the people of Floyd County, and spent every day tirelessly advocating for patients, providing transportation, and ensuring the clinic was run transparently.

She seemed to spend the next three decades racking up awards and honorary degrees, as well. To date, Eula has been recognized by the US Congress and former presidents, and has received honorary degrees, such as one from Berea College where she stood alongside Nobel Peace Prize winner Desmond Tutu. Her story of coming from nothing touched a nerve with those who sympathized with the idea that the poor could take their destiny into their own hands. Eula embodied that spirit, and exemplified the potential of a homegrown activist.

Eula's children didn't fall far from the tree. Dean, manager of the Mud Creek Water District, recently campaigned for Floyd County magistrate against a longtime incumbent. Eulana currently serves as a director of a local senior citizens' center in Betsy Layne. Danny, Troy, and Randy retired as coal miners, but still find ample time to be with their mother. Randy particularly changed his ways and found Jesus in the years after the fire. His born-again mentality makes him a calmer and more likable figure than in years past.

Until 2011, when the eighty-four-year-old Eula's diabetes prevented her from working every day, she would arrive at the clinic at eight a.m. and often worked late into the night. While the doctors changed over the years, the ethos remained the same. As of 2013, the clinic is still part of BSH, and employs twenty staff members, including a full-time doctor originally from Pakistan. They see nearly fourteen thousand uninsured and underinsured patients a year. Robin Holbrook, the current clinic director, and Lou Ellen Hall are, according to Eula, "the lifeblood of this place. They'll carry on the legacy."

There is a separate dental clinic, a full pharmacy, food pantry, and plans to expand. Many of the doctors are foreign-born physicians, and many of the pharmacy and nursing staff are local. In 2006, the road running through Mud Creek, Route 979, was renamed the Eula Hall Highway by the Kentucky state legislature. In 2012, the BSH-operated clinic was officially renamed the "Eula Hall Medical Center."

*   *   *

It was often surreal for me to sit with Eula in her clinic office, surrounded by decades of awards and patient notes, crosses and poems, while listening to stories of her humble beginnings. In an economy and world plagued by difficulty, no one quite knew hardship like Eula, and here she was in her temple telling me she had much more work to do.

"You know what I'm planning to do next?" she asked me, as if she had another lifetime of advocacy left. "Well, my next plan is to build a domestic abuse shelter, 'cause women like me still have nowhere to go and we gotta work hard to fix that." If history is any indication, I have no doubt we'll eventually see it happen in Mud Creek.

Through all of Eula travails and accomplishments— the creation of the Water Board, the clinic, black lung compensation, and ongoing workers' rights—she has helped paint a picture of poverty alleviation seemingly missing from today's discussions about the economy and individual responsibility. Poverty is omnipotent, spatial, violent, and it can attack from many angles. There is no panacea. There is no single market efficiency or lever government can pull. It requires many things—health, safety, jobs, and, most importantly, an understanding of dignity—to overcome. Eula found dignity in her work, and offered it to those around her who wanted to be part of the same struggle and invested in their community. An ethos that rings true throughout Eula's story is one of inclusiveness, community, and a wholesale rejection of libertarian fallacies of the individualistic mantra. Individuals like Eula don't overcome poverty on their own—they do it with help of people like John Rosenberg, Drs. Jim Squire and Eleanor Graham, and Dr. Ellen Joyce. They do it with the help of caring neighbors and family. They do it with the help of government and civil society institutions. If they're lucky, like Eula, they can come out of poverty self-sufficient, without handouts but with self-worth, and a community behind them.

Today, Eula's mind has outlasted her body, and she no longer is able to work at the clinic helping patients with their court proceedings, or finding food or medicine. Her family—her children, patients, friends, fellow activists, and nearly the whole of Kentucky—surrounds her and loves her dearly. In one of my last interviews with Eula, we spoke about the presidential election. She was an early supporter of President Barack Obama, but had since soured on both political parties. She lamented to me about the fact that every politician, left or right, spoke effusively about the middle class. It was a class that nearly every American aspires to join, and every politician offered policy prescriptions to expand its ranks. But Eula thought they missed the point.

"Where the hell are the politicians talking about the poor—the *lower* class—the ones that don't have jobs, food, or shelter?" she asked. "The middle class already made it, and I agree it's gotta grow, but there's still a lot of poor out there. The poor are the ones who desperately want to be middle class."

Her clarity struck me. Perhaps a new generation in a stagnant economy has all but forgotten the poor.

I outlined for her again the reason why I thought her story was important to tell. Appalachia is a region long forgotten by the larger American narrative. Appalachians still hold some of the lowest rankings in major economic, health, and educational indicators. Politicians at the national level, except for the erstwhile John Edwards, rarely discuss Appalachia or poverty. Local leaders continue to skirt around long-term growth issues, and continue to indulge in patronage and play corrupt games that support dwindling industries. Pop culture still relies on an old and outdated stereotype of the region. And yet through all this there has been noteworthy development. There have been many reasons to find hope in Appalachia for a brighter future. But it will take thousands of Eula Halls and many more Mud Creek Clinics to secure prosperity for the region. It will take continued local initiative to rejuvenate the area, and more role models like Eula Hall for mountain youth to imitate.

I told her on her eighty-fifth birthday that she was an inspiration to everyone she came across. Not only because she was an amazing individual, but because she embodies the culture and commonsense wisdom of the mountains like no one I have ever met. Her response to my praise: "You give me too much credit. You see, I'm actually just too damn stubborn to sit by and let the world be cruel to my family and friends."

Exactly, I thought, that's just what I meant.[148]

Acknowledgments

I owe many debts of gratitude to those who directly and indirectly helped me piece together Eula's incredible life. First and foremost, I owe a heartfelt thanks to the Hall family—Dean, Danny, Randy, Troy, and Eulana—and especially to Eula. When I first stepped into her office to ask about writing her story, I had no idea if she would oblige or kick me out. Her family's generous time made this story richer and much more dynamic than it would have been without their input.

I also owe thanks to all of those who put up with my numerous questions, including Robin Holbrook, Lou Ellen Hall, John and Jean Rosenberg, Steve Sanders, Dr. Eleanor Graham, Dr. Arnold Schecter, Dr. John Belanger, Dr. Ellen Joyce, Richard Couto, Ned Pillersdorf, Cathryn Wright, and John Handshoe, among many others. Thanks to various folks at Berea College, the University of Kentucky, the National Archives, and Appalshop for their archival help. A special thanks to those who helped procure pictures, including Mark Taflinger, Earl Dotter, and Caroline Rubens. Thanks especially to Carol Butler who finally saw this project to its end. And thanks to my family and to my partner, Sara, whose tough love and motivation helped me power through the many drafts of the biography.

Finally, thanks to my father, Dr. Rao S. Bhatraju, who brought my family to Eastern Kentucky and worked with Eula Hall in her Mud Creek Clinic years ago. His insatiable appetite for books gives new meaning to the term bibliophile.

About the Author

KIRAN BHATRAJU is a writer and entrepreneur from the mountains of Eastern Kentucky. His father worked as a physician at Pikeville Medical Center and the Mud Creek Clinic for two decades. He currently resides in Boston with his wife Sara.

Notes

CHAPTER 1

1 Eula Hall, interview with author, October 27, 2011.

2 Hardy Smith, *The Company Town: The Industrial Edens and Satanic Mills that Shaped the American Economy* (New York: Basic Books, 2011), 99–100; Crandall A. Shifflett, *Coal Towns: Life, Work, and Culture in Company Towns in Southern Appalachia 1880–1960* (Knoxville: University of Tennessee Press, 1995); Michael Wallis, *The Real Wild West: The 101 Ranch and the Creation of the American West* (London, Macmillan, 2000).

3 William Lynwood Montell, *Killings: Folk Justice in the Upper South* (Lexington: University of Kentucky Press, 1994), 144, 163–65. A hundred years later, the Hatfield and McCoy feud has spawned a persistent identity and still serves as a symbol of family dignity, violence, and vengeance. Today, an eponymous festival takes place every year in the region and in 2003 the families officially signed a truce in Pikeville.

4 Eula Hall, interview with author, October 27, 2011; Ron Eller, *Uneven Ground: Appalachia Since 1945* (Lexington: University of Kentucky Press, 2008). Eller's book looks at the political economy of the region as the primary driver of exploitation and underdevelopment that has plagued the region for so long; also

see Harry M. Caudill, *Night Comes to the Cumberlands* (Ashland, KY: Jesse Stuart Foundation, 2001).

5   Eula Hall, interview with author, May 29, 2009; Troy Hall, interview with author, May 12, 2011; Dean Hall, interview with author, May 12, 2011; "Tribulations Don't Deter Eula Hall," *Louisville Courier-Journal*, December 12, 1982. Eula said of the inequality and the moneyed folks her father sold corn to: "These big coal owners, the way they could strut—but he'd come and look at that corn and he'd pick the biggest pile . . . him with cribs full of money in his pockets, you know, and a car and all that stuff. And we was dirt poor. You can't help but get sick to your stomach."

6   Loyal Jones, *Appalachian Values* (Ashland, KY: Jesse Stuart Foundation, 1994).

CHAPTER 2

7   Eula Hall, interview with author, May 29, 2009; Melanie Beals Goan, *Mary Breckinridge: The Frontier Nursing Service and Rural Health in Appalachia* (Chapel Hill: University of North Carolina Press, 2008), 347. In the absence of doctors, 'granny women' served as caregivers, passing their healing traditions down orally through generations since many women of the time were illiterate. At the turn of the twentieth century, granny women attended nearly half of all Appalachian births. Many of these women were adept at local pharmacology and herbal healing, and often went unpaid for their services.

8   "History of Pikeville Medical Center," Pikeville Medical Center website, accessed in 2011, http://www.pikevillehospital.org/ history.html. Pikeville Medical Center is currently the largest hospital in southeastern Kentucky. The hospital is 535,552 square feet, and has 261 beds, and more than two thousand employees.

CHAPTER 3

9   Anthony P. Cavender, *Folk Medicine in Southern Appalachia* (Chapel Hill: University of North Carolina Press, 2003), 116–118,

149; Eula Hall, interview with author, May 29, 2009. Eula's hair hasn't changed since she was a young girl, and has been her trademark among her friends and patients; some refer to it as a "halo on the head of an angel." Many folks in Floyd County with similar haircuts claim they are sporting the "Eula Hall."

10   Dr. John Belanger, interview with author, May 20, 2011; Christine B. Daugneaux, *Appalachia: A Separate Place, A Unique People* (Parsons, WV: McClain Printing, 1981), 30–35; 63–80; Cavender, *Folk Medicine*, 37–39.

11   Daugneaux, *Appalachia*, 40–48; Cavender, *Folk Medicine*, 38–41; Eula Hall, interview with author, May 29, 2009; Troy Hall, interview with author, May 12, 2011.

CHAPTER 4

12   Eula Hall, interview with author, May 29, 2009; Randy Hall, interview with author, October 8, 2012. Henry Ford, famed industrialist and founder of the Ford Motor Company, established one of his many coal-mining operations in Stone, Kentucky, only a few miles from Greasy Creek. This proved to be his largest and most productive mine.

13   Eula Hall, interview with author, June 1, 2009. With the advent of radio, mountain families were exposed to what life was like for those who lived in the cities and towns outside Appalachia. Eula and the family made the move out of the holler and closer to what is today Harold, Kentucky. Students can still attend and complete elementary school in Greasy Creek, but usually attend middle and high school at nearby Pike County Central or Betsy Layne High Schools.

14   Eula Hall, interview with author, June 1, 2009. For more on Appalachian schools, read Jesse Stuart's *The Thread That Runs So True: A Mountain Schoolteacher Tells His Story* (Touchstone, 1950), or Jesse Stuart, *To Teach, To Love* (Jesse Stuart Foundation, 1992)

15 Cavender, *Folk Medicine*, 122; 1900 Census of the United States. The 1900 census confirms that the southern Appalachian mountain region faced one of the highest death rates per capita due to the whooping cough; http://www.wkyt.com/wymt/home/headlines/Kentucky-has-increased-numbers-of-Whooping-Cough-169842826.html. Pertussis has made a comeback in recent years; more than 380 cases were reported in Eastern Kentucky in 2012. Doctors at the Centers for Disease Control believe that the effectiveness of the vaccine may be diminishing.

16 John Alexander Williams, *Appalachia: A History* (Chapel Hill: University of North Carolina Press, 2002), 383–386. The war would eventually take many of Appalachia's men to be the nation's foot soldiers in the war. Williams notes that six of the top seven states to give men to the volunteer army were found in Appalachia (384). Eula recognized later that many alarmists in the community built up fear—and the recruitment rolls—by insinuating that the war could hit them at home; the reality of such an attack was nearly nonexistent.

17 Eula Hall, interview with author, July 14, 2009; William Leuchtenberg, *The White House Looks South: FDR, Truman, and Johnson* (Baton Rouge: Louisiana State University Press, 2007), 40–45. Leuchtenberg wrote about FDR's appeal to the southern working-class millhands and miners, quoting several of them: "Mr. Roosevelt is the biggest-hearted man we ever had in the White House . . . He's for the common class of folks . . . the only man we ever had in the White House who would understand that my boss was a sonofabitch."

CHAPTER 5

18 Robert Allen Ermentrout, *Forgotten Men: The Civilian Conservation Corps*, (Pompano Beach, FL: Exposition Press of Florida, 1982), 99; Perry H. Merrill, *Roosevelt's Forest Army: A History of the Civilian Conservation Corps* (Perry H Merril, 1984), 9.

19 Eula Hall, interview with author, May 29, 2009. Eula and the other Rileys were Baptist parishioners who attended the Old Regular Baptist Church. For more information on mountain Christianity, see Deborah McCauley, "We Believed in Family and the Old Regular Baptist Church," chap. 4 in *Appalachian Mountain Religion: A History* (Champaign: University of Illinois Press, 1995), 101–112.

20 Eller, *Uneven Ground,* 12: "Appalachian people had always been quick to serve their country in times of war, and enlistment rates were among the highest in the country during World War II"; Williams, *Appalachia: A History,* 383; "Military recruiters targeted Appalachia's surplus manpower, and local draft boards granted deferments and other considerations more often to middle- and upper-income town dwellers than to young men from farming or mining communities."

21 Williams, *Appalachia: A History,* 383. Eula remembers not knowing where they were going, but they probably weren't told. These well-documented trips are referred to by historians as the "day coach migration" of World War II—so called because of the hot and crowded passenger trains that carried men and women from the mountains to military plants and bases.

22 Eula Hall, interview with author, July 14, 2009. Eula, Andy, Buster, and Frank all made it out of the war alive, and for the brothers, like many Appalachians of the time, they were given new avenues for opportunity in factories outside of the mountains in cities such as Cleveland, Detroit, and Pittsburgh.

23 National Canners Association, Communications Services, *The Canning Industry: Its History, Importance, Organization, Methods, and the Public Service Values of Its Products,* 6th ed. (Washington, DC: National Canners Association, 1971).

24 Rosie the Riveter, a fictional character immortalized by posters supporting the war effort and a song of the same name, helped to recruit more than six million women to join the American war effort on the home front between December 1941 and early 1944. Rosie became a cultural and feminist icon and was the result of

the most successful recruitment advertising in American history. The fictional character was inspired by a real life Rosie—Rose Will Monroe, born in Pulaski County, Kentucky, in 1922.

25   Eula Hall, interview with author, July 14, 2009; "Tribulations Don't Deter Eula Hall," *Louisville Courier-Journal*, December 12, 1982.

26   Paul A. C. Koistinen, *Arsenal of World War II: The Political Economy of American Warfare, 1940–1945* (Lawrence: University of Kansas Press, 2004), 410. In contrast, the mineworkers, who did not belong to the American Federation of Labor (AFL) or the Congress of Industrial Organizations (CIO) for much of the war, threatened numerous strikes, including a successful twelve-day strike in 1943. The strikes and threats made mine leader John L. Lewis a much hated man and led to legislation hostile to unions. The war mobilization changed the relationship of the Congress of Industrial Organizations (CIO with both employers and the national government. Both the CIO and the larger American Federation of Labor (AFL grew rapidly in the war years. Nearly all the unions that belonged to the CIO were fully supportive of the war effort and of the Roosevelt administration. However, the United Mine Workers, who had taken an isolationist stand in the years leading up to the war and had opposed Roosevelt's re-election in 1940, left the CIO in 1942. The major unions supported a wartime no-strike pledge that aimed to eliminate not only major strikes for new contracts, but also the innumerable small strikes called by shop stewards and local union leadership for particular grievances. In return for labor's no-strike pledge, the government offered arbitration to determine wages and other terms of new contracts. Those procedures produced modest wage increases during the first few years of the war, but not enough to keep up with inflation, particularly when combined with the slowness of the arbitration process.

27   Eula Hall, interview with author, July 14, 2009: "Tribulations Don't Deter Eula Hall," *Louisville Courier-Journal*, December 12, 1982. It proved difficult to verify this account, as records of

factory worker skirmishes are not well documented. However, many other in Eula's life would recall the story nearly exactly as Eula had recalled it, and it has since become part of the Hall family lore.

CHAPTER 6

28   Elliot J. Gorn, *Mother Jones: The Most Dangerous Woman in America* (London: Macmillan, 2002), 96–98; Judith Pinkerton Josephson, *Mother Jones: Fierce Fighter for Workers' Rights* (New York: Lerner Books, 1996), 63–65. Among the many labor heroes of the generation, Mother Jones was one of the few women to take prominence in the movement. Many times over the course of our interviews, Eula used the refrain, "Pray for the dead, but fight like hell for the living," and even repeated it to clinic staff who needed an extra boost of morale.

29   "The Experiences of a Hired Girl," *The Outlook*, April 6, 1912, 778–780. One of the most compelling passages in all of Great Plains literature is "The Hired Girls," the middle section of *My Antonia* by Willa Cather. In the boy's-eye view of Jim Burden, the immigrant country girls who kept house for the townspeople of Black Hawk, Nebraska, are wonderfully alluring. They include the Norwegian girl Lena and the Bohemian girl Antonia; these older daughters of farm families help their families get out of debt and send younger siblings to school by working for Anglo-American town folk.

30   Eula Hall, interview with author, July 15, 2009. According to Eula, being a hired girl was extremely common and sometimes brought women from all across the region for lucrative paying jobs.

31   Eula Hall, interview with author, July 15, 2009. Eula considered opening a restaurant or catering service in the holler, since so many families were making money boarding. She still cooks big country meals for her family and often for clinic staff and patients.

32   Eula marvels at the advances she's seen in her life, most notably, how technology has enabled housework to become so much easier, stress-free, quick, and most importantly—less dangerous.

CHAPTER 7

33   Eula Hall, interview with author, September 9, 2009.

34   Author's note: Eula and many in her family think she sings poorly, but I've heard Eula sing, and I think she sounds like an angel.

CHAPTER 8

35   Eula Hall, interview with author, September 9, 2009. The word "hillbilly" has been used both with praise and incredulity. Eula often uses the term to describe herself affectionately, but also to deride those she thinks are idle loafers.

36   Eula and McKinley were married without the consent of Eula's parents because she knew they would oppose the union. The Rileys hoped Eula would settle with an established family, or at least a suitor with a steady job. According to Eula, the courts back then also often overlooked age to allow folks to marry, and in her case, the forged note was enough to get a marriage license.

CHAPTER 9

37   The difference between Big Mud and Little Mud is a matter of a few miles of winding mountain roads.

38   Eula Hall, interview with author, September 9, 2009.

39   Domestic abuse in Appalachia is a serious problem that some researchers say may affect as many as one in four women in the region. While Eula herself doesn't like to talk about the abuse in her early life, one of the prime motivations for her to start the clinic was domestic violence and the meager resources for help for her and so many other women. For further reading, see Lettie Lockhart and Fran Danis, "Appalachian Narratives of Survival and Recovery" in *Domestic Violence: Intersectionality and*

Culturally Competent Practice (New York: Columbia University Press, 2010), 351.

Part Two

Chapter 10

40   Some of Eula's brothers would go off for some time after the war to work in bigger cities, but many of them eventually came back to the mountains; Eula Hall interview with author, July 14, 2009. For further reading on John L. Lewis, see Melvin Dubofsky and Warren Van Tine, *John L. Lewis: A Biography* (Champaign: University of Illinois Press, 1986) and Price V. Fishback, *Soft Coal, Hard Choices: The Economic Welfare of Bituminous Coal Miners, 1890–1930* (New York: Oxford University Press USA, 1992).

41   Eula Hall, interview with author, September 15, 2009. According to her many children, Eula was a doting mother in the early years, but then became less involved during the years of her increasing activism and the establishment of the clinic. She also helped raise one of her grandchildren, Nanetta's child Eulana, who all of the other children claim is Eula's favorite along with Dean.

42   Eula Hall, interview with author, September 9, 2009.

43   Ibid. The business of creating, hiding, and selling moonshine provided Eula excitement as well as spirits and income. She describes her early moonshine production days as a time where she felt as entrepreneurial as she did setting up the clinic. Eula still keeps a Mason jar under her desk in case she is having a hard day. For further reading on moonshine, see Gerald Carson, *The Social History of Bourbon* (Lexington: University Press of Kentucky, 2010); Bruce Stewart, *Moonshiners and Prohibitionists: The Battle over Alcohol in Southern Appalachia* (Lexington: University Press of Kentucky, 2011).

44   This was a common line used by moonshiners during and after prohibition.

45   Eula Hall, interview with author, September 16, 2009.

CHAPTER 11

46 Eula Hall, interview with author, September 9, 2009; many women in Appalachia were tethered to their home life, and the ones lucky enough to have access to a car could access a life outside. Eula knew how important that pickup truck was to her ability to help others and get out of the holler, so for years, she meticulously cleaned, refueled, and parked the truck after she used it to ensure that McKinley had no idea she was driving it.

47 In 1956, the United Mine Workers of America (UMWA) and thousands of citizens in the coal communities established ten hospitals under the auspices of the Miners Memorial Hospital Association (MMHA). At the time, the UMWA represented the most extensive union-sponsored medical services in existence. See Raymond Munts, *Bargaining for Health: Labor Unions, Health Insurance and Medical Care* (Madison: University of Wisconsin Press, 1967). The system's hospitals were located in Harlan, Hazard, McDowell, Middlesboro, Whitesburg, Pikeville, and South Williamson, Kentucky; Man and Beckley, West Virginia; and Wise, Virginia. By the early 1960s, MMHA announced its intention to close some of the hospitals and soon after the Presbyterian Board of National Missions formed a new and independent not-for-profit health system, Appalachian Regional Hospitals (ARH) that purchased the Miners Memorial Hospitals. http://www.arh.org/about_us/our_history.aspx. ARH was later renamed Appalachian Regional Healthcare in 1982.

48 Eula Hall, interview with author, January 6, 2010. Although Eula may have taken issue with ARH in its earlier years, today, ARH plays a critical role in Central Appalachia, providing a safety net of uncompensated care. The Eula Hall Medical Center is part of the ARH system, which according to ARH President Jerry Haynes, touches the lives of nearly 350,000 uninsured and under-insured residents across Eastern Kentucky and Southern West Virginia. http://www.arh.org/about_us.aspx.

CHAPTER 12

49   Caudill, *Night Comes to the Cumberlands*; John Cheves and Bill Estep, "Fifty Years of Night," *Lexington Herald-Leader*, December 17, 2012. http://www.kentucky.com/2012/12/17/2444083/chapter-two-the-perfect-man-to.html#emlnl=AM_update. There are few authors as important as Caudill in understanding the socioeconomic plight of the Eastern Kentucky coalfields. He was a descendent of the first settlers of Letcher County, an elected state representative, and author of the groundbreaking 1962 *Atlantic* essay "The Rape of the Appalachians," which many point to as one of the clarion calls for the War on Poverty. Caudill would go on to write many books and later developed a relationship with Eula, commiserating on the sorry state of politics and economics of their beloved Eastern Kentucky. While Cheves and Estep detail Caudill's later deplorable insistence on eugenics and even sterilization as an answer to idleness, Caudill's words on economic colonialism still ring true today.

50   Caudill, *Night Comes to the Cumberlands*, 32; Thomas Kiffmeyer, *Reformers to Radicals: The Appalachian Volunteers and the War on Poverty* (Lexington: University Press of Kentucky, 2008), 113; President Lyndon B. Johnson, "Remarks at the University of Michigan, May 22, 1964," the American Presidency Project website, http://www.presidency.ucsb.edu/ws/index.php?pid=26262.

51   Eula Hall, interview with author, January 7, 2010; Kentucky election results for Kennedy on US Election Atlas website, http://uselectionatlas.org/RESULTS/datagraph.php?fips=21&year=1960&off=0&elect=0&f=0.

52   Cookstove and shoes: Eula Hall, interview with author, January 7, 2010; organizing: Eula Hall, interview with author, January 6, 2010. Eula often said that people in the activist community needed to understand that "the best form of activism is being a good neighbor."

53   Creation of 979 with AV involvement: Appendix II, Details of the
     Kentucky AV Program as Excerpted from the Quarterly Report
     to the Board of Directors (draft: 1967); EKWRO: AV Papers, box
     7; Floyd County 1967, AV Papers box 8; Report on Community
     Action Efforts of AV's from Prestonsburg Office by Flem Messer,
     1966; Eula Hall's personal notes, accessed July 2011; EKWRO
     and 979: Richard Couto, *Poverty, Politics, and Healthcare: An
     Appalachian Experience* (Westport, CT: Praeger Publishers,
     1975), 87–101: "In 1972, EKWRO claimed 400–500 dues paying
     members and up to 1,500–2,000 supporters." Excerpt from the
     Hawkeye, September 9, 1971, 4: "We believe people are poor
     because in this generation and in generation past, they have been
     denied equal opportunity. The resources of our nation should be
     used to correct these injustices of the past and to give adequate
     income, education, and health to Americans whose kin have died
     protecting this country and whose men have given their health
     and lives for the growth for the industrial might of this nation."

54   Eula Hall, interview with author, January 6, 2010; Couto, *Poverty*,
     90–92.

55   Eula Hall, interview with author, January 6, 2010; scene in school
     during lunch: Troy Hall, interview with author, May 29, 2011.
     The politically motivated lack of school lunch guidelines is well
     documented; Bill Peterson, *Coaltown Revisited: An Appalachian
     Notebook* (Washington, DC: Henry Regnery, 1972), 183–86.

56   Eula Hall, interview with author, January 6, 2010.

57   School board politics: Peter Schrag, "The School and Politics"
     in *Appalachia's People, Problems, Alternatives*, compiled by
     People's Appalachia Research Collective, vol.1 (PARC: 1971);
     EKWRO's reputation: Couto, *Poverty*, 92, quote from state
     official: "They're some well-meaning people in EKWRO and
     some revolutionaries . . . But there ain't any other damn way to lay
     it out, except in terms of the present political and social structure,
     they're revolutionary as hell."

58 EKWRO mission statement in the organization's newsletter, *Hawkeye*, September 9, 1971, 4.

59 Fight: Couto, *Poverty*, 90; Anthony J. Salatino, *Will Appalachia Finally Overcome Poverty?* (Kuttawa, KY: McClanahan, 1995), 176–177; Eller, *Uneven Ground*, 139–141; Woodrow Roger, "Sticking Together," *Mountain Life and Work* 49 (1973); Eula Hall, interview with author, January 6, 2010.

CHAPTER 13

60 Eula Hall, interview with author, January 6, 2010. Eula often said it was no wonder that activism in the mountains coincided with the civil rights movement, because much of the white and black poor in Appalachia felt that they too were being denied the civil rights entitled to them in the constitution.

61 Eula Hall, interview with author, March 29, 2010; Troy Hall, interview with author, May 12, 2011. Eula became more and more withdrawn from home life and her older children, Randy, Troy, and Nanetta, saw less of their mother than did Dean and Eulana.

62 Kiffmeyer, *Reformers to Radicals*, 102.

63 Sociotherapy: John Ehrenreich, *The Altruistic Imagination: A History of Social Work and Social Policy in the United States* (Ithaca, NY: Cornell University Press, 1985), 117–119; Caudill quote: Kiffmeyer, *Reformers to Radicals*, 113.

64 For a comprehensive study of the content, compromises, and bureaucratic dynamics of Title VII of the Economic Opportunity Act, see Daniel P. Moynihan, *Maximum Feasible Misunderstanding: Community Action in the War on Poverty* (New York: Free Press, 1969); haughty judgments by outsiders: Kiffmeyer, *Reformers to Radicals*, 106–107, quotes from New York college students, "In a poor society, recreation is irrelevant," "monotony of daily routine" in mountains unlike "sophistication of New York culture"; 150 VISTAs in AV school projects and overlap; Kiffmeyer, *Reformers to Radicals*, 110–111.

CHAPTER 14

65   Signing up as VISTA: Eula Hall, interview with author, March 31, 2010; additional info on sign-up process, Kiffmeyer, *Reformers to Radicals*, 111–112.

66   VISTA Training: Eula Hall, interview with author, March 31, 2010; for background on the culture of poverty theory, which dominated poverty alleviation efforts through the New Deal and early Appalachian Volunteer efforts, see Jack Weller's, *Yesterday's People: Life in Contemporary Appalachia* (Lexington: University Press of Kentucky, 1965). This interpretation of Appalachian poverty, of which even Harry Caudill was an early proponent, precipitated into different interpretations that by the late century included modernization theory, labor issues, and sociology. For a modern, empirical rebuttal of the culture of poverty theory, see Dwight Billing, "Culture and Poverty in Appalachia: A Theoretical Discussion and Empirical Analysis," *Social Forces* 53, no. 2, special issue (New York: Oxford University Press: 1974), 315–323. Modernization theory, describing the virtual control of the region by industrial coal giants, is best described in the scholarly work of Ron Eller, John Gaventa, and John Hevener. In Eller's *Miners, Millhands, and Mountaineers* (Knoxville: University of Tennessee Press, 1982), he describes how absentee ownership, rapid industrialization, and the extraction of natural resource wealth to urban centers led to the impoverishment of Appalachia. For more on the training sessions and theories of the VISTA program, see Kiffmeyer's *Reformers to Radicals*.

67   Governor's and OEO funding: American Academy of Political and Social Science, and National American Woman Suffrage Association Collection (Washington DC: Library of Congress), 1969; VISTA workers in East Kentucky: David Whisnant, *Modernizing the Mountaineer: People, Power, and Planning in Appalachia* (Knoxville: University of Tennessee Press, 1994); "long-haired hippies": Stephen L. Fisher, *Fighting Back in Appalachia: Traditions of Resistance and Change* (Philadelphia:

Temple University Press, 1993), 253; AV funding cut off: Kiffmeyer, *Reformers to Radicals*, 190.

CHAPTER 15

68 Eula Hall, interview with author, March 29, 2010.

69 Eula wrote about what she saw during this survey in an essay: Eula Hall, "The Grass Roots Speak Back," in *Back Talk for Appalachia: Confronting Stereotypes*, eds., Dwight B. Billings, Gurney Norman, Katherine Ledford (Lexington: University Press of Kentucky, 2000)

70 AV Papers, box 8, Flem Messer, "Report on Community Action Effort of Appalachian Volunteers from Prestonsburg Office," 1966; AV Papers, Box 30, "The People of Little Mud Creek"; Eula Hall interview with the author, January 8, 2010.

71 Dean Hall, interview with author, May 12, 2011. Dean currently works for the Water Board and while he wasn't present during the initial days, he and his colleagues acknowledge the tough political fights that existed.

CHAPTER 16

72 John Ehrenreich, *Maximum Feasible Participation: The Altruistic Imagination* (Ithaca, NY: Cornell University Press, 1985) 170–176; Lillian Rubin, "Maximum Feasible Participation: The Origins, Implications, and Present Status," *Annals of the American Academy of Political and Social Science*, 385 no 1 (September 1969), 14–29.

73 Title II programs: Scott Myers-Lipton, *Social Solutions to Poverty: America's Struggle to Build a Just Society* (Boulder, CO: Paradigm Publishers: 2006), 216–217; Maximum feasible participation in legislation without mention in Congressional Record: Rubin, 26; James Jennings, *Understanding the Nature of Poverty in Urban America* (Westport, T: Greenwood Publishing Group, 1994), 139.

74 Big city mayors and conservative critics: William S. Clayson, *Freedom is Not Enough: The War on Poverty and the Civil Rights Movement in Texas* (Austin: University of Texas Press,

2010), 66: quote from Mayor Daley to Bill Moyers in response to OEO funding of activists: "What the hell are you people doing? Does the president know he is giving money to subversives?"; Shriver on health program: Scott Stossel, *Sarge: The Life and Times of Sargent Shriver* (New York: Other Press, 2011); Floyd County Health Statistics: Couto, *Poverty, Politics*, 63; Bureau of the Census, 1970 Census of the Population: General Social and Economic Characteristics, Kentucky, vol. 1, pt. 19.

75   Couto: *Poverty, Politics*, 58–63. Floyd County Health Department Proposal Submitted for Program Year A, see Couto, 63.

76   Carl D. Perkins: Michael Gillette, *Launching the War on Poverty: An Oral History* (New York: Oxford University Press, 2010), 371–73: Donald Baker, OEO General Counsel "He's sort of a countrified gentleman who doesn't seem to have a hell of a lot of energy or seem too bright, talks a bit like a hick. The fact of the matter is, he's one of the most sagacious old gentlemen in the House of Representatives. His greatest concern in life is that of the poor people of Eastern Kentucky." For more on Perkins's early life and Congressional Record, see Andree Reeves, "The Chairmanship of Carl Perkins," chap. 6 in *Congressional Committee Chairman: The Three Men who Made an Evolution* (Lexington: University Press of Kentucky, 1933).

77   Eula Hall, interview with author, February 23, 2010; Couto, *Poverty, Politics*, 60–65.

78   Along with Eula's anecdotes, Couto's history of the FCCHSP as well as the US Government's Boone Report all find that medicine in the mountains worked as a monopoly, with doctors, hospitals, and pharmacists, essentially working together to profit: US Department of Interior, Coal Mines Administration, "A Medical Survey of the Bituminous Coal Industry," (Washington, DC: US Government Printing Office, 1947), vii; Third Quarterly Report of FCCHSP provided to author by Eula Hall, April 1, 1971.

79   Couto, *Poverty, Politics*, 68.

80   Eula Hall, interview with author, February 23, 2010

CHAPTER 17

81 Ernest Glen Hentschel, "Exit Report from STAP Assignment with FCCHSP"; Jerry Sparer, "Site Visit Appraisal of FCCHSP," June 1968 (Washington, DC: Office of Health Affairs, 1968); Dr. Schecter, interview with author, July 22, 2010.

82 Statistics from Hentschel, Sparer report, and "Administration and Conduct of Antipoverty Programs,": Hearings H.R., first session before the House Committee on Education and Labor, 91st Congress, November 13, 1969, 3–4; Couto, *Poverty, Politics*, 72–77, 80–82.

CHAPTER 18

83 Dr. Arnold Schecter, interview with author, July 22, 2010.

84 Park DuValle Community Health Center website, http://www.pdchc.org/. Dr. Jack Geiger is a legendary figure in public health who initiated the community health center model by founding and directing the nation's first two community health centers in the Mississippi and Boston. These centers became models for what is now a national network with federal funding of more than 1,100 CHCs, serving some twenty million low-income and minority patients

85 Kiffmeyer, *Reformers to Radicals*, 180

86 Dr. Arnold Schecter interview with the author July 22, 2010, "I had transformative plans"; Couto, *Poverty, Politics*, 99; "Arnold Schecter and the Outsiders: Proposals for Change."

87 Pikeville Medical Center launched a MedFlight program, but promptly shut it down after a year of expensive losses; Eula Hall, interview with author, July 22, 2010.

88 Couto, *Poverty, Politics*, 110.

89 This predicament led to the creation of an Osteopathic School of Medicine at the University of Pikeville. For further reading, see http://www.upike.edu/College-of-Osteopathic-Medicine/about/mission: "A group of influential businessmen and public officials began to investigate the possibility of establishing a medical

school in Eastern Kentucky in the early 1990s. The supporters believed that creation of an osteopathic medical school was the best way to help alleviate the shortage of primary care physicians in rural Eastern Kentucky. Support of the development of an osteopathic medical school for this region arose from the fact that osteopathic physicians tend to stay in rural areas and in family practice. KYCOM enrolled its first students in 1997."

CHAPTER 19

90   Dr. Arnold Schecter, interview with author, July 22, 2010; Robert Bazell, "OEO Hedges on Kentucky Program," *Science* 172 (1971), 45; Homer Bigart, "Anti-Poverty Programs Imperiled in Appalachia," *New York Times*, June 15, 1971; Couto, *Poverty, Politics*, 150–159.

91   Eula Hall, interview with author, January 10, 2010; Woodrow Rogers, president of EKWRO and Eula Hall, community board member of FCCHSP, letter to Leon Cooper, April 15, 1971.

92   John and Jean Rosenberg, interview with author, January 12, 2010; additional material taken from Arwen Donohue, "John Rosenberg," chap. 8 in *This is Home Now: Kentucky's Holocaust Survivors Speak,* (Lexington: University Press of Kentucky, 2009).

93   AppalRED Mission Statement and History, Appalachian Research and Defense Fund website, http://www.ardfky.org/AboutUs.aspx, accessed 2012.

94   John Rosenberg, interview with author, January 12, 2010. In much the same way that the local medical community created conflict with Dr. Schecter, John Rosenberg faced fierce and immediate opposition from the local legal community.

95   John Rosenberg's illustrious career is detailed in "Personal Reflections of a Life in Public Interest Law: From the Civil Rights Division of US DOJ to AppalRED," *West Virginia Law Review* 96, no. 2 (Winter 1993–94), http://www.ardfky.org/PDFs/AppalRedRosenburg.pdf, accessed 2012.

96   Troy and Dean Hall, interview with author, May 5, 2011.

CHAPTER 20

97 Eula Hall, interview with author, January 10, 2010. Statistics provided to Richard Couto by Dr. Louis Lefkowitz, Vanderbilt coordinator of the health fair. Additional information on health fair from Maxine Kinney, "Why a Health Fair?," *Mountain Life and Work* 47, nos. 7–8, (July–August 1971), 11–12.

98 Trailer: Eula Hall, interview with author, January 10, 2010; Dr. Eleanor Graham, interview with author, November 20, 2012; $1 pay: Couto, *Poverty, Politics*, 122.

99 Clinic set-up and first patients: Eula Hall, interview with author, January 10, 2010; Maxine Kinney, interview with author, April 12, 2011; Dr. Graham, interview with author, November 20, 2012. The organic growth of the clinic mainly relied on the shutdown of the FCCHSP, and the continued effort by EKWRO; Sally Maggard, "Rural Health Care," *Mountain Life and Work* (Council of the Southern Mountains Records, 1970-1989), 31–33.

CHAPTER 21

100 Eula Hall, interview with author, February 10, 2011; Dean Hall, interview with author, January 10, 2010. Eula would eventually get her divorce, but as many women at the time knew, without physical separation, a divorce often meant little in terms of peace at home.

101 Abuse and sleeping at nursing home: Eula Hall and Dean Hall, interview with author, May 12, 2011. Sliding scale payment to keep clinic as safety net: this is the model that many Federally Qualified Health Centers (FQHC) use today in the United States. According to US Department of Health and Human Services, "[All FQHC'] **must provide access to services without regard for a person's ability to pay**. Ability to pay is determined by a patient's annual income and family size according to the most recent US Department of Health & Human Services Federal Poverty Guidelines." Today there are nineteen FQHCs in Kentucky; the program started in the late 1960s. See Health

Resources and Service Administration website, http://bphc.hrsa.gov/about/index.html.

102 Eastern Kentucky UMWA and the Miners Hospitals: Eller, *Uneven Ground*, 45–50: "The UMWA had established its Health and Retirement Funds to provide free health care and other benefits to miners and their families, and in 1954 the union had built ten state-of-the-art Miners Memorial Hospitals in southern West Virginia, Virginia, and Eastern Kentucky that provided medical care for a large percentage of families in the area." For more information on the Miners Memorial Hospitals, see Richard Mulcahy, *A Social Contract for the Coal Fields: The Rise and Fall of the UMWA Welfare and Retirement Funds* (Knoxville: University of Tennessee Press, 2000). For further detail on the ravages of underground coal mining, see "Injury Trends in Mining," US Department of Labor, Mine Safety and Health Administration website, http://www.msha.gov/MSHAINFO/FactSheets/MSHAFCT2.HTM.

103 Eula Hall, interview with author, January 10, 2010. Eula recited her speech as if she had rehearsed it the day before. It was clear that this was one of her favorite, and most eloquent, moments.

CHAPTER 22

104 Eula Hall, interview with author, October 11, 2011; Dr. Eleanor Graham, interview with author, November 20, 2012. Like many activists who came to the mountains in those years, Squire and Graham were leftists who practiced what they believed on poverty alleviation and the adequate distribution of resources. Although Eula spoke about the threatening group they associated with, my conversation with the doctors showed peaceful, caring healers who wanted desperately to change the status quo of poverty that they found abhorrent. Both doctors dedicated their lives to this cause.

105 Eula Hall, interview with author, January 10, 2010.

106 Eula continues to push for a domestic abuse shelter at the Mud Creek Clinic today. For further information on reproductive

health in the mountains, see the Eastern Kentucky Reproductive
Health Project website, http://www.ekrhp.com/?page_id=14.

107 Eller, *Uneven Ground*, 45-50: "Eastern Kentucky, where 43
percent of adults smoked, led the country in lung cancer
mortality rates"; difficulty of receiving black lung benefits: Rep.
Ron Mazzoli's testimony to the House Committee on Education
and Labor, "Black Lung Benefits Eligibility," 1973; the resurgence
in Eastern Kentucky of black lung in the new century: http://
www.publicintegrity.org/2012/07/08/9293/black-lung-surges-
back-coal-country: "From 1968 through 2007, black lung caused
or contributed to roughly 75,000 deaths in the United States,
according to government data. In the decades following passage
of the 1969 law, rates of the disease dropped significantly. Then,
in the late 1990s, this trend reversed."

CHAPTER 23

108 Eula Hall, interview with author, June 7, 2010; Black Lung
Association: see United Mine Workers of America website, http://
www.umwa.org/?q=content/black-lung; 1972 amendments:
William Graebner, "The Black Lung Rebellion" chapter in *Coal-
Mining Safety in the Progressive Period: The Political Economy
of Reform* (Lexington: University Press of Kentucky, 1976), 88;
"Pressure from BLA organizers forced SSA to pay a number of
BLA organizers to participate in the formulation of what came
to be known as the 'interim standards,' a more liberal set of
eligibility regulations." Eula, among other state chapter BLA
presidents, were thus invited to help write the 1972 regulations.

109 Graebner, *Coal-Mining Safety*, 90–93.

110 Graebner, *Coal-Mining Safety*, 103; "The Tragedy of the Miners,"
Washington Post, January 16, 1977. Arnold Miller was one of the
first organizers of the Black Lung Association in West Virginia.
Former Appalachian Volunteers started the organization, with
the help of pioneering West Virginian Dr. Donald Rasmussen's
evidence. Rasmussen started Designs for Rural Action (DRA)
to press for direct pressure on miners' rights issues. Miller, a

disabled former miner himself with black lung, was eventually elected UMWA president in late 1972.

111 "Coal's Chilling Strike," *Time*, November 18, 1974. This twenty-eight-day strike resulted in a nearly 54 percent increase in miner's wage and benefits over the next three years. Miller/Eula altercation: Eula Hall, interview with author, June 7, 2010.

112 Eula Hall, interview with author, June 7, 2010. Eula believed that the mines could prosper even while paying miners living wages and providing health care; others disagreed and the debate still rages in the coalfields. But many like Eula were scared to speak out because of violence and intimidation. Today, as market forces have focused on cheaper fuel sources such as natural gas, coal jobs have been steadily leaving the mountains. In 2012, mines in Kentucky directly employed a little over eighteen thousand people—less than 1 percent of the state's workforce.

113 Eula Hall, interview with author, October 11, 2011; Dr. Eleanor Graham, interview with author, November 20, 2012.

114 Eula Hall, interview with author, February 10, 2011. In the most emotional interview I had with Eula, she admitted that she knew such an attack would come eventually. She continued to have nightmares about this night for the rest of her life.

Chapter 24

115 Eula Hall, interviews with author, February 10, 2011, and October 11, 2011; Maggard, "Rural Health Care," 31–33.

116 Eula Hall, interview with author, June 7, 2010. Bill Worthington, an African American coal miner, became a good friend to Eula and the family. Bullets and threats: Goetz, *Courier-Journal*, December 12, 1982.

117 Eula Hall, interview with author, June 8, 2010; Fred Harris, "Burning up People to Make Electricity," *The Atlantic*, (July 1, 1974): "Lois Scott says that the women organized the Brookside Women's Club and got involved in the strike 'because we knew that if the women didn't come in there would be violence'; Sally

Ward Maggard, "Coalfield Women Making History" in Billings, Norman, Ledford, *Back Talk From Appalachia*; Goetz, *Courier-Journal*, December 12, 1982: "The women keep the mountains going. They may be behind the scenes and the men may get credit for it, but the women won the strike in Harlan County."

118 Lynda Ann Ewen, *Which Side Are You On?: The Brookside Mine Strike in Harlan County, Kentucky* (Vanguard Books, 1979); Alessandro Portelli, *They Say in Harlan County: An Oral History* (New York: Oxford University Press, 2010), 310–340.

119 "Which Side Are You On?" was written by Florence Reese in 1931, and is one of the more famous strike songs of the era. Eula freely sang across the office while I interviewed her.

120 Worthington & UMWA: Portelli, *They Say in Harlan County*, 174.

121 Harlan County USA, Barbard Kopple (1976)

122 Eula Hall, interview with author, June 8, 2010

CHAPTER 25

123 APHA Presidential Citation, http://www.apha.org/about/awards/previouswinners/prescitation/.

124 Eula Hall, interview with author, June 9, 2010.

125 Eula Hall, interview with author, October 11, 2011; Big Sandy Health care http://www.bshc.org/.

126 Eula Hall and Robin Holbrook, interview with author, August 11, 2012; Medical homes, accountable care organizations, and community health center coordination became a central facet of President Barak Obama's 2010 Affordable Care Act that overhauled the nation's health care system. For further reading, see: http://www.pcmh.ahrq.gov/portal/server.pt/community/pcmh__home/1483/pcmh_tools___resources_coordinated_care_v2

127 Dr. Ellen Joyce, interview with author, July 15, 2011.

CHAPTER 26

128 Dr. Ellen Joyce, interview with author, July 15, 2011.

129 Ibid; ARC study http://www.kentucky.com/static/pdfs/ARCreport. pdf.

130 Section entitled: Appalachia Health and Well Being, Richard Couto, 223–226; Dr. Joyce interview with author, July 15, 2011; Low energy and depression: http://www.gallup.com/poll/148787/ appalachia-america-low-energy-zone.aspx

131 Eula Hall, interview with author, September 9, 2012; Conservative opponents of poverty alleviation in Appalachia look to welfare (SNAP, SSI, and other federal income support programs) as causes for cultures of poverty in the region. For reading on this argument of Appalachian dependency, see Paul Salstrom, *Appalachia's Path to Dependency: Rethinking a Region's Economic History* (Lexington: University Press of Kentucky, 1997), Salstrom moves away from the colonial model to discuss the complex web of factors—regulation of credit, industrialization, population growth, cultural values, federal intervention—that he believes has worked against the region. However, modern research shows that SSI payments significantly improve outcomes for poor children, see http://www.cbpp.org/cms/index.cfm?fa=view&id=3875. In a twist of irony, Eula notes how the modern-day tea party, popular in the hollers of Kentucky, also believes this orthodoxy even though many are still struggling for food, shelter, and health care; Eula wins approximately 90 percent of her cases, and at one point was arguing an average of ten a month.

PART THREE

CHAPTER 27

132 Eula Hall, interview with author, October 25, 2011; "Tribulations Don't Deter Eula Hall," *Louisville Courier-Journal*, December 12, 1982: "When you start this you can't give up."

133 "Woman Who Make a Difference," *Family Circle,* January 12, 1993; Eula Hall, "If There's One Thing You Can Tell Them, It's that You're Free," *Back Talk from Appalachia*, 192–199; R. G.

Dunlop, "Fire Ravaged Appalachian Clinic, *Louisville Courier-Journal*, July 5, 1982.

134 Eula Hall, interview with author, October 25, 2011: These are questions that Eula still considers and wonders about today.

CHAPTER 28

135 Michael Winerip, "Kentucky's Godmother to the Poor," *People Magazine,* October 24, 1991.

136 Eula Hall, interview with author, October 27, 2011; quote from Frasure: "Mud Creek Clinic Tries to Recover from Fire" *Louisville Courier-Journal*, July 8, 1982.

137 Eula Hall, interview with author, October 27, 2011; interview with John Rosenberg January 12, 2010; new trailer was donated by the Kentucky State Department of Health and Human Services and is now used by the Water Board that Eula helped start, and currently employs Dean; Letter from ARC pledging new funds: http://www.arc.gov/magazine/articles.asp?ARTICLE_ID=102

CHAPTER 29

138 Peter Kilborn, "In Coal Country, a Home-Grown Clinic," *New York Times,* March 15 1991.

139 Robin Holbrook, interview with author, October 25, 2011; Lou Ellen, interview with author, October 10, 2012; Dr. Ellen Joyce, interview with author, July 16, 2011.

140 Lynda McDaniel, "Appalachian Scene: Eula Hall: Driving force for change," *ARC Magazine*

141 Letter from *Good Morning America* Producer Mellen O'Keefe to Eula Hall, August 6, 1982

CHAPTER 30

142 Eula Hall, interview with author, October 25, 2011

143 Lexington *Herald Leader,* "It's Now Official: Eula Hall is a Wonder Woman," November 23, 1982; List of Eula's awards: http://www.bshc.org/index.php?page=eula-hall-story

CHAPTER 31

144 Eula Hall, interview with author and Dean Hall, interview with author, May 12, 2011

145 Dr. Ellen Joyce and Ron Joyce, interview with author, July 16, 2011

146 Eula Hall, interview with author, September 9, 2009

CHAPTER 32

147 Direct quotes taken from "Mud Creek Clinic" Appalshop Documentary, 1986; Eula Hall, interview with author, January 7, 2010.

EPILOGUE

148 Eula Hall, interview with author, June 13, 2013